# _____... and education for all_

## Public Policy and Handicapped Children

**Roberta Weiner**
**Maggie Hume**

Education Research Group
Capitol Publications, Inc.
1101 King Street, Alexandria, Virginia 22314

Also published by the Education Research Group:

*From Birth To Five: Serving The Youngest Handicapped Children*
*The Child Abuse Crisis: Impact on the Schools*
*P.L. 94-142: Impact on the Schools*
*AIDS: Impact on the Schools*
*Teen Pregnancy: Impact on the Schools*
*Education Directory: A Guide to Decisionmakers in the Federal*
  *Government, the States and Education Associations*
*Education Regulations Library*
*The Education Evaluator's Workbook:*
  *How to Assess Education Programs*

Copyright © 1987 by the Education Research Group,
  Capitol Publications, Inc.

Helen Hoart, Publisher
Roberta Weiner, Executive Editor

Printed in the United States of America

**Library of Congress Cataloging-in-Publication Data**

Weiner, Roberta.
  And education for all.

  Rev. ed. of: P.L. 94-142 / by Roberta Weiner.
  Bibliography: p.
  1. Handicapped children — Education — Law and
legislation — United States.   2. Handicapped children —
Education — United States.   I. Hume, Maggie, 1961-
II. Weiner, Roberta.   P.L. 94-142.   III. Title.
KF4210.W44   1987       344.73'0791        87-6049
                        347.304791
ISBN 0-937925-31-4 (lib. bdg. : alk. paper)
ISBN 0-937925-26-8 (pbk. : alk. paper)

Roberta Weiner, Maggie Hume
  *. . . And Education For All:*
    *Public Policy And Handicapped Children*

Cover design by Linda C. McDonald

*Second Edition*

# About The Authors

Roberta Weiner, executive editor of Capitol Publications' Education Research Group (ERG), has been an education writer and editor for eight years. Before taking the helm of ERG when it was formed in 1986, Ms. Weiner was managing editor of *Education Daily* and *Higher Education Daily*. She is also the author of *AIDS: Impact on the Schools* and co-author of *From Birth to Five: Serving the Youngest Handicapped Children*.

Ms. Weiner began her career at the *Middlesex News* in Framingham, Mass., where she was an education reporter. She has a bachelor of science degree in journalism from Boston University.

Maggie Hume is editor of *Education of the Handicapped*, a biweekly Capitol Publications newsletter on public policy and handicapped children, and a reporter for *Education Daily*. Ms. Hume previously edited *School Law News*, a sister newsletter on developments in school law. She is the author of *The Supreme Court and Education: The 1985-86 Term* and was a contributing writer to *AIDS: Impact on the Schools*. Prior to joining Capitol, Ms. Hume worked for Fairchild Publications in New York and Washington, D.C. She has a bachelor of arts degree in literature from Yale University.

# Table Of Contents

## Part Two:
## Where Special Education Is Going

**Part Three:
Appendices**

# Introduction: A Free Public Education For All Handicapped Children

It's important to remember, as debate continues to rage over how best to serve handicapped children, that virtually all handicapped students are now being served by the public schools.

That blanket statement can be made thanks to federal special education law, whose single most important contribution has been to guarantee access to education for all handicapped children.

Since the Education for All Handicapped Children Act, P.L. 94-142, was enacted in 1975, the number of handicapped children served has increased from 3.7 million to more than 4.1 million. Federal funding for special education has increased from $246 million to $1.2 billion. And the education of handicapped children in the United States has improved either "greatly" or "somewhat," said more than 97 percent of school administrators the Education Research Group surveyed in 1985 for the first edition of this book.

"Those of us who remember the days when there was no law are in a position to make comparisons," said Alan Hofmeister, a special education professor at Utah State University. Hofmeister, who recalled working with the families of handicapped children turned away by schools in the 1960s, said "their heartbreak and frustration just compounded the other sorts of problems" posed by a child's disability.

Children today have access to services "with a level of dignity and ease not conceived of" before the law's passage, Hofmeister said.

Intensive "child find" searches conducted by states to comply with P.L. 94-142 have spurred widespread provision of services for handicapped children in schools, according to Frederick Weintraub, assistant executive director of the Council for Exceptional Children. "It's hard today to find handicapped kids sitting at home." Thus while "debates and struggles" continue over how best to implement programs, "the basic thrust of the law has been achieved," he said.

* * *

9

But . . .

■ Money remains the single biggest problem with special education. The problem was made more intense by the 1986 amendments to the Education of the Handicapped Act, which gave states added requirements for serving preschoolers and infants.

■ There is no end in sight to the high costs of litigation. And 1986 legislation to allow parents to collect attorneys fees if they win special education cases — an enactment that was heralded by parents and advocates — is causing high levels of consternation in school districts, which fear soaring legal costs. (When we surveyed school administrators in 1985, a full 72 percent opposed the then-pending attorneys fees legislation.)

■ Children are still being placed in classrooms for the learning disabled even though they may have another handicap or no disability at all.

■ Schools officials are drowning in paperwork.

\* \* \*

The first edition of this book was published in 1985 on the 10th anniversary of P.L. 94-142. At that celebratory time, optimism reigned. We found educators and parents demonstrating some frustrations, of course, but always found an undercurrent of positive feelings about what they were accomplishing. Two years later, advocates are once again celebrating, this time over a banner legislative session in the 99th Congress. The preschool legislation takes special education into what we predicted in 1985 to be the next frontier: the youngest handicapped children. And the attorneys fees legislation was another major victory for advocates.

But school administrators are not so happy. They fought the attorneys fees bill and, while they concurred with the need for early childhood education, they want to know where the money is going to come from. They see it happening all over again: the banner legislation, the initial rush of attention, and then schools left out in the cold to cope without adequate funding.

It's unclear how it will all turn out. Once again, the ball has been handed off to the states, and we'll be watching them eagerly. Education for handicapped children continues to be one of the most exciting areas of public policy in this nation.

\* \* \*

We'd like to acknowledge Jane Koppelman, editor of *Report on Preschool Programs,* who contributed to the chapter on the new preschool programs, Laurie Evans, who assisted with the copy editing, and James Buie, assistant editor of the Education Research Group, for his many helpful suggestions in critiquing the manuscript.

Thanks also go to Deborah L. Gold and Susan Landers. Much of their contribution to the first edition of this book has stood the test of time and remains in this edition. Debbie, a reporter for *Education Daily* and editor of *Report on Education of the Disadvantaged*, researched and wrote about advances in curriculum and teaching. Susan, former editor of *Education of the Handicapped*, helped research the history of P.L. 94-142 and its regulations.

Production of this report was coordinated by Leslie A. Ratzlaff, managing editor of the Education Research Group. Proofreading was done by Christopher Grasso and Susan B. Abkowitz. Thanks also to production manager Rosette Graham, typesetter Cynthia Peters, graphic artist Linda C. McDonald, and our marketing and circulation staff: Kristan S. Winters, Tammy Vagias, Ellen Carroll, Allison Sator, Barbara L. Davis, Gloria Smith, Joan Rodriguez and Robin Carey.

Roberta Weiner and Maggie Hume

# Part One

# Where Special Education Has Been

# 1

# Legislative History

*"We can all agree that all handicapped children should be receiving an education. We can all agree that that education should be equivalent, at least, to the one those children who are not handicapped receive. The fact is, our agreeing on it does not make it the case. There are millions of children with handicapping conditions who are receiving no services at all."*

— *Sen. Robert Stafford, R-Vt., June 18, 1975, Senate debate, S. 6, later to become P.L. 94-142*

On Nov. 29, 1985, President Gerald Ford boarded an airplane for China. Left behind in the White House was a bill he had just, reluctantly, signed into law.

After the president was airborne, his aides announced that Ford had signed the Education for All Handicapped Children Act, P.L. 94-142.

Ford had planned to veto the bill because he thought its price tag — estimated at $3 billion to $4 billion — was too high. Instead, after Ford's aides apparently convinced the president his veto would be overturned, Ford put his name on the landmark legislation.

The reaction of advocates whose every waking hour had been spent pushing the bill through Congress and then through the White House?

Relief, ecstasy, and especially . . . exhaustion.

"Thanksgiving morning of 1975, I had escaped, I was dead tired, to the Conrad Hilton Hotel in Chicago. No one knew where I was. I had my family there," said Phil Jones, who was president of the Council for Exceptional Children (CEC) at the time. Somehow, one of Ford's domestic policy advisers caught up with Jones and warned him the president was close to vetoing the bill.

"That whole Thanksgiving weekend, we were in contact three or four times," Jones said.

Meanwhile, the entire CEC Political Action Network, made up of 50 or 60 state CEC representatives, was meeting at the council's headquarters in Reston, Va., right outside Washington, D.C., recalled Joseph Ballard, CEC associate director of governmental relations. "They were all calling" the White House, plus they were phoning home so state people would call, too.

When the word came that the president had been persuaded, and the law signed, the action network had gone home and Ballard was in the CEC offices with other CEC officials.

"I think it was probably the greatest moment of personal relief in my life. We all had tears in our eyes," Ballard said. "We felt a great thing had happened." Looking back on the battles recently, Jones said the struggles were all worth while. "I'm proud to be a special educator, proud of 94-142. . . . The law has had tremendous impact," said Jones, a professor of special education administration and supervision at Virginia Polytechnic Institute and State University in Blacksburg, Va.

"I look back and say, 'Has it been 10 years?' There has been tremendous progress, but there's still progress to be made," said Jones.

### Back to The Beginning

P.L. 94-142, like any major piece of legislation, did not spring into life from a vacuum. Its roots were in legislation enacted over the previous 10 years.

The congressional push to open schools to handicapped children began in 1966, when lawmakers added Title VI to the Elementary and Secondary Education Act, passed a year earlier. Title VI launched a grant program to help states educate handicapped children and created within the then-Office of Education (OE) a Bureau of Education for the Handicapped (BEH).

Title VI was added after congressional hearings in 1966 revealed horror tales of handicapped children excluded from school or sitting idly in regular classrooms biding time until they were old enough to drop out.

Edwin Martin, staff director in 1966 of the then-Ad Hoc House Subcommittee on the Handicapped, and later, head of BEH, recalled how painful it was to see disabled children denied an education or placed in inappropriate programs. But then, Martin said, he was able to help draft legislation to correct the situation.

Four years later, Congress went a step further and replaced Title VI with the Education of the Handicapped Act (EHA), which kept BEH and the state grant program and added funds to help schools buy equipment and build needed facilities.

The 1970 law added grants for regional resource centers, centers for deaf-blind children, experimental early education programs and personnel training, and established research and demonstration projects.

The House and Senate both proposed legislation in 1972 and again in 1973 to extend these provisions of EHA and create a new Part B of the act that would be permanent, an entitlement program with no need for reauthorization. But neither bill went anywhere.

### Section 504

Meanwhile, advocates for handicapped people had won a major victory with the enactment Sept. 26, 1973, of the Rehabilitation Act. The act included the historic Section 504, the first major civil rights statute to protect the rights of the handicapped.

Section 504 states: "No otherwise qualified handicapped individual in the United States . . . shall solely by reason of his handicap be excluded from participation in, be denied the benefits of, or be subjected to discrimination under any program or activity receiving federal financial assistance."

And action in the federal courts helped push Congress into action. Cases such as the 1971 *Pennsylvania Association of Retarded Citizens (PARC) v. Pennsylvania* and the 1972 *Mills v. Board of Education of the District of Columbia* had established the right of handicapped children to receive a free public education *(see Chapter 3)*.

### 1974 ESEA Amendments

But the true precursors of P.L. 94-142 were the 1974 amendments to the Elementary and Secondary Education Act. The amendments pulled together all the elements that would become P.L. 94-142, including due process protections for handicapped children and their parents and requirements that children be taught in the least restrictive environment possible.

The key omission from the 1974 amendments was a timetable. Under the amendments, each state could set its own deadline for providing an appropriate education to its handicapped students.

Rep. John Brademas, D-Ind., then-chairman of the House Select Education Subcommittee, believed there was a need for federal mandates to the states and a need for a greater federal commitment to handicapped children.

So on May 21, 1974, Brademas introduced H.R. 7217, which set a deadline of Oct. 1, 1978, for states to provide an appropriate public education for their handicapped children. Combined with S. 6, introduced in the Senate Jan. 15, 1975, by Sen. Jennings Randolph, D-W.Va., chairman of the Handicapped Subcommittee, the bill would become P.L. 94-142 the next fall.

In an opening statement at an April 8, 1975, hearing on S. 6, Randolph said, "In all, 3.9 million children are waiting for the fundamental equal educational opportunities on which our nation is based. This is not right and it is an emergency situation."

### The 1975 Senate Hearing

Testifying before the Senate panel in 1975 was then-OE Commissioner Terrel Bell, who was to become, five years later, President Reagan's education secretary. During hearings on S. 6, Bell told Randolph the federal government had a heavy responsibility to increase its commitment to handicapped children. But, Bell continued, the administration thought states were in better fiscal condition than the federal government and should shoulder more of the cost.

Amendments were added to S. 6 in both subcommittee markup and markup by the then-Labor and Public Welfare Committee to require states, to qualify for federal dollars, to spell out how they would reach the goal of providing all students a free appropriate public education.

The bill, after full committee markup, also set out specific due process guarantees for handicapped children in identification, evaluation and placement. A requirement was also added that handicapped children be educated alongside their nonhandicapped peers to the maximum extent appropriate.

Initially the bill called for annual individualized educational programs (IEPs) for every handicapped child, but the full committee replaced IEPs with a requirement that schools hold three planning conferences a year with the teacher, parents and child.

The subcommittee reported out an S. 6 that would give the states a flat $400 payment for each handicapped child they educated. The allotment dropped to $300 per child in full committee markup.

The Senate bill would have limited to 10 percent of a state's school-age population the number of handicapped children for whom states could receive federal funds. And to monitor compliance with the law, S. 6 called for each state to set up a board or commission to evaluate programs and receive complaints from individuals on compliance with the law.

S. 6, after markup, also said 40 percent of the money given to a state had to pass through to local education agencies with the remaining 60 percent allotted by the state: first for children who were not being educated at all and second for the most severely handicapped children.

### Senate Floor Action

The full Senate passed S. 6 on June 18, 1975, by a vote of 83-10. During debate that day, senator after senator rose in support of the measure. Their sentiments ran much like this comment from the late Sen. Hubert Humphrey, D-Minn., who said, "I believe a profound injustice has been suffered by these handicapped children of school age who are excluded from public schools."

Dissent came mainly on the high projected cost of the measure. Sen. Howard Baker, R-Tenn., said, "I feel that enactment of S. 6 . . . would be a step backward in our efforts to hold down federal spending." Baker said he intended to vote against the bill, but he then had to leave, and was one of six senators who did not vote on the measure.

### House Action

While the Senate was reporting its bill out of full committee, Brademas's House Select Education Subcommittee was marking up its companion bill, H.R. 7217.

The House bill set a formula for distributing money rather than a flat grant system. Under the formula, states would receive payment for each handicapped child equal to 50 percent more than the amount it cost to educate a nonhandicapped child.

H.R. 7217 also specified that no more than 12 percent of all children aged 5 to 17 could be counted as handicapped; the comparable Senate level was 10 percent.

The House bill also would have required that all federal funds flow straight through to local school districts, much to the chagrin of the Council of Chief State School Officers. The chiefs pushed for allocating funds to the state agencies because the state was responsible for monitoring local schools.

The House Education and Labor Committee, under the leadership of the late Rep. Carl Perkins, D-Ky., finally decided to let states distribute federal money to local districts with the understanding that funds would "flow through the agency responsible for compliance" to the local schools.

The full committee also retained the subcommittee's funding formula. Brademas successfully shepherded his formula through the markup by promising to make it clear in the report accompanying

the bill that the committee did not necessarily expect that the estimated $3 billion to $4 billion it would take to fully fund the bill
would be forthcoming from appropriations committees.

The House bill included a cap within a cap. Along with a 12
percent limit on the numbers of handicapped children for which a
state could receive funding, it placed a limit of 2 percent on the
number of learning disabled children for whom a state could receive
funding until OE more clearly defined learning disability.

The House July 29, 1975, passed H.R. 2717, 375-44, rechristen-
ing it S. 6 to conform with the Senate measure. Debate ran much as
did the Senate discourse; members rose one after another to praise
the bill. Again, only budgetary concerns were raised.

### Conference Action

Although the bills carried the same number, there was a wide gulf
between them. Among the issues needing discussion was the essential matter of money. Just how many dollars would schools get to
educate their handicapped children?

The Senate bill, if fully funded, would carry a price tag of $1.2
billion while the House version carried a potential check of between
$3 billion and $4 billion.

House and Senate conferees had to resolve the House's 12 percent
cap on the number of children age 5 to 17 who could be counted as
handicapped versus the Senate's 10 percent cap on children age 3 to
21. Also needing resolution was the House's 2 percent cap on the
number of learning disabled students, as the Senate bill contained
no such ceiling.

The report that emerged from the conference — later to become
law — entitled states and schools to payment for all handicapped
children aged 3 to 21 through a formula that based federal payments
on a percentage of average per-pupil expenditures ranging from 5
percent in 1978 to 40 percent in 1982. The report, however, let states
decide whether they would provide education to handicapped children aged 3-5 and 18-21.

The conference report also required that by 1978, 50 percent of a
state's money be passed through to school districts with the local
share increasing to 75 percent in 1979, and states keeping the
remaining 25 percent for administration.

It also called for a $300 incentive payment for every child 3 to 5
years old served in special education and set 1980 as the year when
a free, appropriate public education would have to be available to
all handicapped children if states wanted to keep getting federal
money under the law.

### "*P.L. 94-142 Was Law*"

The conference report sailed through the House Nov. 18 on a 404-7 vote and through the Senate Nov. 19 on an 87-7 vote. Rep. Robert Michel, R-Ill., chairman of the House Appropriations Committee, went along with the bill's enormous potential price tag of $3 billion to $4 billion but warned against falsely raising hopes that all the money ever would be appropriated.

The House's cap of 12 percent on a state's 5- to 17-year-old population being classified as handicapped remained in place, as did its 2 percent cap on the numbers of learning disabled children for whom a state could receive funding.

The report also kept the House requirement that every handicapped child have an individualized education program to be reviewed annually.

\* \* \*

When President Ford, to everyone's surprise, signed the bill, he wrote at length about its high price tag. The law "promises more than the federal government can deliver" and contains "many unwise provisions," including "a vast array of detailed, complex and costly administrative requirements . . . under which tax dollars would be used to support administrative paperwork and not educational programs."

"Even the strongest supporters of this measure know as well as I that they are falsely raising the expectations of the groups affected by claiming authorization levels which are excessive and unrealistic," Ford said. "The funding levels proposed in this bill will simply not be possible if federal expenditures are to be brought under control and a balanced budget achieved over the next few years."

Ford went on to say that because the law would not become fully effective until 1978, there was still time to revise it and come up with an "effective and realistic" program. "I will work with the Congress to use this time to design a program which will recognize the proper federal role in helping states and localities fulfill their responsibilities in educating handicapped children."

But Congress had no intention of going back to the drawing board. P.L. 94-142 was law and it was time to move ahead.

# 2

# Regulatory History

*The original P.L. 94-142 regulations were "never really controversial" because "compromises were developed as we went along."*
— *Edwin Martin, former head of the Bureau of Education for the Handicapped*

The most memorable event in the history of P.L. 94-142 rule-making came not, as with most laws, in the struggle to write those original rules, but in a politically costly attempt to rewrite them.

Nowhere in the annals of Education Department history have so many people complained so loudly as they did after President Reagan, two months into his term, ordered massive government deregulation that was to include special education.

ED officials tried to do everything right. Before starting their rewrite, they asked for guidance from educators in the field. The response they received—educators urged cutting some reporting requirements and limiting the related services that schools must provide handicapped children—convinced ED officials to go on.

But they underestimated the passion out there.

In February 1982 an internal draft was circulating that called for dramatically streamlining the rules, deleting, for example, the list of related services for handicapped children.

Public outcry began immediately. As Reagan sent his 1983 budget to Congress, 350 lawmakers drafted a plea asking him to maintain federal support for P.L. 94-142. Two months later, delegates to a Council for Exceptional Children convention overwhelming voted to oppose administration policy on special education.

On Aug. 4, 1982, ED published its proposals, which were nearly identical to the draft, and received 30,000 written comments, the most ever received for any ED proposal. The vast majority—insiders said up to 99 percent—opposed the proposals.

The outcry continued at hearings around the country. In Portland, Maine, advocates filled a wheelbarrow with copies of the regulations, set them on fire and dumped the ashes in front of ED representatives, who have privately described the road show as the low point in their careers.

The political damage was complete and then-ED Secretary Terrel Bell dropped the regulations. Former ED Undersecretary Gary Bauer, assessing the first Reagan term, said the experience had "so poisoned the well" that another deregulation attempt "would be politically impossible to accomplish."

### Drafting The Regulations

Back in 1976, when officials at the then-Office of Education (OE) started drafting those regulations, no one could have foreseen that an effort to change their handiwork would result in so much chaos.

Even though the law did not have the solid support of the Ford administration, OE staff began work immediately after the bill was signed on a package of regulations to implement P.L. 94-142.

By January 1976, the office had contracted with the Council for Exceptional Children to develop three slide presentations geared, alternately, to parents, general audiences and school administrators, explaining the massive new law and seeking suggestions for regulations to enforce it.

In March 1976, OE took the law to the field and brought to Washington, D.C. — for the first of six meetings — 70 representatives of school and advocacy groups to gather advice on drawing up regulations.

Other meetings were conducted throughout 1976 with representatives from governors' offices and state legislatures and with colleges and universities that received special education training grants.

Rumors were flying that some states would opt out of the federal plan because of the complexities of the law, and OE's Bureau of Education for the Handicapped (BEH) was trying to offset that by gathering as much information on state concerns as possible before sitting down to write the rules.

BEH also tried to stem states' growing fears by reassuring them that the new regulations would be kept "free of educational, legal and bureaucratic jargon."

Edwin Martin, who headed BEH at the time, said in a recent interview that the regulations were "never really controversial" because "compromises were developed as we went along."

### The Proposed Rules

OE was under particular pressure to come up with rules for identifying learning disabled students because only after an acceptable definition was developed would Congress eliminate its 2 percent cap on the numbers of learning disabled handicapped children for whom a state could receive funding.

So officials decided to split the regulatory package in two. Proposed regulations for evaluating learning disabilities were published in the *Federal Register* on Nov. 29, 1976. A 120-day comment period was allowed and OE received more than 980 letters.

Many of the comments criticized the proposal for relying on a formula based on a child's intelligence quotient, or IQ, to determine if a 50 percent discrepancy existed between the child's expected and actual achievement. If such a discrepancy existed, the child could be counted as learning disabled under the proposal.

The main body of the proposed regulations were published in the *Federal Register* Dec. 30, 1976, 13 months after P.L. 94-142 became law.

The proposed rules covered seven specific areas: general provisions of the law, annual state plans, provision of a free appropriate public education, participation of private school children, due process procedures, state administration of funds and conditions for allocating state grants.

OE received more than 1,600 comments on the proposal, with many of those requesting a delay of the Sept. 1, 1978, deadline imposed on states for providing appropriate education to its handicapped children.

Educators also suggested that the requirement to provide each handicapped student with an individualized education program be deleted from the requirements unless more federal money was made available to pay for them.

Rumblings from the state were getting louder and in March 1977 the Florida state legislature voted to refuse federal money under P.L. 94-142 because it thought the law and accompanying regulations forced "those states with established ongoing quality programs to either compromise state laws and existing programs or to refuse money which is badly needed."

The Florida appropriations committee said, "Until such time as the federal government recognizes that unless the civil or legal rights of individuals are violated, the state and not the federal government is best qualified to direct its total system of public education."

### Final Regulations

Despite state concern over the proposed regulations, few substantive changes were made and final regulations were signed Aug. 15,

1977, by Hale Champion, undersecretary of Health, Education and Welfare, and published in the Aug. 23 *Federal Register.*

Immediately after publishing those rules, OE went back to the drawing board to refine the learning disability rules and published a final version in the *Federal Register* on Dec. 29, 1977.

The new rules defining learning disabilities relied heavily on the evaluation of a multidisciplinary team consisting of a child's classroom teacher and at least one person qualified to conduct individual diagnostic examinations of children, such as school psychologists, speech pathologists or remedial reading teachers.

Publication of those rules paved the way for Congress to lift the cap in February 1978 on the number of learning disabled students a state could count for federal reimbursement.

* * *

The requirement that states provide a free appropriate public education to all handicapped children went into effect Sept. 1, 1978, and all states except New Mexico had filed plans by October 1977 to receive federal money under the new law. Despite its concerns, Florida, like most other states, could not resist the lure of added federal money. New Mexico joined the rest of the union six years later, and signed on to P.L. 94-142.

Although nearly all the regulations were published except those on the removal of architectural barriers and handicapped Indian or military children, OE was not out of the regulatory game.

November 1977 found BEH head Martin writing to the Council of Chief State School Officers, with a clarification that schools must provide handicapped children with the services they need, not just those that were available in the schools. Martin's letter was intended to clear up any confusion created by a change in language from the proposed rules to the final rules that some schools had misinterpreted.

Included among those services, explained Martin, were transportation needs and the corrective and supportive services required by a handicapped child.

OE reported in August 1978 that "anxiety" was high as states approached the Sept. 1 deadline for providing a free, appropriate public education to all handicapped children.

OE officials said some states had to rewrite education codes, change state board policies, establish interagency agreements and ask for new state legislation. In addition, some states had to make major changes in their due process procedures in order to comply with P.L. 94-142.

# 3

# Litigation History

*"In these days, it is doubtful that any child may reasonably*
*be expected to succeed in life if he is denied the opportunity*
*of an education. Such an opportunity . . . is a right which*
*must be made available to all on equal terms."*
— *U.S. Supreme Court,*
*Brown v. Board of Education, 1954*

Two decades before Congress enacted P.L. 94-142, the U.S.
Supreme Court cleared a path for special education law, in a case in
which the students who sued were not handicapped: the racial desegregation decision in *Brown v. Board of Education* (347 U.S. 483).

"In these days," wrote the justices, in a passage quoted by congressional authors of P.L. 94-142, "it is doubtful that any child may
reasonably be expected to succeed in life if he is denied the opportunity of an education. Such an opportunity, where the state has undertaken to provide it, is a right which must be made available to all
on equal terms."

In the late 1960s, handicapped rights advocates brought the principle of *Brown* — the bold application of the Constitution's equal protection clause — to their own clients' cases. Results at first were
mixed or limited.

Then lightning struck in 1971 with *Pennsylvania Association of
Retarded Citizens (PARC) v. Commonwealth* (334 F. Supp. 1257).
In a consent decree that settled a class action for mentally retarded
children, Pennsylvania discarded a state law that relieved schools of
the responsibility to enroll "uneducable" or "untrainable" children.
On the basis of extensive expert testimony, the federal district court
in Philadelphia entered a "finding" that mentally retarded children
can benefit from education and are entitled to it.

"The groundbreaking lightning bolt there was [the notion] that
these kids could learn. Up until then we warehoused our kids in institutions, because 'those poor kids aren't educable, God bless
them,'" remembered Reed Martin, an attorney with Advocacy Inc.

27

in Texas. "*PARC* was a consciousness-raising; it wasn't just a legal decision. It printed the bumper stickers" for disability rights.

But *PARC* may have gone further than the case warranted, some school lawyers say. "I think we could have come to where we are without *PARC*," said Gwen Gregory, deputy general counsel at the National School Boards Association (NSBA). "We may have come a lot further [by litigation] than we had to come."

Just one year after *PARC*, the federal district court in Washington, D.C., went further in *Mills v. Board of Education* (348 F. Supp. 866). While admitting it was not living up to its duty to provide special education for handicapped children, the city school board pleaded lack of funds as an excuse. But the court quoted *Brown*'s "equal terms" language and said the board had to educate all pupils, whatever their handicaps, even if funds were tight. Constitutional rights are rights even if they are costly, the court said, ruling that handicapped students should no more bear the brunt of the district's financial or administrative shortcomings than nonhandicapped students do.

The *PARC* agreement and the *Mills* ruling laid not just the foundation but some of the building blocks of P.L. 94-142. Not only did handicapped children win access to school, but the state had to locate and evaluate them and design for each an individual program. Schools could not change placements without due process, and integration was favored over more restrictive placements.

The two cases later were credited with establishing the right of handicapped children to special public education, but still, "there wasn't a clear precedent" that could be transferred to every state beyond Pennsylvania and the District of Columbia, said Martin. "So when you took a case between '71 and '75, you knew you could win; you just had to be creative." Between *Mills* and the passage of P.L. 94-142, special education advocates pursued at least 46 suits in 28 states.

Courts at first were loath to involve themselves in the day-to-day operations of schools, their hands already full with desegregation, busing and equal education for women. In that atmosphere, some school districts thought they had nothing to fear, according to Martin, while others were struggling to figure out exactly what was required of them and how they were expected to pay for it.

Congress passed P.L. 94-142 in 1975, and "From '77 to '80, there was this very heady time when you could win any case," if you represented the handicapped child, said Martin. "It was like shooting fish in a barrel."

As schools adjusted to the act, the pace of litigation steadied. Meanwhile, implementation of the rulings handicapped students won was sometimes slow: eight years after *Mills,* the Washington, D.C., school board was held in contempt of court for failing to meet the timetables set out in the decision.

Once handicapped students had access to school, by and large, litigation turned to the questions that arose there and the definitions of terms under P.L. 94-142: discipline, payment for private placements, racially discriminatory testing, related services, extended services, the definition of "appropriate" education and other issues.

The year P.L. 94-142 became law, the U.S. Supreme Court spoke on students' rights during disciplinary action in *Goss v. Lopez* (419 U.S. 565), which was the basis for later discipline rulings concerning handicapped students. Calling the right to a public education a protected property interest, which cannot be revoked without due process, *Goss* overturned an Ohio law allowing suspensions of up to 10 days with no hearing.

For any suspension, a student has the right to "notice of the charges against him" and some hearing, "at least an informal give-and-take between student and disciplinarian, preferably prior to the suspension," the Court said. Suspensions longer than 10 days or expulsions "may require more formal procedures;" on the other hand, "in unusual situations," even a short suspension may require "something more than the rudimentary procedures."

Special education raised special questions, answered in disparate rulings that culminated finally in two federal appeals court decisions. In 1981, the 5th U.S. Circuit Court of Appeals ruled in *S-1 v. Turlington* (635 F.2d 342; cert. denied, 454 U.S. 1030) that expulsion is a change of placement demanding a hearing and due process consistent with P.L. 94-142, provided the misbehavior is a manifestation of the handicap. Also, the child must continue receiving some services after an expulsion, *S-1* said.

The court also assigned to the school the burden of determining whether the misconduct is a manifestation of the student's handicap. School officials often are not qualified to determine whether misbehavior is caused by the child's handicap, and a specialist may have to make that judgment, the court added. The 6th Circuit reached the same conclusion the next year in *Kaelin v. Grubbs* (682 F.2d 595).

Meanwhile, Pennsylvania, home of the landmark *PARC* case, became the scene of another groundbreaking ruling, when the 3rd Circuit in 1980 affirmed a decision in *Battle v. Commonwealth of Pennsylvania* (629 F.2d 269) that overturned a state policy against offering summer school. The court said a 180-day limit on the public school schedule violated P.L. 94-142 because it precluded proper determination of what constitutes an appropriate education.

NSBA predicted an $830 million jump in the yearly cost of special education, nationwide, after *Battle*. Despite the association's pleas, the Supreme Court let the ruling stand (452 U.S. 968). Court after court came to the same decision, requiring extended programming where it would benefit a child. The principle disturbed the schools. "I think the potential was there for tremendous problems," Gregory said, "but I don't think that has happened."

The Supreme Court did not take a case under P.L. 94-142 until 1981, when it heard *Hendrick Hudson v. Rowley* (458 U.S. 176), in which parents sued the school system to obtain a sign-language interpreter for their deaf daughter. Amy Rowley was well-adjusted and performing above average in her first grade class, and the school had gone to considerable lengths for her, but she would have been doing better if not for her handicap, noted the district court. The court said an appropriate education is one that provides "an opportunity to achieve [a child's] full potential commensurate with the opportunity provided to other children."

"The handicapped groups were not happy about that case going up, because the facts were so good for the school district," NSBA's Gregory said. "Really, it was almost a situation where you couldn't lose it."

In its 1982 ruling, the Court said P.L. 94-142 guarantees handicapped students an educational opportunity, but not an equal educational opportunity. The school is not required to "maximize each [handicapped] child's potential 'commensurate with the opportunity provided other children,'" the Court said, noting that schools cannot even equalize nonhandicapped students' chances of maximizing their potential.

The justices also told courts to limit themselves to two questions in special education cases. The first is whether the state has complied with the procedures in the act, including adopting — through the district — an individualized education program (IEP) conforming to the law. The second asks whether the IEP is "reasonably calculated to enable the child to receive educational benefits." For a child mainstreamed in a regular classroom, the IEP "should be reasonably calculated to enable the child to achieve passing marks and advance from grade to grade," the Court added.

Joe Scherer, associate executive director of the American Association of School Administrators at the time, was relieved. "We don't want to deny the opportunity [of] adequate education," he said then, "but we don't want to be providing the Cadillac of the line." For schools, the ruling meant the courts would defer more to their educational judgment.

Handicapped rights advocates initially were unsettled by the limits imposed by *Rowley*. Finally, however, "everybody claimed a win," Gregory said. The decision, after all, upheld the basic tenets of P.L. 94-142. Things could have gone a lot worse for handicapped children, advocacy groups said.

The Supreme Court two years later in *Irving Independent School District v. Tatro* (468 U.S. 883) said Amber Tatro was entitled to catheterization at school. Tatro, who could catheterize herself by the time her case reached the high court, had the service performed by a school nurse every three to four hours because delaying it could cause kidney damage.

The school district argued, "Catheterization today, kidney dialysis tomorrow." But the unanimous Court quoted P.L. 94-142's definition of free appropriate education as "special education and [such] related services . . . as may be required to assist a handicapped child to benefit from special education." Catheterization for Tatro amounted to access to school; without it, her IEP would not conform to the act.

The district pointed out that the act excludes medical services other than diagnostics, but the Court responded that catheterization does not require a licensed physician, the crucial factor established in the Education Department regulations. In fact, a layperson with less than an hour's training could do the job in a few minutes.

Later that year, the Supreme Court without comment refused to review a 3rd Circuit decision in *Piscataway Township Board of Education v. T.G.* (cert. denied, 53 U.S.L.W. 3436) that said psychotherapy for an emotionally disturbed student qualifies as a related service under P.L. 94-142. *Piscataway* is one of a line of cases that distinguish psychological services by a licensed physician — not provided under the act — from those of a psychologist, who is not a medical doctor.

The lower courts meanwhile continued working out the special education response to generic education questions. In *Debra P. v. Turlington* (644 F.2d 397 and 730 F.2d 1405), the 5th and 11th circuits found Florida's minimum competency test — a prerequisite for graduation — racially discriminatory because black students failed in disproportionate numbers as a result of prior segregation. The courts also said a state must give students timely notice of the requirement (probably upon entering high school), establish the validity of its test and guarantee that the material on it was presented in the curriculum.

As *Goss* did in the discipline area, *Debra P.* laid the groundwork for judicial standards on graduation requirements for special education students. In 1983, the 7th Circuit upheld the right of a school district to require handicapped students to pass examinations before receiving diplomas, in *Brookhart v. Illinois State Board of Education* (697 F.2d 179). And in 1984 the Supreme Court refused to review a New York school board's challenge of the use of competency tests as a graduation requirement for handicapped children, in *Board of Education v. Ambach* (458 N.Y.S., 2d 680, 684 [N.Y. App. Div. 1982]). The state has since created special education diplomas for students completing their IEPs.

While the lower courts enforced the school district's responsibility for the costs of private placement under an IEP, the Supreme Court went further in 1985, in a ruling that surprised even some special education advocacy workers.

The Court decided unanimously, in *Burlington School Committee v. Department of Education* (53 U.S.L.W. 4509), that parents who unilaterally place their handicapped children in private schools are entitled to reimbursement if a court later finds the placement is more appropriate than what the public school had offered.

"I think a lot of the reason people were surprised [by *Burlington*] was that they had lived with the *Stemple* doctrine," Gregory said, referring to a 1980 ruling by the 4th Circuit, *Stemple v. Board of Education of Prince George's County* (623 F.2d 893). *Stemple* said parents who unilaterally transfer their child are not necessarily entitled to tuition reimbursement, and the Supreme Court declined to review the case.

*Smith v. Robinson* (468 U.S. 992), the Supreme Court's only other decision so far under P.L. 94-142, immediately was "appealed" — to Congress — and overruled. In *Smith* a divided Court held that P.L. 94-142 is the exclusive avenue for relief in special education complaints, and because the act, in all its detail, did not provide for attorneys' fees for parents who win their cases, parents cannot collect fees from schools by adding claims under Section 504 of the 1973 Rehabilitation Act or other federal civil rights laws.

The 1986 bill that overturned *Smith,* the Handicapped Children's Protection Act, P.L. 99-372, states it is Congress's intent that fees be allowed under P.L. 94-142. Under P.L. 99-372, once parents have exhausted all administrative routes to resolving a special education dispute, they may sue a district not only under P.L. 94-142 but under the Rehabilitation Act, the Constitution and the statute allowing for suits that allege a deprivation of a federal right by a state or local agency.

But the issue is not ready to rest in peace. With the ink barely dry after the president signed the measure, school attorneys were questioning the law's retroactivity and its provision for fees for legal work in cases resolved at the administrative levels. Their questions are sure to have a day in court.

Meanwhile the Supreme Court announced its fifth foray into P.L. 94-142: The justices in early 1987 agreed to review the law's "stay put" provision as it applies to discipline of students whose handicap is responsible for violent misbehavior. In the lower court ruling, the 9th Circuit said that apart from imposing a limited disciplinary suspension, a school district cannot change a violent student's special education placement over parental objections without going through the normal due process steps to adopt a new education plan.

Although that case, *Honig v. Doe* (55 U.S.L.W. 3569), just reached the Supreme Court, and other cases certainly may follow, the federal courts in more than a decade of P.L. 94-142 litigation have issued guidance on many of the most important and commonly occurring issues.

"There's still going to be lots and lots of little, annual battles, but hopefully we've got some standards," said Martin. "What I worry about is, somewhere some kid is going to be getting catheterization, get an infection, get kidney damage, and sue the school."

## P.L. 94-142: LEGAL MILESTONES IN THE EDUCATION OF HANDICAPPED CHILDREN

### 1954
*Brown v. Board of Education of Topeka,* 347 U.S. 483

The U.S. Supreme Court ruled that the opportunity of an education, where the state has undertaken to provide it, is a right that must be made available to all on equal terms.

### 1971
*Pennsylvania Association for Retarded Children (PARC) v. Commonwealth of Pennsylvania,* 334 F. Supp. 1257 (E.D. Pa. 1971) and 343 F. Supp. 279 (E.D. Pa. 1972)

Settling a class action suit for the right to education for retarded children, the court-approved consent decree stated that all mentally retarded persons are capable of benefiting from education, and they have a right to a public education. The case overturned a Pennsylvania statute relieving the state of responsibility to educate students classified as uneducable or untrainable.

**1972**

*Mills v. Board of Education of the District of Columbia*, 348 F. Supp. 866 (D.D.C. 1972)

The federal district court ordered that if the school system's funds are insufficient for all the programs that are needed and desirable, then the available funds must be spent equitably so that no child is entirely excluded from education consistent with his or her needs and ability to benefit. The financial or administrative inadequacies of the school system should not bear more heavily on handicapped children than on nonhandicapped children.

**1975**

*Goss v. Lopez*, 419 U.S. 565 (1975)

The U.S. Supreme Court ruled that students suspended for 10 days or fewer have the right to an informal conference, and that suspensions longer than 10 days may require a formal hearing. Though the students involved here were not handicapped, the decision became the basis of later discipline rulings in special education.

**1975**

*Passage of P.L. 94-142*

**1980**

*Battle v. Commonwealth of Pennsylvania*, 629 F.2d 269 (3rd Cir. 1980) [on appeal of the decision in *Armstrong v. Kline*, 476 F. Supp. 583 (E.D. P.A. 1979)]; cert. denied, 452 U.S. 968 (1981)

The circuit court overturned a Pennsylvania state policy against offering summer school, saying that a 180-day limit on instruction precludes proper determination of what constitutes an appropriate education under P.L. 94-142.

**1981**

*S-1 v. Turlington*, 635 F.2d 342 (5th Cir. 1981); cert. denied, 454 U.S. 1030 (1981)

The circuit court ruled that expelling a student for reasons related to his or her handicap is a change of placement, which requires a hearing consistent with P.L. 94-142 due process procedures; that services cannot cease completely even if a student is expelled; and that determining whether misbehavior is related to a student's handicap typically is not within the expertise of school board members. Followed by a similar circuit court decision, *Kaelin v. Grubbs*, 682 F.2d 595 (6th Cir. 1982).

**1981 and 1984**
*Debra P. v. Turlington,* 644 F.2d 397 (5th Cir. 1981) and 730 F.2d 1405 (11th Cir. 1984)

The circuit courts ruled that a state must establish the validity of its minimum competency tests and, if the tests are a prerequisite for graduation, ensure that the material on the tests was included in the curriculum. Though the *Debra P.* students were not handicapped, the decision became the basis of later special education rulings on testing.

Similar rulings applying those principles to special education, mainly on the basis of the Constitution's equal protection and due process clauses and Section 504 of the Rehabilitation Act, included *Anderson v. Banks,* 520 F. Supp. 472 (S.D. Ga. 1981), modified, 540 F. Supp. 761 (1982); *Northport-East Northport Union Free School District v. Ambach,* 458 N.Y.S.2d 680, 684 (N.Y. App. Div. 1982); and *Brookhart v. Illinois State Board of Education,* 697 F.2d 179 (7th Cir. 1983).

**1982**
*Hendrick Hudson Central School District v. Rowley,* 458 U.S. 176 (1982)

Reversing the district and appeals courts, the U.S. Supreme Court ruled 6-3 that federal law does not guarantee that handicapped students' individualized instruction will maximize their potential commensurate with the opportunities provided other children. The ruling strengthened earlier lower court decisions, such as *Bales v. Clarke,* 523 F. Supp. 1366, 1370 (E.D. Va. 1981), which said P.L. 94-142 does not require that the "best" program be selected, only that the selected program be appropriate.

**1984**
*Irving Independent School District v. Tatro,* 468 U.S. 883

The U.S. Supreme Court unanimously held that catheterization is a "related service" that schools must provide to students who need it during the school day, and the Court buttressed Education Department regulations defining "related services" to include school health services that don't have to be performed by a licensed physician.

**1984**
*Smith v. Robinson,* 468 U.S. 992

The U.S. Supreme Court ruled 6-3 that parents who win their cases under P.L. 94-142 cannot collect fees for their cases merely by adding claims under the 14th Amendment, Section 1983 of the 1971 Civil Rights Act or Section 504 of the 1973 Rehabilitation Act.

**1985**
*Burlington School Committee v. Department of Education*, 53 U.S.L.W. 4509

The U.S. Supreme Court ruled unanimously that parents who unilaterally place their handicapped children in private schools are entitled to receive tuition reimbursement if the placement is ultimately deemed proper in court.

**1987**
*Honig v. Doe*, 55 U.S.L.W. 3569

The Supreme Court agreed to review a 1986 decision by the 9th Circuit (called *Doe v. Maher* [793 F.2d 1470]) saying that — apart from a limited suspension set by state law — a school cannot change a violent student's special education placement without adopting a new education plan and giving the parents a chance to challenge it; courts may order exceptions in "truly exigent" cases, however. *Maher* also said the state education agency must serve an individual handicapped child directly if that pupil's school district has failed to provide a free, appropriate public education. The Court was likely to rule on both questions by July 1988.

# 4

# Advances In
# Teaching Methods

*In place of the Dick and Jane series that for years was
standard reading fare for handicapped children even into
their teens, publishers now produce low-ability level
readers featuring everything from rock stars to news
events.*

Money allocated under P.L. 94-142 has bolstered research that
dramatically changed common conceptions of how disabled people
learn, leading to changes in teaching, publishing and technology for
the handicapped.

The "fad diet" approach to special education learning theories
prior to the law represented "an honest search by a frustrated group
of people grasping for straws," said Alan Hofmeister, a special education professor at Utah State University. It resulted from a lack of
coordinated research efforts on the part of "anxious, diverse people
reaching out for solutions."

Despite special educators' good intentions, however, "if you consider that hundreds of thousands [of them] were taking kids' time
doing things that didn't work," the damage to children was considerable, Hofmeister said.

As recently as the mid-1970s, many special educators believed
"structural deficits" made it impossible for a mentally retarded or
learning disabled child to learn to read, said Ellen Peters, director
of training for the Council for Exceptional Children's (CEC) Department of Professional Development.

But what arose out of P.L. 94-142-funded research was a body of
data to support the once-controversial theory that "handicapped kids
are a lot more similar" to their nonhandicapped peers than they are
different, said Hofmeister.

The approach supported by research focused not on handicapped
children's limitations but on their potential to succeed, Hofmeister

37

said. Rather than concentrating on "what is wrong with the way handicapped children learn," Peters added, researchers began to look at "how to change their environment" to encourage learning.

Hofmeister said research studies funded under the law concluded that the popular perceptual-motor approach, intended to strengthen a child's mental processes by improving hand-eye coordination, was largely ineffective in improving academic performance.

While advocates of this approach believed exercises such as "throwing beanbags at a target" would eventually improve reading, research showed "if you wanted to teach a child to read, you better teach him directly," Hofmeister said.

In addition, said University of Pittsburgh researcher Margaret Wang, studies conducted with funds generated by P.L. 94-142 disclosed that handicapped children perform as well or better in regular classrooms than in segregated ones.

In 50 studies Wang reviewed that compared the academic performance of integrated and segregated handicapped students, the mean academic performance of the integrated group was in the 80th percentile, while the segregrated students scored in the 50th percentile.

Ellen Peters, who received her Ph.D. in special education from Arizona State University in 1983, said today's special education majors are learning "many more precise skills" for assessing children's needs, designing and delivering individualized lessons, monitoring children's progress and evaluating their performance. Today's teacher trainees are learning "how to teach as opposed to how to weave baskets," Peters said.

### The Publishers Respond

When Laurie Batchelor of Grolier Electronic Publishing taught mentally retarded students in the early 1970s, the prevailing theory among publishers was that general education products that "work well with kindergarteners will satisfy sixth-grade special education students. The only materials available for special education were some perceptual motor products." Batchelor is director of educational microcomputer software for the New York-based firm.

But schools' increased spending power for special education under P.L. 94-142 has provoked a strong response from publishers, said Batchelor, who believes "we've gotten away from teachers going home at night and spending four, five and six hours developing ditto masters" they can now buy for their students.

In 1975, according to the Education Department's Office of Special Education Programs (OSEP), only 12 textbook publishers marketed special education textbooks, guides and other classroom materials. In 1985, more than 100 commercial vendors supply special education products, according to LINC Resources, an OSEP-funded clearinghouse for special education materials.

Since P.L. 94-142's enactment, the number of materials available for special education has increased by more than 500 percent, according to OSEP's Patty Guard.

Besides prodding publishers to depict handicapped people in textbooks, Batchelor said, the law has prompted them to produce more "low-ability level, high-interest products." In place of the Dick and Jane series that for years was standard reading fare for handicapped children even into their teens, publishers now produce low-ability level readers featuring everything from rock stars to news events. Some issue a new reader as often as once a week, Batchelor said.

But Kathy Hurley, Grolier's vice president of microcomputer software, maintains the law has had little effect on textbook publishers, who she said are "not very concerned" with catering to the special education market. She said P.L. 94-142's impact has been most significant on publishers of supplemental materials such as workbooks, teachers' guides and worksheets. Before moving to Grolier in April 1984, Hurley worked for one such publisher, Developmental Learning Materials, for 11 years.

"I definitely have seen a much more enthusiastic response" from supplemental publishers than from textbook publishers as a result of P.L. 94-142, agreed Judy Wilson of Kansas's Microcomputer Information Coordination Center. Wilson said the law prodded publishers to create supplementary materials that could be used with students at either end of the ability scale instead of aiming products at "the mid-point child."

Supplementary classroom materials for secondary school special education students have improved "by leaps and bounds" under the law, said Batchelor, who pointed to the proliferation of filmstrips, workbooks, guides and computer programs that teach these students "survival skills for daily living."

### Technology In The Classroom

Ten years ago many simple science experiments would have been considered too dangerous, impractical or physically demanding for many handicapped students. Today, even students with severe physical disabilities can blend volatile chemicals or dissect a frog with ease and safety using a microcomputer.

The technological revolution occurring in today's classrooms was not ignited by special education legislation. But P.L. 94-142 funds have helped outfit handicapped students with microcomputers and fueled research efforts to explore how computers affect learning.

Though the verdict is not in on the long-term effects of computerized learning on handicapped students, the computer is a powerful tool for teaching handicapped students both basic skills and complex problem solving.

Because they do not tire or become frustrated, computers are uniquely suited for learning disabled children, whose often-slow learning processes can try a teacher's patience. And because they are "versatile enough so you can build in programs that meet a wide range of students' abilities, computers offer unique possibilities for individualized instruction," said Susan Elting, who directs CEC's Center for Special Education Technology.

Louise Appell of Macro Systems Inc. predicted that as the well of general education funds, already drained by school microcomputer purchases, runs dry, software publishers will eye the special education market with a keener interest. These publishers will find that "when the rest of education gets soft, special education still has money to spend and is thirsty for high quality materials," Appell said. "When they catch on, they'll get religion very fast."

Alan Brightman, director of Apple Computer's special education unit, argues that the point may be moot. "In my opinion, there shouldn't be special education software: only good educational software made better by sound education practices" in special education.

Brightman said the "growing reliance that there will be disks in the world branded for special education" is at odds with the purpose of P.L. 94-142. "It is wrong to keep building walls between regular and special education," said Brightman, who believes the question should not be "what is the best special education software, but what are the best teaching processes" for using quality software of any kind in an integrated classroom.

Though Brightman's sentiments may seem controversial to some special educators, they are shared by many of the law's advocates. "Many of us have come to the conclusion that the special education software market is not going to develop to the extent we thought it would," CEC's Susan Elting said. As she and her colleagues learn to use existing software more effectively, however, "we are finding it has applications for our kids."

Hofmeister said research funded under the law has spawned "widespread breakthroughs" in technology tailored for education. Under a 1978 OSEP grant, for example, Utah State University engineered the "very first link" between a microcomputer and a laser videodisc player, Hofmeister said.

Laser-driven videodiscs are more durable than other audiovisual devices, produce higher-quality sound and images and allow users to scan thousands of frames in seconds, freeze the action and repeat frames at any point.

When a videodisc player is linked to a microcomputer, "interactive" lessons combining features of both technologies can be designed. The powerful application of computer and laser technology Utah researchers used to teach severely handicapped students to recognize colors and shapes became a prototype for more sophisticated military training programs, Hofmeister said.

For handicapped children unable to communicate through the channels most nondisabled persons take for granted, the most meaningful technological development in the last decade has been a host of devices that lend even those with severe disabilities a way to express themselves. Linked to a microcomputer, apparatus such as voice synthesizers, Braille printers and touch pads have helped handicapped persons compensate for impairments in speech, hearing, sight and manual dexterity. Such devices make composition possible even for "the child who couldn't ever hold a pencil," Wilson said.

These "powerful sensory interpretation systems," now a "standard part" of treatment programs for the sensory impaired, "have only come into being since P.L. 94-142," Hofmeister said.

But some experts, including Batchelor, argue that the earliest work on such devices preceded P.L. 94-142 and was initiated by "a bunch of dedicated people" who emanated not from special education but from the rehabilitation field.

Either way, funds allocated under P.L. 94-142 "allowed us to invest in technology and enhance what we were able to do with it," noted Wilson, who said that before the law, technological experimentation was limited to "trial and error and best guess."

### Breaking Down Stereotypes

Though enriched classroom materials from textbooks to software have improved the quality of education since P.L. 94-142 was passed, they are not the best measure of progress achieved under the law.

"Textbooks are not necessarily a major force in instruction anyway," maintained Hofmeister, who believes "the most important variable is the quality of the teacher's behavior."

And despite headway made in harnessing the computer's power for special education in the last decade, Brightman does not believe technological breakthroughs should be seen as a "central focus of P.L. 94-142. There are hundreds of examples where the integration of computers in the classroom has made a difference," he said, "but it's easy to hype that."

Instead, both Brightman and Hofmeister argue, P.L. 94-142's real success rests in raising public awareness of "who disabled kids are." And besides broadening teachers' and administrators' knowledge of how to work with handicapped students, the law has had a sweeping effect on the general public, advocates say.

Since P.L. 94-142's enactment, said Patty Guard, all forms of the media, from magazines to movies, have contributed to a "significant awareness and understanding of the handicapped individual."

And an "unexpected result of the law" has been its effect on non-disabled schoolchildren, said Brightman. "A very important and easily overlooked component" of P.L. 94-142 has been in breaking down children's stereotypes about their disabled peers, he said. "They are no longer seen as those strange kids down the hall."

While some expectations underlying the passage of P.L. 94-142 have not been met, Brightman concluded, "Those who billed it as the most sweeping legislation" in the history of special education "have not been let down."

# Part Two

# Where Special Education Is Going

# 5

## Money:
### The Special Education Problem That Won't Go Away

*"Districts are on the verge of bankruptcy because of special education."*
— *H. Robert McNiel, director,*
*Cluster 5 Special Education Cooperative,*
*Uvalde, Texas*

Money. Federal policymakers groan when you ask them about it, but it's the special education problem that just won't go away.

P.L. 94-142 promised educators they would receive a sizable percentage of the cost of special education: a full 40 percent of the average per pupil cost by 1982. Instead, the percentage has never exceeded 12 percent.

And many educators feel cheated.

Special education has escaped the massive budget cuts other education programs have experienced; in fact federal spending for P.L. 94-142 state grants has grown from $100 million in fiscal 1976 to $1.34 billion in fiscal 1987.

But the special education increases in recent years have simply kept the program at the 12 percent level; that is, the program, again doing better than other education programs, has stayed just about equal with inflation.

In a survey conducted in 1985 for the first edition of this book, educators agreed overwhelmingly that P.L. 94-142 was placing a financial burden on their jurisdiction: 73.2 percent of the 691 persons responding to that question said yes, while 26.8 percent said no (*see Appendix A*).

When asked to name a solution, 42.5 percent said more federal money, 39.7 percent said more state money, 10.3 percent said raising local taxes, 6.3 percent said reducing services to handicapped students and 1.2 percent said reducing services to nonhandicapped students.

Realistically, though, significantly more federal money is not a possibility. And the nation's top special education policymaker says there's really nothing wrong with that.

When people ask her about money, "the first thing I say is my program has grown," said Madeleine Will, the Education Department's assistant secretary for special education and rehabilitative services. "It may not be increasing at the rate at which people at the state level would like, but it has grown."

And, she added, "It is also the case that when [P.L.] 94-142 was passed . . . it is clear the act was intended to stimulate the development of services at the state and local level, not to create a huge federal program to fund education. And I think that 94-142 seen in that context has been very successful. As an example I would cite early childhood programs, I would cite some of the discretionary programs, the funding of which has allowed for innovative programming to develop."

\* \* \*

No one is arguing that P.L. 94-142 has not had a significant "seed money" affect that has stimulated research and development, curriculum planning and advanced teacher training.

But state, local and regional school administrators say the day to day education of these youngsters takes cold, hard cash that they just don't have.

Bruce Hunter of the American Association of School Administrators put it bluntly: "The federal funding really has slipped to the point where it's really outrageous what a low percentage it is."

Diane Sydoriak, state director of special education in Arkansas, agreed. "Money? Yes, it's a problem. We still have not received from the federal level that which we were promised. There are a lot of requirements that take a lot of money. If it weren't for state funding, 94-142 could not have been implemented."

Hunter adds: "The law has been successful. There's no doubt about that. The only problem people have with the statute is that there is a lack of clarity that has caused schools to incur costs and caused other state agencies to get out of the business of helping handicapped children altogether. Schools shoulder the costs that mental health [and other] agencies used to. Schools can't do that forever."

\* \* \*

Local and regional school administrators have a hard time talking about any aspect of P.L. 94-142 without bringing up money.

Bob White, superintendent of the Gateway Regional High School District in Woodbury Heights, N.J., said, "You're constantly kept up in the air in reference to funding. It's very difficult after your budget is made up and you find out the federal dollars you'd hoped for will not be there. It creates a lot of problems."

Those problems, White said, frequently revolve around administrators' relationships with parents, who may have been promised a certain kind of program when administrators were expecting a certain level of funding. "For example, you say to parents, 'Okay the money is not available, there's a strong possibility we're going to have to cut back.' It causes the school district unnecessary concern. It's a more difficult job being in education today than ever before. . . . Administrators realize everyone wants a share of the pie."

Charles Fields, executive secretary of the Indiana Association of Public School Superintendents, said, "It's a case of government coming forth with a set of priorities and not providing the financial wherewithal."

"There's no question there is a need there, a need that should be met. The education needs and other needs are being met," he said.

But, Fields added, P.L. 94-142 "has placed us in a financial dilemma. The answer basically is [for federal, state and local policymakers] to carefully try to place a price tag . . . on what a program costs and to say this program is important enough to fund at this dollar level. School officials should not testify against meeting the needs of special education youngsters."

\* \* \*

H. Robert McNiel, director of the Cluster 5 special education cooperative in Uvalde, Texas, was one of dozens of local and regional school administrators who used the survey done for this book to voice his concerns about funding.

"The federal requirement placed on school districts to provide service for the more severely handicapped (residential type) will soon 'break' small school districts," McNiel wrote.

In an interview, McNiel expanded on his fears for the rural southwestern Texas districts he deals with every day.

In Texas, as in many other states, small school districts are combined under the umbrella of cooperatives, aided by state funds, for special education. "A smaller district," McNiel explained, "cannot provide all the different kinds of services in serving a handicapped child. We band together to provide diagnosticians, things that one district couldn't possibly afford."

For instance, McNiel's cooperative might hire one speech therapist to serve students from the 11 districts it represents. "A school district with maybe 25 handicapped children would have five that need speech [therapy] and cannot afford a speech therapist," he explained.

But the cooperative approach breaks down when all 11 districts only have, say, one three-year-old with spina bifida and the cooperative has to hire a teacher just for that child. A larger city such as San Antonio will have 10 of these same kinds of children, McNiel said. "They can form one class with one teacher and a couple of aides. It's much more cost-effective."

That is not an isolated example, said McNiel. "We're looking at schools on the verge of bankruptcy anyway."

McNiel and many educators are frustrated over the issue of education versus custodial care. "We need 94-142 to soften requirements where school districts are concerned regarding custodial care. Schools are supposed to focus on education. More and more medical and custodial things are being dropped on school districts. That's okay for big rich ones but not for poor little ones. Three districts [in my cooperative] are on the verge of bankruptcy because of special education."

McNiel and other educators interviewed put much of the blame for high costs on private schools. "We're looking at school districts that may have residential placements that may cost as much as $40,000 and $50,000 for one child," McNiel said.

Representatives of those schools, however, maintain that they are no more costly than public schooling.

"Those are isolated figures they are pulling out," said Frank Kleffner, president of the National Association of Private Schools for Exceptional Children, which represents about 650 of the some 2,700 private special education schools in the country. "There have been a number of local area and state area comparative studies and the data collected in those really doesn't substantiate that it's any more costly in private schools than in the public schools, and in some cases public schools are more expensive."

Kleffner, however, said he could not provide any data on average private school costs. "It's hard to give an average figure. There are so many different categories" of children, he said.

### Regular Education Losing Out?

Other administrators are concerned that special education funding is diverting funds from regular education programs.

Orvin Plucker, superintendent of the Kansas City, Kan., public schools, agrees that something must be done about skyrocketing special education costs.

"It's placed a tremendous strain on resources available for education and there are still needs unmet," said Plucker, whose 23,000-student district includes 3,000 in special education. "The question is whether mandatory service regulations for handicapped children have reached the point where they tend to divert highly important funding to other aspects of school programs. There's a high potential that is taking place in some instances."

The only way to prevent such a situation, he said, "is that any programs that are mandated by either the federal or state government need to be also adequately funded to meet whatever criteria is established. That has not happened. So there is an inevitable diversion of funds."

The solution? "Perhaps there's not a solution, but it's always evolving, compromises are always necessary. It is important we establish priorities — where we allocate funds for education. The priority establishing needs to be done by those responsible for the funds — state legislators are an illustration. That is a state legislative responsibility."

Plucker is among those who think the solution is to look at the entire national budget, not just the education budget, to find more money. And he wouldn't stop with the defense budget, arguing that the nation's youth are losing out to the nation's elderly. "Certainly one of the key questions is whether or not we are neglecting the development of American youth to provide additional security for large numbers of senior citizens who already enjoy large levels of security."

Margaret Burley, director of the Ohio Coalition for the Education of Handicapped Children, also takes a broader look at spending, seeing special education dollars, as most advocates do, as an investment.

"I understand the school systems' position" about money, said Burley, herself the mother of a handicapped child. "But from a cost-benefit point of view to the taxpayer, the spending would be offset by lessened costs on the outside: families able to stay together, reduced child abuse, reduced alcoholism and wife-beating, a number of other social issues. Today, there are a high number of handicapped children who are victims of child abuse. You have to look at the total family, the total problem."

For instance, said Burley, "if we provided early intervention for learning disabled children to develop good behavior management plans early on, we would probably lessen the amount of time they spend in special education, so you're probably going to reduce the number of students who end up in the juvenile justice system."

The question, she said, "is how do taxpayers want to spend their money, in proactive, productive types of activities [such as education] or jails and institutions?"

### Backlash Predicted

It's almost impossible to find an education observer willing to say that P.L. 94-142 is not only too expensive to carry out, but it's good money being thrown after bad legislation.

One who is not only willing but eager to say just that is Scott Thomson, executive director of the National Association of Secondary School Principals.

"It establishes pretty much an ideal program for special education regardless of the cost or regardless of the impact of those expenses to other programs," said Thomson. "So what happens is that money is taken — is stolen — from a mediocre program for average students to pay for an ideal program for special education students. Where's the fairness in that?"

All the reasonable standards that have been set for services to students in other areas of education, Thomson said, "are thrown out the window" by special education, whose students are the only ones "who have the club of federal legislation to beat schools into submission."

So what happens, he said, is the standards for regular education get thrown out the window to make room for the high standards of special education. "You don't have a blindfolded lady of justice trying to keep everything balanced. You have government imposition on one side of the scale and basically no rules or regulations on the other side, only professional knowledge and judgment. It's an unbalanced scale."

Principals, Thomson emphasized, must educate all students, not just some students. "So we have an unfair situation. We have seen class size increase in math classes, social studies, science, to pay for extra teachers who are hired for special education."

Thomson would like to see P.L. 94-142 rewritten to set up a formula that would provide additional money for special education students but also take into account the resources available to the school district. Under such a formula, "wealthy school districts, yes, could spend more on special education, but an average school district would not be stealing from 90 percent of students."

\* \* \*

Thomson admits his position is an unpopular one: "Educators by and large are a faint-hearted lot and they don't like to be engaged in any controversy that would seem to criticize students or cast themselves as not being 100 percent for students.

"No one likes to be seen as a scrooge. No one likes to be seen as callous or insensitive to handicapped kids." So why is he up front about it? "I think it's a bigger issue than that."

While acknowledging that few will support his campaign to drastically reduce the power of P.L. 94-142, Thomson predicts changes will occur anyway.

Communities where resources are "really tight" for the average student will see a backlash from parents of nonhandicapped children, he predicted.

"You're going to have parents saying no one's taking care of my kids, so I'll send them to private school. . . . At the point the average kid's education gets damaged, when nothing is happening for them, parents are going to seek other schools, going to seek a remedy elsewhere, by pulling their kids out of school."

# The Future Of Special Education Litigation

*"Parents and guardians will not lack ardor in seeking to ensure that handicapped children receive all of the benefits to which they are entitled by the Act."*
— *U.S. Supreme Court,*
*Hendrick Hudson Central School District*
*v. Rowley, 1982*

The mandate to educate all handicapped children is simple: "It is the purpose of this Act to assure that all handicapped children have available to them . . . a free appropriate public education which emphasizes special education and related services designed to meet their unique needs," states the 1975 Education for All Handicapped Children Act, P.L. 94-142.

But implementing the mandate means defining what is appropriate, establishing the related services and ensuring that unique needs are met for 4.4 million children each year. The issues are so complicated and provoke such intense — sometimes bitter — emotions that P.L. 94-142 is known as one of Congress's more intricate and heavily litigated pieces of legislation.

While litigation through the first years under P.L. 94-142 focused on access to education and the appropriateness of education, it has since graduated to a second generation of issues. Many suits relating to only one child's placement or services have little transferability to other students.

In contrast to the early role of litigation in winning access to education, "I see litigation in the future less as a vehicle for solving problems . . . [and] more a tool for resolving policy," said Frederick Weintraub, assistant executive director of the Council for Exceptional Children (CEC). Educators agree special education is good policy; the chief problems now relate to lack of resources to implement the policy, Weintraub said. "I don't think advocacy lawyers —

though I don't think they would admit it — like 94-142; it doesn't provide room for class action suits."

But a number of advocacy lawyers maintain that important legal
questions remain to be answered, and they do not rule out class
action litigation. Arlene Mayerson, directing attorney for the Disability Rights Education & Defense Fund (DREDF), said more
judicial guidance is needed on "appropriateness" and related services questions. As the state of the art of special education evolves,
litigation also will confront new issues; yesterday's unimaginable
related service may be feasible tomorrow.

Mayerson also insists litigation remains a needed and valid tool
in securing full implementation of P.L. 94-142. Suits may focus,
for example, on enforcement of a few areas of the act throughout
a state or major school system, particularly the areas that received
least attention during the law's first years. Advocacy groups say
some of those areas are secondary and vocational education; placement and services for the most severely retarded and institutionalized children; due process; and services for incarcerated handicapped youth.

New issues have come up as well: services for children with
acquired immune deficiency syndrome (AIDS); the award of attorneys' fees to parents who prevail in administrative due process
hearings on their children's programs; 1986 amendments to the Education of the Handicapped Act (EHA), which extend services to
infants and preschoolers and include new financial arrangements;
and the U.S. Supreme Court's 1987 announcement that it will consider discipline in special education.

And in the trenches of administrative hearings and litigation,
as one school lawyer says, "we continue to rehash the same issues"
of placement and services. As regular education in the 1980s
has emphasized "achieving excellence in education, . . . the question in special education is whether these kids can achieve that
[and] whether there's going to be continuing commitment to
giving these kids education," added Jane Stern, who until early
1987 was executive director of Advocates for Children in New
York City.

"The question [during such litigation] is, what are the issues
people are most likely to go to the wall for?" said Martin Gerry,
Washington-based advocacy attorney who, from 1975 to 1977, led
the Office for Civil Rights in the old Department of Health, Education and Welfare. "It's not necessarily the most important thing. It's
often the one with the most money involved," such as residential
placement or expensive related services, said Gerry, who is president of the Fund for Equal Access to Society.

## A Free Appropriate Public Education

Many of the legal questions arising under P.L. 94-142 concern the core requirement that states offer each handicapped student an "appropriate" public education.

The U.S. Supreme Court's 1982 ruling in *Hendrick Hudson Central School District v. Rowley* (458 U.S. 176) and federal appeals court rulings supply broad guidance on what constitutes appropriate education and what does not, but to some experts, the word "appropriate" always can use further clarification. Still others expect some currently accepted definitions of "appropriate" to be reconsidered and narrowed in light of *Rowley*.

In *Rowley,* the Court denied a bright and well-adjusted deaf student a sign language interpreter and said it is not a requirement of an appropriate education under P.L. 94-142 to "maximize each [handicapped] child's potential 'commensurate with the opportunity provided other children.'"

Districts must, however, obey any state standards that exceed the federal requirements, two federal appeals courts agreed in 1985: the 1st Circuit in *David D. v. Dartmouth School Committee* (775 F.2d 411; cert. denied, 54 U.S.L.W. 3716) and the 3rd Circuit in *Geis v. Board of Education of Parsippany-Troy Hills, Morris County, N.J.* (774 F.2d 575).

\* \* \*

Year-round programming and extended school days have been among the most frequently raised "appropriate" education questions. In a trend-setting ruling in *Battle v. Pennsylvania* (629 F.2d 269), the 3rd Circuit in 1980 overturned a state policy against offering summer school. While summer services are not automatically required for handicapped students, the 3rd Circuit said a 180-day limit on the public school schedule violated P.L. 94-142 because it precluded proper determination of what constitutes an appropriate education.

That ruling came in 1980, but some parents and schools have continued clashing over extended services, according to Reed Martin, a leading handicap advocacy attorney. "The approach [courts have] taken up to now has been, 'you can't say automatically that you won't do more than 180 days,'" Martin said. But "that doesn't leave [schools] with a very workable standard for what a child needs" and what a school should provide, he said.

"So what we see is schools saying, 'Okay, for multihandicapped kids facing severe regression, we'll do two hours a day, five days a week for the month of June,'" Martin said. "That doesn't in any way address the need for summer services."

Martin attributed disputes over extended services to a tendency of schools and parents to write the student's individualized education program (IEP) with sketchy goals. "It's not unusual for an IEP to have a goal of 'mathematics' or a goal to 'improve motor performance.' That's it, no short-term objectives," he said. Parents and educators could avoid the disputes and litigation, Martin indicated, by "real concrete goal setting, saying 'Johnny is now at [step] 3 and we want to get him at 19. And if June comes and Johnny is only at 7, then we need summer programming.'"

Now, according to Advocacy Inc., where Martin practices in Austin, Texas, "Virtually every court to examine the issue of summer programming has struck down public school policies that deny summer services." Courts that have followed *Battle* in a spate of rulings include:

■ the 11th Circuit in 1985 ruling in *Georgia Association of Retarded Citizens v. McDaniel* (716 F.2d 1565; cert. denied, 53 U.S.L.W. 3599);

■ the 8th Circuit in 1986 in *Yaris v. Special School District of St. Louis County* (780 F.2d 724); and

■ the 5th Circuit's *Alamo Heights Independent School District v. Texas Board of Education* (790 F.2d 1133) in 1986.

The same principle has been applied to the number of years a handicapped student stays in public school. The 10th Circuit in 1985's *Helms v. Independent School District No. 3* (750 F.2d 820; cert. denied, 105 S.Ct. 2024) said districts could not apply to handicapped students a state policy of never providing more than 12 years of public education.

The "court found that the graduation of handicapped students was a sham designed to terminate the school system's responsibility at the earliest possible moment," observed Nancy Jones, a legislative attorney for the Congressional Research Service (CRS).

P.L. 94-142 requires decisionmaking on the basis of individual students' needs, Advocacy Inc. emphasized in a 1986 briefing paper for parents. "Any policy that attempts to be categorical . . . breaks the law," according to the group.

\* \* \*

But Jean Bilger Arnold, a Blacksburg, Va., attorney who represents school districts in special education cases, said courts should hone down the situations in which extended services are required. Arnold said the 1980 *Battle* decision, which required schools to consider year-round programming, may have been read too broadly at first. Fine-tuning is required, she said.

Some experts look at *Rowley* as a basis for that fine-tuning, saying the decision may encourage courts to think twice before requiring a school to offer year-round courses or longer school days to a special education student.

In a similar vein, Arnold saw a trend toward questioning the point of educational services for the most severely handicapped students or those some consider uneducable. The question has been "in the mind of educators since the passage of the act," she said. "Schools have been serving children even though the services are almost noneducational — students that are almost nonfunctional, where you may have a teacher going in and turning them over on a mat."

The problem may be that community health services have shifted quasi-medical, barely educational services to the schools. "But the educational question is, is there a point at which an individual is so handicapped that he can't benefit from education?" Arnold said. "There may be a tendency toward further action there — not a lot, but some — especially as federal and state budgets get tighter and tighter."

* * *

Another area that may become a subject for litigation on "appropriate" education is program quality, with advocacy lawyers arguing that poor programs, even if the hours are ample, are not "appropriate."

"An area where I think you're going to see a lot of action, and I'm trying to go out there and stir some up, is secondary programming," Gerry said. While the first years of P.L. 94-142 saw "an enormous pressure from both parents and school districts" to implement effective elementary education programs, secondary education lagged, Gerry said. Ironically, litigation grows more likely as more schools implement good programs of secondary education and transition to life after school, he added. "The more [good programs] there are, the less satisfied parents will be" if their children are left out.

Of those not receiving an adequate secondary education, some seem to drop from the IEP rolls, even though they may still need special education, while others move into residential institutions that may "warehouse" more than educate them, attorneys charged. Finally, a number of retarded or learning disabled children who remain in high schools with IEPs suffer through irrelevant programming, Gerry contended.

"Too many schools very simplistically reason, if they learned A through L in elementary school, they should learn M through Z in secondary school," he said. "But there's no way you're going to teach a real learning disabled kid M through Z, and no reason to since he wouldn't be using it. There's no point in trying to teach the alphabet to someone who's not verbal when he really needs to learn to cross the street."

Where secondary programming is insufficient, retarded and other handicapped children may receive no meaningful preparation for independent living, advocates say. "If you want your child to live in something other than an institution, and have a job perhaps, you have to develop skills," Gerry said.

"I think we'll see a new generation of cases on what kind of education poor, inner city, minority students are getting," he said. "Consigning kids to dead-end programs" by classifying them as mentally retarded on the basis of unsound intelligence exams, he said, is "rearing itself again as an issue."

Dropouts could be the subject of related litigation. "We see the dropout problem as an access issue," said New York's Stern. "If programs and services are not structured in a way to maintain [handicapped students in school], and there is poor attendance, they are denied access. A system that actually encourages kids to leave . . . goes beyond the latitude allowed in the *Rowley* case. That violates the spirit of the law."

\* \* \*

Critics say the greatest gap in secondary programming usually is vocational education, which they have called "a very, very, very big problem," a "systemic" problem and "minimal or useless." Predicting that the first secondary education suits would erupt in that area, Gerry added, "I think the schools are far from ready for it."

Even CEC's Weintraub, who otherwise downplayed litigation, said vocational education could produce class action litigation against schools, districts or state education agencies. Since P.L. 94-142 was enacted, there has been "greater access to vocational education, but we don't have access to those parts of voc ed that are meaningful: apprentice programs and the other kinds of programs that lead to jobs," he said.

A consistent, widespread pattern of poor or sparse vocational education for handicapped students could make a state liable for a suit on the grounds it is not providing an appropriate education, said Paul Weckstein, director of the Center for Law and Education's (CLE) Washington, D.C., office.

"You may make the case that at least for every kid who is not going on to college it may be appropriate," Weckstein suggested, adding that only a small percentage of those students do receive vocational education. "It's not clear to me that [the law's provision for vocational education] has ever been adequately enforced," he said.

But P.L. 94-142 may not be the best vehicle for vocational education cases. More effective laws would be Section 504 of the 1973 Rehabilitation Act and the 1984 reauthorization of federal vocational programs (the Carl Perkins Vocational Education Act), civil rights lawyers said. Discrimination claims, rather than "appropriate education" claims, could be brought under those acts, Weckstein said.

"The handicapped have been denied access to the best programs and shunted to sheltered workshops," Weckstein charged. Section 504, which forbids discrimination against handicapped individuals seeking access to federally funded activities, would apply because many schools receive federal grants under the Vocational Education Act: The Perkins Act ensures that each state will spend an amount equal to 20 percent of its federal vocational education grant on handicapped students, and it encourages schools to educate handicapped students alongside nonhandicapped students.

* * *

New York's Stern, who worked for years on enforcement of a ruling against New York City, named other areas where school districts have had great difficulty complying with the law. It is hard for multilingual districts — New York at least — to meet the "very stringent requirements in P.L. 94-142 for involving [non-English-speaking] parents in the full spectrum of due process rights," she said.

Stern also said enforcement action is needed to serve homeless children, a disproportionate number of whom will be eligible for special education, and undocumented aliens. The parents of those children, if they are available, cannot be expected to spend hours in "middle-class-oriented due process hearings," she said.

Another problem, touching fewer children, is that the surrogate parent provision of P.L. 94-142 is "just something that hasn't been implemented," said Kathleen Boundy, an attorney in CLE's Boston office. The act entitles any child without parental representation to a surrogate parent, but many times it is not clear who is responsible for filling the role.

The confusion is deepest in the cases of institutionalized children, she said. Who should the surrogate be? "Are we talking about the directors of these institutions? Or are the children wards of the state?"

The issue overlaps the problems incarcerated handicapped children may face, Boundy said. One difficulty is that the intended duration of their stay often is unclear. Also, many have had no testing and lack an IEP. "Incarcerated youth have a higher rate of disability, especially learning disability, and they're not being served," Boundy said. Even where there is an IEP, another lawyer said, it often is not implemented.

### Placement In The Least Restrictive Environment

Because placement can be a very emotional and costly decision, the issue is likely to remain at the center of many suits. Advocacy groups have been focusing more and more of their attention on implementing the law's "mainstreaming" provision, which calls for placement in the least restrictive environment (LRE).

"To the maximum extent appropriate, handicapped children, including children in public or private institutions or other care facilities, [must be] educated with children who are not handicapped," P.L. 94-142 mandates.

A number of advocacy lawyers say LRE has not been enforced, especially for older children, and the Education Department's 1986 report to Congress on P.L. 94-142 particularly faults implementation of LRE for seriously emotionally disturbed youths.

"There's no way you can bus a mentally retarded child from the warehouse to a public school for six hours a day and get him socialized," said Martin. "What's the good of sending a child to school six hours a day when he's trashed by the other 18 hours?"

"For example, self-toileting: it's very hard to teach six hours a day and then let the kid do what he wants 18 hours a day. Or feeding with utensils" when a child may use his hands at home or be fed by a staff member or by gastronomy tubes, said Martin. "These are kids who could, with proper attention, learn to feed themselves, learn to toilet themselves."

LRE "is an entitlement to be placed in their neighborhood to the maximum extent appropriate, where support systems would exist, and they would be involved in the community as opposed to being shipped to a facility for the handicapped," Boundy said.

Stern said mainstreaming is the crux of the enforcement battle in many districts, including the New York case she monitored, and Mayerson, of DREDF, anticipated more litigation toward integrating handicapped students with their nonhandicapped peers. The law requires schools to have a "compelling educational reason" for segregating students in an institution or in daytime special education centers, she said, but parents often find themselves in the position of proving the child should be mainstreamed, Mayerson maintains.

"Some say integration is just an educational technique, at the discretion of the school district, or that there is a preference for integration, but not a mandate," Mayerson observed. "I feel it's clear" there must be a compelling reason for separation, "but unfortunately it hasn't been implemented that way."

She cited the 1983 6th U.S. Circuit Court of Appeals decision in *Roncker v. Walter* (700 F.2d 1058; cert. denied, 464 U.S. 864), which said integrated placement is mandatory if possible, and the burden of proof for doing otherwise is on the school.

"In a case where the segregated facility is considered superior, the court should determine whether the services which make that placement superior could be feasibly provided in a nonsegregated setting," said the 6th Circuit. "If they can, the placement in the segregated school would be inappropriate under the Act."

* * *

Ironically, Mayerson added, some children miss out on mainstreaming for the sake of another fundamental special education right: related services. Central schools for handicapped students may be the most efficient way to meet special education and related services needs, but the arrangement can backfire against a child, Mayerson said. "Provision of related services [such as therapy available in a special school] is often used to deny integrated placement."

In the same way, providing private or residential placements where appropriate "and the concept of mainstreaming or placement in the least restrictive environment could be seen as contradictory policies," CRS's Jones noted in a 1987 paper on special education law.

"However, they can also be seen as complementary. The two provisions can be seen as reflecting congressional intent to produce a broad definition of what is 'appropriate' placement," that is, placement that provides both education and the opportunity to participate in society, Jones wrote.

Jones said the 3rd Circuit reconciled the principles in 1981 in *Kruelle v. New Castle County School District* (642 F.2d 687). It is clear that if "residential placement is the only realistic option for learning improvement, the question of 'least restrictive' environment is also resolved," said *Kruelle*. If the more restrictive facility is better, the question is whether the public school program can provide the same services feasibly, *Kruelle* said. If so, the private placement would be inappropriate.

Although 93 percent of all handicapped students are educated in at least some regular classes, there have been "persistent problems in providing an appropriate educational program within the LRE for all handicapped children," according to the Education Department's report to Congress.

The department reports that about 7 percent of all handicapped children in the 1983-84 academic year were educated outside of regular school environments, in special schools or at home, and another 25 percent were educated mainly in separate classes within public schools. Both of those groups are obvious candidates for LRE disputes. But disputes can arise even over the placements of the remaining 69 percent of students, who spent most of their time in regular classes with supplementary aids and services. (The total does not add to 100 percent because the figures are rounded.)

With special education advocates concerned about mainstreaming, desegregation suits are a possibility, said Gerry. "There is still massive separation in secondary schools, and even segregation," he said.

But the opposite placement battle occurs frequently, too. Parents sometimes ask the school to pay for a child's institutionalization, while the school believes it can offer a better program in the regular system. While parents say they need or want to put their children in a 24-hour residential placement, the reasons are not always educational, and school districts are not required to pay for any strictly residential portion of the placement.

"The distinctions between care and residential services, who makes what decisions about placement, when the placement is for noneducational services, and who has the primary financial responsibility" need to be resolved, Weintraub said.

### AIDS

Students with AIDS have been some of the toughest to place. The syndrome does not automatically make a child handicapped within the meaning of P.L. 94-142, but the argument can be made that when children with AIDS fall under the act, they should be educated in the least restrictive environment.

"For most infected school-age children, the benefits of an unrestricted setting would outweigh the risks of their acquiring potentially harmful infections in the setting and the apparent nonexistent risk of transmission" of the virus that can cause AIDS, state the guidelines published by the federal Centers for Disease Control (CDC).

Given the possibility — however remote — of transmitting AIDS to others, and given the risk an AIDS patient will catch infections from other students, however, school officials must consider each child with AIDS separately. CDC advises a more restricted environment for preschoolers, "for some neurologically handicapped children who lack control of their body secretions or who display behavior such as biting and [for] those children who have uncoverable, oozing lesions."

Jones argues that, balancing the mainstreaming imperative of P.L. 94-142, there are precedents for making an exception to integration where there is a danger to other students. Citing two discipline cases in which students were moved after threatening other students — the 11th Circuit's 1984 ruling in *Victoria L. v. District School Board of Lee County, Fla.* (741 F.2d 369) and *Jackson v. Franklin County, Miss., School Board* (765 F.2d 535) from the 5th Circuit in 1985 — Jones argues the rationale of the 11th and 5th circuits in those cases could apply to a biting student with AIDS.

The federal district for central California, however, in 1986 issued a preliminary injunction ordering the mainstreaming of a child with AIDS who bit another student. In *Thomas v. Atascadero Unified School District* (No. 86-6609-AHS[BX]) (C.D.Cal. Nov 17, 1986), Ryan Thomas bit another pupil, without breaking the skin, allegedly while a group of other students were bullying him. The school put Thomas in a home instruction program, but the court said that would violate Section 504 of the Rehabilitation Act, which prohibits disability-based discrimination in federally funded programs.

Individual consideration also is required to determine whether a child with AIDS even fits under the P.L. 94-142 rubric. AIDS may accompany other potentially handicapping conditions, such as hemophilia or birth defects related to a mother's drug use while pregnant.

But whether a student with AIDS is handicapped under P.L. 94-142 depends on if the syndrome is hurting his or her educational performance. Madeleine Will, the Education Department's assistant secretary for special education and rehabilitative services, has advised educators to ask, on a case-by-case basis, "What is it about that condition that would require the child to be placed in special education? Is the child cognitively impaired?"

"I think the burden of proof would be on the system of regular education, which needs to identify exactly what it is this child requires that cannot be delivered in the universe of regular education. Because the separation of a child from the world of regular education is a very serious matter, and it should be done only if it's clear the child will benefit," Will said.

Queens County, N.Y., Supreme Court Judge Harold Hyman agreed with that assessment in his 1986 ruling in *District 27 Community School Board v. Board of Education of the City of New York*

(502 N.Y.S.2d 325). A child with AIDS or the less severe condition, AIDS-Related Complex (ARC), "could become handicapped as a result of deterioration in his or her condition," but such children are not handicapped under P.L. 94-142 "merely because they have AIDS/ARC or are infected with the virus," he said.

When Ryan White, an Indiana teenager and hemophiliac with AIDS, was kept out of school and his mother filed suit in 1985 to force a school district to readmit her son, a U.S. district judge in Indianapolis at first treated the case as though White automatically was handicapped under P.L. 94-142 because he had AIDS. Other courts, however, have not followed the lead of *White v. Western School Corp.* (IP 85-1192C), which came in one of the first legal battles over a student with AIDS before the classification issue had been debated.

But even if a student with AIDS is not handicapped under P.L. 94-142, he or she might be handicapped under Section 504 of the Rehabilitation Act, under a 1987 Supreme Court ruling, *School Board of Nassau County v. Arline* (55 U.S.L.W. 4245), that said a contagious disease may be a handicap if the victim is or has been impaired by it or is perceived as impaired. The Section 504 regulations set up educational standards very close to those schools must meet under P.L. 94-142, guaranteeing an "appropriate education" with "regular or special education and related aids and services . . . designed to meet individual educational needs."

### Related Services

Despite *Rowley* and *Irving Independent School District v. Tatro* (468 U.S. 883), in which the Supreme Court required a district to have an employee catheterize a student at school, gray areas linger in interpretation of related services.

"It was expected that the definition of related services in the act would suffice, but litigation history shows more clarification is needed," the National Association of State Directors of Special Education said in testimony on the 1986 Education of the Handicapped Act Amendments. In a "free appropriate public education," related services are half the game, with "special education" itself doing the rest.

Encompassing everything from transportation to speech pathology to catheterization, in Amber Tatro's case, related services are those "required to assist a handicapped child to benefit from special education," except for nondiagnostic medical services. The line between medical services schools need not provide and nonmedical services that may be demanded is fuzzy, however, particularly when it comes to psychological services for emotionally disturbed children. "The education and the therapy service are really intertwined, and you can't separate them," said Gerry.

In *Tatro,* the Court stressed that without catheterization, Tatro could not stay at school and would lose access to her education; the decision also relied upon the fact that the service could be done by a nurse or layperson rather than a licensed physician. Because of that, some school lawyers credit *Tatro* with causing lower courts to begin "to acknowledge that school districts are not required to provide medical services," as Bobbie Albanese, counsel to the Orange County, Calif., superintendent, put it.

"However, the courts have struggled with the distinction between a service that is 'purely medical' and one that may qualify as a related service necessary to provide a child with a free appropriate public education," Albanese said in a 1986 paper written for publication by the Council of School Attorneys, an arm of the National School Boards Association (NSBA), and for presentation at the council's 1987 school law seminar.

For example, consider "general intense ongoing psychotherapy for a schizophrenic child," Gerry said. "We're talking about 70, 75, 80, 85 bucks an hour, and kids who need a lot of it." Open-heart surgery also may be necessary for a child to benefit from education but clearly does not qualify, he pointed out. Mayerson added that the circumstances under which a given service is delivered can provoke conflict among legal experts about whether the service qualifies.

Said Warren Kreunen, a Milwaukee attorney who represents school districts in special education cases, "The problem is, psychological treatment [includes] many of the same things psychiatrists do, except prescribing medicine. That's a broad range of things to include."

Even before *Tatro,* the courts have distinguished between mental health services provided by a psychiatrist—a licensed physician—and those that can be performed by others, notes CRS's Jones. Those cases included:

■ *Darlene L. v. Illinois State Board of Education* (568 F.Supp. 1340), in which the federal district court for northern Illinois in 1983 said psychological services by a licensed phsyician are not a related service, but the services of psychologists—who are not medical doctors—can be;

■ the U.S. district court for the District of Columbia's ruling in 1983 in *McKenzie v. Jefferson* (566 F.Supp. 404), saying that a child's psychiatric hospitalization was not a related service if the placement was made for the sake of medical treatment; and

■ the 3rd Circuit's 1984 decision in *Piscataway Township Board of Education v. T.G.* (cert. denied, 53 U.S.L.W. 3436), which said psychotherapy for an emotionally disturbed student qualifies as a related service under P.L. 94-142; half a year after *Tatro,* the Supreme Court without comment refused to review it.

But the rules still are not rigidly set, Albanese noted. In a 1986 ruling in *Max M. v. Illinois State Board of Education* (629 F.Supp. 1504), the federal district court for northern Illinois said the nature of the service, not the personnel providing it, determines whether it is a reimbursable related service. But the court added that the district should be held liable for only "the costs of those services as if they had been provided by the minimum level health care provider recognized as competent to perform the related service," Albanese added.

Albanese said she was shocked by two recent cases in which hearing officers ordered districts to pay for psychiatric services provided to students in psychiatric hospitals:

■ *Clovis Unified School District v. California Office of Hearings* (CV-F-85-479 EDP), in which the federal district court for eastern California in 1986 upheld the hearing officer's ruling. The case now is on appeal to the 9th U.S. Circuit Court of Appeals (86-2742); and

■ *Orange Unified School District v. Boggus* (Nos. 46-97-63 and 47-41-76), which was pending as of March 1987 in the Superior Court of California for Orange County.

On the other hand, in *Detsel v. Auburn Enlarged City School District* (637 F.Supp. 1022), the U.S. district court for northern New York in 1986 said a district did not have to provide constant supervision of a child with severe physical disabilities, even though a doctor was not required for the service. The court said the monitoring amounted to medical care that the district did not have to provide. The regulations on medical services, the court said, quoting *Tatro,* were meant to "spare schools from an obligation to provide a service that might well prove unduly expensive and beyond the range of their competence."

But as *Detsel* shows, the fine line between medical and nonmedical services poses problems aside from psychological services, too. Some decisions "have required school staff to clean out tracheotomy tubes, because these are not medical services requiring a doctor. That's a pretty broad range" of services considered nonmedical, Kreunen said.

"You have school personnel worried about that" and afraid of malpractice liability if, for example, they are called upon to administer emergency medication and err somehow, he said. "The question is, how far must schools go to educate the very severely handicapped?"

"You're starting to get kids in [breathing equipment] mainstreamed in the classroom," Kreunen said. "The kid may be benefiting, but maybe not as much as possible. And you may start to diminish the education of the other kids in the classroom" by diverting the teacher's energy and the attention of the other students. "That's an unpopular thing to say," Kreunen acknowledged.

\* \* \*

Related services questions come up not only in the psychologist's office but also on the athletic field. In a 1986 ruling in *Rettig v. Kent City, Ohio, School District* (788 F.2d 328; cert. denied, 54 U.S.L.W. 3859), the 6th Circuit said school districts do not have to provide handicapped children with "an equal opportunity" for participating in extracurricular activities, even though a P.L. 94-142 regulation requires that.

Ruling that the regulation is in conflict with *Rowley,*the 6th Circuit said schools only have to ensure that the IEP, "when taken in its entirety, is reasonably calculated to enable the child to receive educational benefits." The court also said the weekly hour of activities that the parents sought in *Rettig* would have provided no significant educational benefits. The Supreme Court let that decision stand.

\* \* \*

The costs of different placement alternatives and related services can be an issue when educators write IEPs. With the determination of an appropriate placement being the first question, it is not common for cost to be an explicit issue in litigation, but it has happened.

"You're starting to see more cases that recognize the validity of cost considerations in public schools," commented Arnold. "Over the past few years I'm beginning to see cases where the judge says, 'Yes, you can consider cost.' That's almost surprising to me."

In *Kruelle,* for example, courts have said cost is a proper factor because excessive spending on one handicapped student deprives other handicapped children of appropriate education funds, or deprives students in regular education classes. The idea is the flip side of the D.C. District Court's reasoning in 1972 in *Mills v. Board of Education of the District of Columbia* (348 F. Supp. 866), which said schools should not withhold spending on handicapped students to spend more on nonhandicapped students.

CLE's Boundy conceded that courts may have become "increasingly aware" of the costs as an issue. But even where cost is great, courts should consider the appropriateness of differently priced options, she said. She quoted a 1984 case, *Clevenger v. Oakridge School Board* (744 F.2d 514), in which the 6th U.S. Circuit Court of Appeals said, "Cost considerations are only relevant when choosing between several options, all of which are for an appropriate education. When only one is appropriate, there is no choice."

### The 1986 EHA Amendments

With the 1986 EHA amendments — early intervention for infants and the preschool special education mandate — still in their own infancy, only a sketchy outline of the legal questions they may raise was possible as of March 1987. Some are apparent by analogy to problems in existing preschool and school-age programs, however.

One educator anticipated conflicts over the level of services schools are willing to write into a 3-year-old's IEP. Once a service is in an IEP, it is difficult to drop even if the student outgrows it, and the younger the student is to start, the more likely the special education provided will bring progress that outdates services in the IEP. A district might offer some summer school without prescribing it in the IEP, for example, as a way to avoid making a lengthy and formal commitment to it, said that educator.

Some other questions that have been raised so far include:

■ What does least restrictive environment mean for preschoolers, given that many states and districts do not offer preschool for non-handicapped students? Must districts make efforts to integrate handicapped preschoolers in Head Start programs or day care centers?

Although the new preschool program incorporates by reference the LRE requirement of P.L. 94-142, Gray Garwood, who was staff director for the House Select Education Subcommittee when it wrote the House version of the amendments, said he sees the requirement as not generally relevant for preschoolers. A district certainly cannot be expected to create a nonhandicapped preschool just for the sake of mainstreaming, he added.

The 8th Circuit, in its 1986 ruling in *Mark and Ruth A. v. Grant Wood Area Education Agency* (795 F.2d 52; cert. denied, March 23, 1987), made the same point in upholding a district's decision to put a preschooler in an all-handicapped classroom in a public school. The parents had advocated placement in a private program designed to integrate handicapped and nonhandicapped students.

■ For infants, is the "individualized family service plan" (IFSP), which states must develop for the family of each child served, a binding contract between the family and state agencies?

■ Does the IFSP continue after the child turns 3? If so, who pays for family services? Will infants suddenly lose eligibilty for accustomed services on their third birthdays? Will some classified as at risk of developmental delay be edged from the program altogether?

■ How will information on infants and families remain confidential in the interagency web?

Also, for infants and toddlers, the new program provides only the skeleton of the P.L. 94-142 due process system and leaves most of the procedures and rights for states to devise. Under P.L. 94-142, Garwood said, "it is clear what the individual has a right to: special education and related services which are definable, identifiable and providable." Services for infants are far less clearly understood, however. "There is no right yet," Garwood said. "Once the states are participating fully, then there can be some other effort" to make sure the due process procedures suffice.

Iowa, which has served all handicapped children from birth since 1980, applied the same P.L. 94-142 due process requirements to its infant program "with a minimum of problems" and controversy, according to Joan Turner Clary, early childhood special education program consultant to the Iowa Department of Education.

Garwood anticipated little litigation under the infants' and preschool programs. Seven years ago the extension of services "would have been a catastrophe, but the system [now] is much better able to absorb this," he said. "It'll just burp and go on with it. I don't think it's going to create as many problems" as some people think.

### The Medicaid Conflict

The 1986 amendments to EHA created a new conflict that may have to be resolved in the courts. Congress said state agencies other than the education agency must pay for related services in an IEP if they would have paid for them in the absence of an IEP. The amendments direct states to develop interagency agreements to allocate costs among the various public agencies that have responsibilities for handicapped children.

"That's going to be a really important battleground, and on this issue parents and school systems have exactly the same interests," at last, Gerry said. The provision for reimbursements from other agencies applies to special education for students of all ages, not just the new infant and preschooler provisions. Given the timing of development of the interagency agreements, "the real impact will be felt in the fall of '88," Gerry predicted.

The new interagency agreements must define each agency's financial responsibility and set policies and procedures for resolving disputes, including procedures by which school districts can seek reimbursement for health and social services they provide according to students' IEPs.

"Of course the other agencies aren't going to go down without a fight," Gerry said. "But if you look at the overall structure, that's just not fair to make public schools the deep pocket for every kind of service that child needs."

He expected the "biggest areas" for reimbursement battles to be Medicaid (Title XIX of the Social Security Act) for children from low income families; Community Mental Health; and Vocational Rehabilitation, for which youths become eligible at age 16. Other areas will include Maternal and Child Health Block Grants (Social Security Title V); Early and Periodic Screening, Diagnosis and Treatment; Child Welfare Services; Head Start; and the Developmental Disabilities program.

The 1986 amendments say the state education agency's responsibility for P.L. 94-142 "shall not be construed to limit the responsibility of [other agencies] . . . from providing or paying for some or all of the costs of a free appropriate public education to be provided handicapped children." The amendments add that the EHA "shall not be construed to permit a State to reduce medical and other assistance or to alter eligibility under titles V and XIX of the Social Security Act with respect to the provision of a free appropriate public education."

The biggest fight might be with the federal government, at least under the Reagan administration. The Health and Human Services Department, which runs Medicaid, strongly opposes Medicaid reimbursements for services in an IEP, arguing that position in administrative opinions and in comments on a July 1986 General Accounting Office report on the issue.

Under a Connecticut interagency agreement foreshadowing the 1986 EHA amendments, GAO reported that local school districts receive about $5 million per year in Medicaid reimbursements for school-based health services provided to handicapped children. HHS said the program "ignores long-standing Medicaid statutory provisions, regulations, and the State Medicaid Manual which precludes Federal Medicaid reimbursement where other funding is available." In a September 1985 policy statement in the state manual, HHS's Health Care Financing Administration declared Medicaid coverage unavailable for services described in an IEP.

"Ultimately, it's going to be settled," albeit with "stress, groans and tensions," observed Garwood. Assuming Health and Human Services does not give in and Congress does not amend the Social Security Act — or EHA — to resolve the issue, "somebody's going to file a lawsuit, maybe a school district [unable] to recover funds from other agencies."

There has been one ruling on the issue, in which a federal district court in Massachusetts found residential institutions for mentally retarded students eligible for reimbursement of health services even though the services were educational in that they were listed in an IEP. HHS has appealed that ruling, *Massachusetts v. Heckler* (616 F.Supp. 687), to the 1st Circuit.

Gerry was optimistic that schools would see a tangential benefit in addition to the financial relief once reimbursement is resolved. "A lot of due process hearings have been fights over resources, so if you take some of the financial pressure off school districts, there's a good chance [conflicts] will get resolved without hearings," he said. "If school systems respond creatively, they can turn some disputes into collaborative efforts with parents," although "I'm not saying it's going to solve everything," he added.

### The Supreme Court Takes Up Discipline

Another issue that attracted keen attention during 1987 was discipline. P.L. 94-142 says nothing directly about it, leaving parents and educators to read between the lines. Several cases have pitted parents protective of an unruly child's educational placement against district officials afraid the child will hurt someone or disrupt education at the school.

Discipline calls several parts of P.L. 94-142 into play: the procedures for a change of placement, the meaning of "mainstreaming" and of "appropriate" education, and the "stay put" provision keeping the child in her or his current placement until the parents and school agree on a change.

Some advocacy lawyers fear parents' lawsuits are scaring schools away from enforcing needed discipline, and others say schools have too much latitude in disciplining handicapped students. While some school lawyers feel the due process procedures courts have required schools to follow are too strict, an equal problem is that the case law so far does not answer all questions about a school's responsibilities and rights in discipline.

Gwen Gregory, deputy general counsel of NSBA, and others have been hoping for a Supreme Court ruling on the issue, and the Court took a step toward answering their wishes when it agreed to hear a California case regarding suspensions. That case, *Honig v. Doe* (55 U.S.L.W. 3445), is likely to be decided in 1987.

Under the precedents that set the stage for *Honig*, handicapped students, like other pupils, have a right to a hearing if they are to be suspended, under the Supreme Court's 1975 decision in *Goss v. Lopez* (419 U.S. 565). Overturning an Ohio law allowing some

suspensions with no hearing, *Goss* said students have a constitution-
ally protected interest in public education that cannot be revoked
without due process.

*Goss* established minimal due process rights for brief suspensions: the student's right to "notice of the charges against him" and
some hearing — "at least an informal give-and-take between student
and disciplinarian, preferably prior to the suspension."

The chief discipline ruling for special education followed that
lead. In *S-1 v. Turlington* (635 F.2d 342), the 5th Circuit in 1981 held
that expulsion of a handicapped student is a change in placement and
that, after an expulsion, services cannot cease altogether. The 5th Circuit echoed other courts' opinions that a student cannot be expelled
for behavior that is a manifestation of his or her handicap. Since *S-1*,
"Short suspensions are generally allowed if there is a danger to other
students, but that is a trend, not an absolute," Jones said.

In *Honig v. Doe,* the Supreme Court agreed to decide whether a
school may change the placement of a handicapped student who is
a danger to him- or herself or others without drafting an entire new
education plan for the child. The Court will review a 1986 decision
by the 9th Circuit that said districts may suspend handicapped pupils
for the duration allowed by state law for their nonhandicapped
peers; in California, where *Honig* originated, that is 20 consecutive
days or 30 consecutive days for students being transferred to a
new placement.

Apart from that suspension, though, a school cannot change a
violent student's placement over the parents' objections without
adopting a new IEP because doing so would violate P.L. 94-142's
stay put provision, the 9th Circuit ruled in the case, then called *Doe
v. Maher* (793 F.2d 1470).

Instead, educators confronted with a violent handicapped student
may resort to "the gamut of lesser disciplinary measures and program variations that do not rise to the level of changes in placement," the 9th Circuit said. In extraordinary cases in which parents
resist an immediate placement change school officials consider
imperative, officials may seek a court order, the court added.

California schools chief Bill Honig contends the 9th Circuit's
approach could have "disastrous consequences." As parents help
draft IEPs and can challenge a school's plan, it can take months or
years to put a new IEP in place, he argues.

Toby Fishbein Rubin, a lawyer for the students, was "shocked"
that the Court accepted the case. But if the 9th Circuit is affirmed,
"the impact will be tremendous for students," she said. Currently,
she said, "the easiest way for schools to deal with difficult students
is to remove them."

The case began in 1980 when an emotionally disturbed student tried to choke another pupil and broke a plate glass window, and a second handicapped student engaged in theft and extortion and made sexual advances on other students. The San Francisco Unified School District suspended both students indefinitely but provided home instruction.

Attorneys for the students contend Honig exaggerates the impact of the 9th Circuit ruling, because that ruling does allow suspensions of as long as 20 days without an IEP evaluation. "The exception sought . . . would override entirely the Congressional purpose behind [P.L. 94-142]: to guarantee an education to handicapped students regardless of the nature or severity of their handicaps," the students' attorneys said, contending Honig wants to give districts "unbridled discretion."

Atlanta school lawyer Charles Weatherly counters that applying the 9th Circuit ruling elsewhere would be even tougher on schools, because most state laws do not allow suspensions as long as 20 days; Georgia's limit is 10 days, he said. Weatherly added that discipline cases account for about half the legal problems he handles.

Arguments in *Honig* may consider the meaning of mainstreaming. "If you look at LRE as an entitlement, how can you justify expelling handicapped children? How can you justify suspensions?" CLE's Boundy has asked. "There is no problem with removal in an emergency. What the regulations and the act don't provide for is this extended exclusion from school," especially through serial suspensions, none of which alone is long enough to justify invoking the due process proceedings for a change of placement.

NSBA's Gregory advocated the opposite approach, a Supreme Court ruling that a suspension or expulsion is not a change of placement. "It's a part of being mainstreamed. They could also say it's an exception [to the stay put rule] that must have been intended because any other reading" would verge on nonsensical, she said.

The possibility of an emergency court order to remove a violent student does not dispense with the practical problems educators face, say school lawyers. "You could have a situation where it's not an emergency in terms of safety, but the kid is so disruptive that no one is learning. It's an educational emergency," Gregory said. She was considering arguing in *Honig* that school officials should have the flexibility to make a quick change of placement even for students who are merely disruptive, not dangerous. If parents object, it can be they who seek judicial intervention, she said.

Gregory thought judges too easily attribute misbehavior to a handicap, an important factor because that connection is what brings

P.L. 94-142 into play during discipline. Although *Honig* does not directly raise the question, Gregory hoped the Court would define more clearly — and more narrowly than some courts have — the relationship between misbehavior and a student's handicap.

She and Weatherly supported the 9th Circuit's application of the stay put rule only to "conduct that is caused by, or has a direct and substantial relationship to, the child's handicap." The 9th Circuit added that "a handicapped child's conduct is covered . . . only if the handicap significantly impairs the child's behavioral controls." That definition "does not embrace conduct that bears only an attenuated relationship to the child's handicap," the court said. The stay put rule would not apply, for example, if a physical handicap causes a child to lose self-esteem, and the child consciously misbehaves to gain the attention, or win the approval, of peers.

"True, an emotionally disturbed kid is going to be more of a discipline problem," Gregory said. "But when you put them in the mainstream program, that's part of the program." The threat of discipline "is a teaching tool: living in society you have to abide by the rules," she added. "Some attorneys suggest you write discipline into the IEP."

Lashing out during an epileptic seizure certainly is related to the handicap, but most cases are less clear, she said. Gregory argued that if the handicapped student "knows the difference between right and wrong and is capable of refraining from the misbehavior," then the student should be disciplined as his or her nonhandicapped peers are. An inflexible rule on discipline from the Supreme Court would only discourage mainstreaming, she said.

Like some school attorneys, Gerry found courts' discipline standards sometimes a bit alarming. "I have this nightmare of a kid running around school stabbing people and they can't take the knife away from him and send him home because he hasn't had a case conference" to see whether he might have a handicap that is responsible for his behavior, he said.

But Gerry suggested that the Supreme Court might allow exceptions to the stay put rule, and he noted that the justices have narrowed the provision before, in a different context. In a 1985 ruling in *Burlington School Committee v. Department of Education* (53 U.S.L.W. 4509), in which parents unilaterally transferred their child to a private school, the Court held that a parental violation of the stay put provision did not waive their right to reimbursement.

"Clearly, after *Burlington*, the stay put provision is in some jeopardy," Gerry said.

Questions are likely to remain even after *Honig*. For example, the courts have not yet dealt with serial suspensions of less than 10 days each. Seeing "lots of room for improvement" and for a clear judicial standard, Boundy looked for more judicial restraints in disciplining handicapped students. Suspension or expulsion "is only appropriate when there is an emergency," she said.

It is also not clear whether educational services must be delivered during a suspension; and while *S-1* said services cannot cease altogether after an expulsion, it is not clear what level of service the school system must provide after a child has been expelled.

Appeals court precedents diverging from the 9th Circuit's approach include the 11th Circuit's 1984 ruling in *Victoria L. v. District School Board of Lee County, Fla.* (741 F.2d 369), which invoked the school's duty to provide a safe environment and upheld the immediate transfer of a handicapped student who threatened other pupils with a razor blade.

\* \* \*

Also in *Honig*, the justices will review the 9th Circuit's decision that the state education agency must serve an individual handicapped child directly if that pupil's school district has failed to provide a free appropriate public education. Honig argues P.L. 94-142 requires the state to serve students only when a district is unwilling or unable to operate a special education program or when students "can best be served" by the state — in a school for the deaf, for example. Requiring the state to provide direct services if a district falters in its duties to an individual student would "place an intolerable burden on the states," he contends.

The 9th Circuit, however, said that whenever a district falls short of P.L. 94-142 standards — and the "breach must be significant" — the student "can best be served" by the state. The state has a duty to monitor districts' performance, and the point of monitoring is to ensure the proper services, the court added, finding California's procedures inadequate.

### Due Process

On a more routine level than the emergency issues in *Honig v. Doe*, implementation of the procedural safeguards of P.L. 94-142 concerns those on both sides of the courtroom.

"The procedural safeguards of P.L. 94-142 are some of the most significant and most litigated provisions in the Act," CRS's Jones has observed. Important issues include the nature of the due process hearing; mediation; legal avenues of relief for parents and advocacy groups; damages for failure to serve students properly; and the availability of attorneys' fees for parents who prevail in IEP disputes.

Congress settled one of those issues in 1986, including a provision in the Handicapped Children's Protection Act to allow parents to sue not only under P.L. 94-142 but also under civil rights laws such as the Rehabilitation Act, provided they exhaust the administrative hearings first.

The provision reversed the Supreme Court's 1984 ruling in *Smith v. Robinson* (468 U.S. 992), which said P.L. 94-142 was the only avenue for relief in special education cases. By allowing suits under civil rights statutes such as the Rehabilitation Act, HCPA rebroadened the types of special education suits parents can bring, including class action suits, which can be brought under the Rehabilitation Act but not P.L. 94-142.

Another issue on which there has been little guidance is the question whether courts may order compensatory services for inappropriate special education, particularly for students past their 22nd birthdays, the age at which services normally stop. Few courts have ruled on the issue, but the 7th Circuit in a 1983 ruling in *Timms v. Metropolitan School District of Wabash County* (722 F.2d 1310) suggested that such a compensatory damage award may be legitimate. According to CRS's Jones, the few lower courts that have considered compensatory education generally have allowed it. But there is ample room for clarification of the circumstances under which it might be ordered.

Other questions regarding procedural safeguards focus on the administrative due process hearing that parents may request if they object to a proposed change in their child's IEP or if they want a change that the school refuses.

"The IEP is seen as the foundation document" of a child's education, said DREDF's Mayerson. "The biggest problem in practice is that parents can't get anything they want into the IEP" in services, placement or goals. "The school district has the final say. There are so many parents who have to swallow whatever the school districts give them. So a lot of parents are forced into hearings."

Unfortunately, Mayerson said, when the parents reach hearings, some hearing officers will consider only whether the IEP is being implemented, not whether it is appropriate or whether the placement is the least restrictive possible.

Leonard Rieser, an attorney with the Education Law Center in Philadelphia, saw no such problem with the formulation of IEPs or the scope of the hearing examiner's review, but big problems with the hearing process otherwise.

"This 'simple' due process hearing is so complicated that many people simply forgo their rights," Rieser said. "I think the due process hearing is unworkable most of the time, so mediation is a really good option" when parents and schools agree to it voluntarily, he added.

NSBA's Gregory was "troubled" that many hearing examiners informally act as mediators in the due process hearing, effectively making it an extension of the IEP conference. That means that schools — and parents — are pushed to compromise where it is not necessarily in their interests to do that, she said. Hearing officers "won't admit it openly [though], because they're supposed to be judges," she added. Kreunen, however, saw no problem with some hearing officers' attempts to mediate.

CLE's Boundy added more fuel to the fire. All too routinely, she said, hearing examiners are not impartial, and she predicted more attention will focus on that issue in the future.

In 1984, the 11th U.S. Circuit Court of Appeals tackled the impartiality issue head on in *Mayson v. Teague* (749 F.2d 652), Boundy said. The court observed that while a hearing examiner employed in another district or another area of the student's district had no personal interest a case, the officer may well have had professional interests. An examiner may fear retaliation, for example, or set certain standards with the intent that the same standards would be observed in his or her own districts.

### *Mediation*

While there were disagreements about whether hearing examiners should act as mediators, most attorneys supported the growing movement toward mediation at some level, to save on valuable good will as well as on money, time, paperwork and ever costlier liability insurance.

Mediation is taking hold because the due process hearing is "long and complicated, and nobody wins," said Linda Singer, executive director of the Center for Dispute Settlement in Washington, D.C. About 30 states report offering some form of mediation assistance, said Singer, although the standards vary, even within a state, because many programs are locally administered.

Some attorneys were cautious about mediation. Even if no lawyers will be in the hearing room, Boundy said, parents might be smart to talk to a lawyer or legal aide before bargaining away rights they are not even aware of having. Gerry and others stressed that mediation must be voluntary for all parties.

"Formal mediation I have considerably less confidence in," said Gerry. "You can't compromise rights. Either [the mediation] won't be effective, or we'll lose the sense of what the child's rights are." There are times when either the school or the parent should back off from an overly strong demand, he added, and the hope of a mediated compromise may discourage that concession.

On the other hand, Singer said, there may be room for such compromise. "There are enormous gray areas" in what constitutes appropriate education, for example. Also, mediation allows parents "to participate in fashioning the plan," something that may not happen if lawyers take over the case, she said. "Courts are not satisfying people."

Mediation has always played a part, said Pat Wright, director of governmental affairs for DREDF. But it is "not a panacea."

### *Attorneys' Fees*

Of the many issues litigated in this heavily litigated law, one of the most bitter is irrelevant to the handicapped child. That issue, starting not with education but with the due process hearing, is attorneys' fees.

Until 1984, schools routinely were required to pay the legal fees of parents prevailing in IEP disputes. P.L. 94-142 had no "fee-shifting" provision, but courts ordered the payments under other federal rights statutes that do offer fee-shifting provisions.

The Supreme Court brought that to an abrupt stop with its 1984 ruling in Smith, saying P.L. 94-142 is the exclusive route for challenging a school's special education program, and parents therefore could not win fees by augmenting their P.L. 94-142 suits with claims under the Rehabilitation Act, for example.

Congress reversed *Smith* in a pithy bill — HCPA — that fills less than a page of the *Congressional Record,* but not without two years of delay and debate. Much debate concerned the merit of fee awards for work done in the administrative proceedings where parents and schools must begin resolving disagreements. The final version of HCPA, P.L. 99-372, provides for administrative fees.

In the debate before HCPA became law, legislators and school lawyers opposed to administrative fees predicted they would twist educational decisionmaking. Kreunen said that, faced with the threat of lawyers newly attracted to due process hearings, "a lot of schools aren't going to fight. They're going to throw in the towel. It's so expensive that a lot of the smaller districts are reluctant to try these cases." That capitulation is "not always in the best interest of the child," he said.

Just as undesirable, others suspected schools would litigate more. "Look, if we're going to be faced with parents bringing attorneys [to the hearing or even the case conference], our attorneys will be there," one superintendent said. The fear was that "attorneys will do the talking," while parents and school officials "sit in the back," said those cautious about the fees provision.

And the costs of litigation can be numbing. Defending a school district against one family's intricate complaint, Kreunen said he ran up legal fees of close to $20,000, and the parents' fees were probably greater; that case never even came to trial. Fees in a class action are even more impressive. A federal judge in 1986 awarded $200,000 to three attorneys who brought a class action suit against the Rochester, N.Y., City School District and settled it before trial, after a year of negotiations. The city is appealing that award.

With such fears and figures on their minds, school board members fought the administrative fee provision, and no sooner did Congress approve it than their lawyers attacked it on two fronts.

First, although special education advocates consider fees available even if a parent prevails at the administrative level without going to court, many school lawyers say the bill's plain language does not provide for that. Secondly, school lawyers protest the law's retroactivity to *Smith;* the act covers all actions and administrative proceedings pending on or after July 4, 1984.

Plaintiffs have been awarded retroactive fees under HCPA, but as of March 1987 experts knew of no court that had been asked to review the retroactivity. As for cases resolved at the administrative level, no court was known to have dealt with a school arguing the statute did not provide those fees.

It was only a matter of time, though. Within three months of HCPA's passage, school lawyers had marshalled their arguments in two thorough articles in *Inquiry & Analysis,* the newsletter of the Council of School Attorneys.

Authors of HCPA "may very well have intended to provide attorneys' fees to parents who prevail in due process hearings," Fort Lauderdale, Fla., attorney John Bowen notes in an article in the September 1986 issue. "But such an intent does not create a right unless it is somehow expressed in the law."

"In any action or proceeding brought under this subsection," HCPA says, "the court" may award fees. Bowen notes that the subsection of P.L. 94-142 in question—subsection (e) of Section 1415—concerns court actions and state administrative appeals from hearing decisions, not due process hearings themselves; the section does not provide fees for those prevailing in due process hearings, he contends.

Gray Garwood, who directed House work on HCPA, sounds slightly exasperated when he is asked about that argument. "Despite that obscure . . . reference" to different subsections of P.L. 94-142, "it is clear from the legislative history and the language of the [HCPA] statute that parents who prevail at the administrative level" without going to court may win fees, he says.

Henry Cohen, a legislative attorney with CRS, agrees, and he argues that legislators on both sides of the debate over fees for proceedings understood that.

In a September 1986 CRS paper, Cohen concludes that while the reference to subsection (e) arguably precludes fees for hearings, that reference likely "would be regarded by the courts as loose wording that should not be construed narrowly to defeat the clear purpose of the Act."

Bowen also focuses on the words "the court" and says they mean hearing officers cannot award fees. And parents who have prevailed in IEP hearings cannot get around that by going to court for fees alone, Bowen argues, because neither P.L. 94-142 nor HCPA provides for such a visit.

NSBA staff attorney Naomi Gittens, in a later *Inquiry & Analysis* article, argues the Supreme Court followed the same reasoning in a November 1986 ruling denying administrative fees under Title VI of the 1964 Civil Rights Act.

But critics of the argument say that ruling, *North Carolina v. Crest Street Community Council* (55 U.S.L.W. 4001), is irrelevant because administrative hearings are optional under Title VI but not under P.L. 94-142. It makes sense to deny fees for an optional proceeding, they say.

CRS's Cohen adds that parents arguably could sue to recover fees alone because P.L. 94-142 allows suits "under" the statute, not necessarily suits "to enforce" the statute. If the Courts reject that argument, Cohen added in a November 1986 paper on *Crest Street,* then HCPA's legislative history "apparently would be the only basis for construing EHA to permit court actions solely to recover attorneys' fees incurred in administrative proceedings."

Cohen and other critics of those statutory construction arguments emphasize the words "action or proceeding" and quote Rep. Pat Williams, D-Mont., chairman of the Select Education Subcommittee during action on HCPA, who said the "proceeding" is the due process hearing.

Gerry went further. "I don't think the [statutory construction] argument passes the 'risibility test,'" he said, referring to one of the first legal standards lawyers learn: an argument must be deliverable without making everyone laugh. The argument against HCPA's retroactivity, on the other hand, "has a glimmer of respectability," Gerry said.

Gittens argues the retroactivity is unconstitutional. The Supreme Court has said that when Congress ties program funding to compliance with certain conditions, "these conditions must be unambiguously stated so that a state may be aware of the contract terms before making a decision as to whether to enter into the agreement," Gittens noted in the November 1986 *Inquiry & Analysis*. Even if HCPA were retroactive, it cannot be used to reopen orders denying fees before HCPA passed on Aug. 5, 1986, she argues.

But Cohen contends in a January 1987 CRS paper that HCPA's retroactivity is legitimate because passage of the fee provision came as no surprise.

School officials are putting HCPA's retroactivity to the test in *Georgia Association of Retarded Citizens v. McDaniel* (78-1950) in U.S. district court in northern Georgia and in *Barbara R. v. Tirozzi* (Civ. Action No. H-83-991-PCD) in federal district court in Connecticut.

\* \* \*

Those issues aside, HCPA will give districts and parents new grounds for conflict, Advocacy Inc.'s Martin predicts. For example, the law denies fees to parents who have "unreasonably protracted the final resolution of the controversy." Even if parents protract the proceedings, however, schools may have to pay if their officials also drag the case out.

The IEP hearing "can be nasty enough," Martin says. "I can't wait to see the proceeding over who 'unreasonably protracted' more." Also, parents may win some but not all the points they raise, making it difficult to determine who prevailed or what legal time was spent on each claim. Those provisions "contain some ambiguities which will most likely be clarified by judicial action," Jones predicts.

\* \* \*

Meanwhile, tentative and anecdotal assessments of life under HCPA are surfacing. As some districts review all IEPs at year's end, rather than staggering them throughout the year, the jury was still out in March on the impact of the fees. But half a year after its passage, "The statute has had a significant impact already," Gerry said. It is "beginning to change the climate in which school districts make decisions." From witnessing a few instances he hopes indicate a trend, Gerry said "you don't get that defiant, 'we're going to take this thing all the way up' [attitude]. There is more of a conciliatory tone; officials less automatically go to a hearing" for a decision on their disagreements with parents.

Not all school attorneys dislike the fee law or think it will distort parental involvement or bring about "the Armageddon that some people had projected," as one lawyer said.

On the other hand, another lawyer who preferred not to be named commented, "When HCPA passed, I said we ought to get [our state] to pull out of the federal program; forget the due process" procedures mandated by P.L. 94-142 and provide special education without them.

"I'm not sure due process — when everybody is at each other's throats — is benefiting the kids," that attorney added. Special education conferences originally were not envisioned with lawyers in on the process, but lawyers will be there more often when fees are available for administrative cases.

### The Shortcomings Of Litigation

Lawyers and advocates alike say litigation is not always in a child's best interests, and court can be a bad place to settle disputes.

"The legal aspect [of P.L. 94-142] tends to make very bitter adversaries out of parents and administrators," said Kenneth Brown, executive director of special education at the Spring Branch School District in Houston. "When someone names you in a federal lawsuit, you don't feel like going out to dinner with them."

Litigation can exacerbate a situation that is too prone to being adversarial in the first place. Some school attorneys talk about parents manipulating educators and judges with "the tyranny of tears." In a 1986 report, Will, of the Education Department, notes that the decision of a student's placement can be a "battleground. Parents naturally want the best for their children, a desire that leads some parents to interpret rigid rules and eligibility requirements of special programs as indications that school officials are unwilling to help."

"For their part, schools are often ready to fall back on the stereotype of the 'pushy parent,' especially when requests for services and the insistence on a stronger voice in decisionmaking create inconvenience, embarrassment, and confusion," Will wrote in "Educating Students with Learning Problems — A Shared Responsibility." "As a result, a potential partnership is turned into a series of adversarial, hit-and-run encounters."

"These are emotional cases," said Kreunen. "I've had judges with handicapped children [in special education cases], and they won't excuse themselves from the case. The sympathy factor is worked to the hilt." And while sympathy for a handicapped child may be used, ultimately, Kreunen said, "the bill tends more to be a parents' rights bill than a handicapped children's rights bill."

"The lawyer represents his client and the client is that child, not the parent," Gerry agreed. "I think lawyers [on both sides] ought to point this out more. The child often has to go back to the same school afterward."

People should ask themselves, "'What is the environment going to be like for the child in that building, with that principal?' You have to look at the realistic effect on the child, and I don't see that very often," concluded Gerry. "It is a good area to demonstrate that the legal resolution of human problems should be a last resort."

# 7

# Square Pegs In Round Holes:
## Are Children Being Misidentified?

*"A disorder in one or more of the basic psychological processes involved in understanding or in using language, spoken or written, which may manifest itself in an imperfect ability to listen, think, speak, read, write, spell, or to do mathematical calculations. The term includes such conditions as perceptual handicaps, brain injury, minimal brain dysfunction, dyslexia, and developmental aphasia. The term does not include children who have learning problems which are primarily the result of visual, hearing, or motor handicaps, of mental retardation, of emotional disturbance, or of environmental, cultural, or economic disadvantage."*
> — *P.L. 94-142 regulations, defining learning disability*

The numbers show clearly that more and more children are being identified as learning disabled each year.

What the figures don't explain is why.

In fact, educators don't even agree on whether the increasing numbers are a problem, never mind figuring out why they are increasing.

The number of students classified by states as learning disabled has gone up every academic year since 1976-77, when the federal government first required states to count their special education students for reimbursement under the Education for All Handicapped Children Act, P.L. 94-142.

Of the 3.7 million handicapped children counted that first year, 797,213 were said to be learning disabled. The 1985-86 total was 4.1 million, of which 1.85 million were said to be learning disabled.

That means that while the total special education growth comes to 400,000, the growth for the learning disabled category is a whopping 1.1 million.

### A Continuing Problem

The problem is not new. Concern about overidentification of children as learning disabled was rife in 1975, when Congress put a cap of 2 percent on the number of children who could be so classified.

The cap was lifted in February 1978, two months after the then-Office of Education published revised learning disability regulations.

But the problem — and the debate — refuses to go away.

### Someone Else's Problem

In a survey done for this book, educators saw overplacement as a problem, but a problem that was happening somewhere else.

Some 66.3 percent of the 722 who answered the question said overplacement is not a problem in their jurisdiction, while 33.7 percent said it was a problem (see Appendix A).

But when asked if overplacement is happening in other jurisdictions "that you know about," 56.2 percent of the 681 who responded to that question said yes, while 43.8 percent said no.

Of those who said it was a problem either at home or somewhere else, 85.4 percent said the learning disabilities category has experienced the worst problem with overplacement. Another 10 percent said the emotionally disturbed category, 2.4 percent said mentally retarded and 2 percent said speech impaired. A total of 450 respondents answered the question.

When asked what causes overplacement in their jurisdiction, respondents placed the blame squarely on their peers, with 50.7 percent saying the cause is overburdened regular education teachers and 30.1 percent citing improperly trained personnel. A little less than 20 percent blamed higher financial reimbursement for handicapped students.

The nation's top special education policymaker, while calling the possibility of overidentification "a continuing concern," says the massive increase was not unexpected.

"It's a very complex disorder and it's one that we're learning a great deal about, that professionals are learning more about daily. And that leads to — and should lead to — identification of children who were heretofore unidentified," said Madeleine Will, the Education Department's assistant secretary for special education and rehabilitative services.

### Controversy Over "Slow Learners"

The totals, however, are causing a great deal of consternation for the Association for Children and Adults with Learning Disabilities (ACLD), which fears public pressure to cut back the numbers will force out children who qualify for special help.

"There are a lot of people who question the tremendous growth of the numbers of children with learning disabilities in the last 10 years. It's become the largest category of handicap, so people say why and how and wherefore," said ACLD President Anne Flemming. "And we're afraid because there's a lot of discussion about cutting the number, cutting back on l.d., and depending on how the cuts are made, it may cut even students who deserve to be there.

"Our concern is that—not that we don't want every child to have an appropriate education, because we don't want to kick anyone out—but we also want to protect our population. If the classes fill up with other problems, then some of our population won't be served."

Fleming, a parent of adult children with learning disabilities, said the largest category of students wrongly placed in classes for the learning disabled "is what we call the slow learner. They are not mentally retarded but are having trouble in the regular classroom."

Such students, Fleming said, "need more remedial types of programs rather than the highly specialized l.d. program."

### Link To Mentally Retarded Students

The other major theory is that students with handicaps other than learning disabilities—mental retardation in particular—are being placed in the wrong category. As evidence, educators cite the decreasing numbers of children counted as mentally retarded, which has gone hand in hand with the learning disabilities increase.

Although Will dismissed a question about the theory, saying there is no evidence to link the two trends, the seventh annual report to Congress from her office, the Office of Special Education and Rehabilitative Services, talks about it at length.

A look at the department's child count data over the past decade shows "significant shifts in the categories in which the nation's handicapped are receiving services," says the report.

"The most dramatic example is the contrast between a continual decline in children counted as mentally retarded (from 969,547 for school year 1976-77 to 650,534 in school year 1983-84) and the substantial and continuing increase in the number of children counted as learning disabled (from 797,213 in school year 1976-77 to 1.8 million in school year 1983-84)."

It is likely, said the report, "that the decreases in the mentally retarded count are in part related to increases in the learning disabled count."

It also is likely, the report said, that decreases in the number of children classified as mentally retarded "are the result of an increasing sensitivity to the negative features of the label itself and to reaction on the part of local school systems to allegations of racial and ethnic bias as a result of the use of discriminatory or culturally biased testing procedures.

In some cases, courts have ordered schools to end their disproportionate placement of minority children in classes for the mentally retarded, said the report. Schools then re-evaluated the children and "in many instances it is likely that such a re-evaluation resulted in the assignment to a different handicapping condition."

Another reason the learning disabled numbers could be up, said the report, is that some states are emphasizing noncategorical programming, in which handicapped children are placed in programs on the basis of the services they need rather than strictly by labels.

Finally, the report found "no persuasive evidence" that large numbers of nonhandicapped children are being purposefully identified as handicapped to qualify for special services. "The data more persuasively argue for a shifting of handicapped children among the handicapping categories . . . to find the most appropriate services for the children without sacrificing instructional benefits."

The National Association of State Directors of Special Education (NASDSE), after surveying its members in 1983, came up with many similar reasons for growth in the learning disabled numbers:

- Greater public awareness of learning disabilities.
- Wider availability of assessment techniques.
- Liberal eligibility criteria.
- Budget reductions in other remedial programs.
- Perception that the learning disabled criteria is less stigmatizing than the mentally retarded classification.
- Court orders to re-evaluate minority placement in the mentally retarded category.

"Increasing numbers of youngsters are being covered under the handicapped law, said Gary Makuch, state director of special education in Pennsylvania.

"There's a lot of discussion of whether there is overidentification or overinclusion of youngsters, particularly in the category of learning disability. We need to look at that again.

"One of the things we maybe lost sight of when focusing on

special education, we forgot about the fact that other kids need help. That's part of what has to happen . . . to ensure that the accommodations and adjustments that can be made in regular education but not in the name of special education can be made."

### A Range Of Opinions

If one thing is clear, it's that this is an area where there is no single answer. To demonstrate the range — and ferocity — of opinions, here is a sampling of comments from the written surveys and from interviews:

■ Richard Yoakley, director of pupil personnel, Knox County, Tenn., Schools wrote, "The current standards for identifying l.d. [learning disability] are atrocious. They deny services to students who need them and give them to students who don't need them — aren't l.d.! We were better off when school psychologists were allowed to use their professional judgment to certify l.d."

■ Harold Patterson, superintendent of schools, Spartanburg, S.C., said the use of categories as a "social solution" still exists. He said in an interview, "If you're black and poor, you're likely to be labeled EMH [educable mentally handicapped]. If you're white, you're likely to be l.d. . . . It depends who does the testing, how well they are trained." Patterson's 10,000-student district is 48 percent black and has a special education population of 13 percent.

■ Wayne Shatswell, director of special education, Marysville Unified School District, Calif., wrote, "The pendulum seems to be swinging the other way: special education at the expense of the nonhandicapped. This is especially true with 'learning handicapped' where being 'handicapped' is no longer a stigma; having a 'learning disability' is becoming a status symbol."

In the survey, Shatswell said the Education Department should again try to deregulate P.L. 94-142, particularly its eligibility criteria.

In an interview, Shatswell said eligibility, especially learning disability criteria, is the biggest problem with P.L. 94-142.

"We had a meeting this morning that made the problem even more evident. A parent wanted me to know her child had a learning disability and wanted him in a program. The kid is functioning on the borderline but is head and shoulders above most of the kids in l.d.," he said.

Shatswell thinks that parent, like others he's seen, consider a designation of learning disabled as a "status symbol that has with it a certain amount of privileges. If you're learning handicapped you can get certain materials, you can modify your graduation requirements."

A few years ago, he said, "telling parents their child was a slow learner or retarded was the worst thing you could tell them. Now that we don't use those terms, more parents are interested. There's a certain kind of prestige to being special, almost like they're gifted."

On the other hand, he said, "the good thing is you don't have to fight tooth and nail with parents to get kids in the classes. It's much less threatening. Now when a child is e.m.r. [educable mentally retarded], the old term, we say learning handicapped. We say he's slow to learn the material, he probably will not be a good college student. That glosses it over, but it's not dishonest."

■ Frederick Weintraub, assistant executive director of the Council for Exceptional Children, said the excellence movement has contributed to the overplacement problem. When academic standards are pushed up, he said, more students become classified as "learning disabled."

"The people who invested in excellence," he said, are not concerned with the plight of special education. "When you up the reading level of textbooks, you end up with more kids classified as handicapped. If a system does not have alternatives, the only alternative becomes special education."

### The Incredible Gains

With all the fuss about overidentification, it's easy to forget the incredible gains made in helping children who truly have learning disabilities. Before the law came around, learning disabled children were often thought to simply be troublemakers, or stupid.

Joan Tellefsen, director of TASK (Team of Advocates for Special Kids), in Orange, Calif., recalled that her son — now in his mid-20s — had a learning disability that wasn't diagnosed throughout his school years.

Her son went through school with dyslexia, a condition in which an individual with normal vision has trouble interpreting written language and therefore has trouble reading, but he was never in a special education course until he was a teenager. At that point, his school district decided that he would be placed in a residential placement "because his behavior was bizarre. No one had ever diagnosed him as having a learning disability," she said.

"Unless it's a very severe learning disability, it's not obvious," said Tellefson. "My son is very bright, he never let anyone know he couldn't read well. He was exceptionally verbal. I had two other children who were doing just fine. They were in the gifted program. I thought he just wasn't behaving too well. So did the school district."

Today, she said, "kids have a better chance of being identified early on. But children with learning disabilities often get shortchanged. You don't always notice them early on. Their self-esteem is sometimes shot down."

Indeed, parents of learning disabled children who are in school today say they couldn't have coped without P.L. 94-142.

"Thank God it was there. I don't know what I would have done. When you are faced with a handicapped child, you need professional help. Obviously you can go the doctor route and if you are lucky you can do the doctor route. I couldn't have done it at home. A regular education teacher couldn't have done it," said Leslie Barnes Hagan, a parent of a learning disabled child and chairwomen of the Special Education Advisory Committee in Alexandria, Va.

When Hagan put her son in special education at age three and a half, professionals told her to institutionalize him. Ten years later, he is able to "function in the real world."

"He can talk, he has the same interests as his peer group. He's doing a lot of age-appropriate school work," she said. "This is an absolute miracle. Because of the law, he's getting speech therapy, occupational therapy, reading specialists, classes with 10 or fewer children. All of his needs have been met and only because of the law. There's no way anyone can afford a private school to get the services at close to $20,000 a year for a day school. No one has that kind of money."

"I look at all of these children I know who would not have done anything. Our son is not retarded, he's actually very bright. He will be a functioning member of society. . . . We will not be caring for this child the rest of our lives."

An end note: The National Center for Education Statistics, the Education Department's fact-gathering arm, says not enough evidence exists to judge why the numbers of learning disabled are going up while other categories are going down.

The center's 1985 statistical report, *The Condition of Education,* put it bluntly: "Until more evidence can be gathered, the issue will remain in debate."

# 8

# Paperwork:
## Is Help On The Way?

*"I'm looking at one file of a three-year-old. Her file is 20 pages long. Can you imagine how big it will be by the time she's in high school?"*
— *Peter Chester,*
*supervisor of learning disabilities,*
*Meridien, Conn., public schools*

School officials consider P.L. 94-142 to be the most proscriptive piece of federal education legislation ever written. When you add in its regulations, it runs nearly 300 pages.

And they say they spend hours filling out what seem to them like endless forms.

The advocates and congressmen behind the act say it was crucial to include so many rules and regulations to ensure state compliance with P.L. 94-142.

In fact, the Education Department has been criticized for being lax on monitoring state compliance. In July 1984, an investigation by the House Select Education Subcommittee found evidence that ED was failing to comply with P.L. 94-142 requirements that it review state plans every year. The panel also found that ED had changed its policy of visiting states for on-site reviews every three years—in some cases only showing up every four or five years—without telling advocates.

Those charges were denied at a congressional hearing in August 1984 by Madeleine Will, the Education Department's assistant secretary for special education and rehabilitative services. Will said monitoring guidelines were "ill-defined" when she took office in 1983, and vowed to strengthen them.

Ironically, ED's strengthened guidelines then raised the ire of state special education directors, who said they were too time-consuming to comply with.

A June 1985 test of the system in South Carolina prompted complaints that the paperwork was out of control. To comply, the state had to send ED 11,989 pages of documents. And state officials had to keep duplicates of every page for their records, making a grand total of nearly 24,000 sheets of paper, according to Robert Black, state director of special education.

ED is working to refine the system. "I think we have seen some excellent suggestions come forward from state directors and local staff about data, about monitoring . . . so yes, there are clearly ways to" reduce paperwork, Will said in an interview. "It's an open question."

"We're always willing to work with states to streamline the process of data collection. I think it's fair to point out that a lot of the paper is required by the state, not the federal government, and I think it's also fair to point out that Congress asks us to gather the data," said Will.

### Computerized IEP Systems

Studies show that computerized systems both for data collection and for writing individualized education programs (IEPs) are cheaper and more efficient for schools.

One of the most recent was done by Lynne Ryan, an assistant professor at Providence College in Rhode Island. For her doctoral dissertation at the University of Connecticut, Ryan compared six randomly selected Massachusetts school districts with manually developed IEPs and six with computerized IEPs.

She found the manual system cost $84 per IEP, including teacher time, while the computerized system cost $66. Teachers spent 118 minutes writing an IEP manually, as opposed to 64 minutes on the computer.

Not only that, Ryan said in an interview, but "there was a significant difference between the attitudes of the teachers toward the value of IEP," with teachers in the computerized group having a more favorable attitude.

The Great Lakes Regional Resource Center has been working with the state of Pennsylvania to develop a computerized IEP system.

"The whole idea behind the computerized IEP is to make available in computerized form what the experts in the field think are the whole range of options available for various handicapping conditions," said Luis Torres, program assistant specialist at the center, which is one of ED's six regional resource centers.

Without the computer, educators may not be aware of the range of options available, he said.

And of course, the savings in paperwork is enormous. "You don't have to generate as much paper. Once you do compile all your decisions, it's a matter of saying [to the computer], 'Print,' and looking at your printout. . . . It's a great timesaver."

If school personnel include all the pertinent information about a student at the time they write an IEP, their jobs will be much easier when their school district or state asks for data to meet federal compliance requests, Torres said. "Your report is done in a matter of minutes, rather than hours or days."

He added, "If you have all your information on a database, you can easily retrieve it. If you have 600 kids with 600 files . . . you can readily see the advantage" of computerization.

Torres, whose center serves Pennsylvania, Ohio, Indiana, Illinois, Michigan, Wisconsin and Minnesota, said the computer software, at about $1,400, is not too expensive for schools, as long as they have the proper hardware.

### *"The Paperwork Burden"*

But most schools don't have the software yet, and there is a lot of hostility out there about the amount of paperwork they have to do — to fulfill both federal and state requirements.

"I feel the paperwork burden is the biggest complaint regarding the federal bureaucracy," Kenneth Brown, executive director of special education for the Spring Branch School District in Houston, wrote in the survey.

"When we have to apply for funds each February or March, we have to apply through the Texas Education Agency," Brown explained in an interview. "To get funds the federal government has granted to us, we have to fill out a 50-page form. Our comptroller and I spent a couple of days on it.

"Then what happens is later, after funds are spent and expended, you are monitored on how well you spent the funds. I feel what happens is like the 'Gotcha' game, like the shaving commercial, if you don't spend the money on what you said you were going to spend the money on, and you don't amend your request, which takes another 50 pages, you have to show them why.

"The money is already given through the federal government through 94-142 for each child and the state comes along and puts on inordinate regulations. The state tells me the federal government monitors them closely. What happens is the local education agency is saddled with it. It's very complicated and not needed."

A similar story is told by special educators in Meridien, Conn. On his survey, Robert Wodatch, coordinator of pupil personnel for the

Meridien public schools, wrote, "The federal and state governments have underestimated the tremendous volume of paperwork, files, compliance items that must be done."

A call to Wodatch found him out of the office but produced Peter Chester, supervisor of learning disabilities for the district, who was eager to discuss the problem.

"Since 94-142, there has been a proliferation of paperwork. The paperwork that is involved now we didn't complete prior to the law. There's a letter to parents, a letter for permission, then the IEP. An IEP can be six pages long, and you make four copies of each page. There are reports, follow-up reports, follow-up letters. All are done annually.

"I'd say there are at least 12 forms for each child, some more than one page. There are 20 pieces of paper, easy, for each child each year. Then the reports — they can be five, six, seven pages. I'm looking at one file of a three-year-old. Her file is 20 pages long. Can you imagine how big it will be by the time she's in middle school, high school?

"You have to have more than one file for one child because the state comes in and looks at our files. One copy in the school, one copy in the central office, and parents have a copy. I don't think the kid gets any more service, it takes time away from delivery."

Chester estimated that IEPs take teachers at least six hours to prepare and write. "I'm not in favor of doing away with the paperwork, but modify it. I don't want any child unserved, but the proliferation of paperwork is ridiculous."

A day after the conversation with Chester, Wodatch called, just to be sure the point has come across. He gave a litany of extra examples, and ended the interview by saying, "The bottom line of course, is are kids getting any more instruction from it? And the answer is no."

\* \* \*

Other educators, however, say it's not so simple.

Complaints about paperwork are "a common problem. Certainly there could be some streamlining and of course this is a criticism I often get as I go around the state," said Wendy Cullar, state director of special education in Florida.

Cullar, who was director of special education for ED in 1984-85 during the monitoring rewrite, said the problem is that "when you look at the specifics of details behind the generalities, however, you find that local school districts have either added on forms, or that additional paperwork is in fact items the local school district has decided they need. The local school district does need additional paperwork because it is making decisions."

\* \* \*

With computers far down the road for many districts, one theme that resounded throughout the interviews was frustration, and some resentment. Local school officials feel put upon, and singled out.

Brian McNulty, state director of special education in Colorado, offered this explanation: "A lot has really been forced on schools. I think very clearly schools did not demonstrate leadership in this area. The reason there are programs for handicapped kids is that parents took the initiative. It was a system that was forced upon the schools. There is some resistance to the level of funding handicapped kids get as opposed to nonhandicapped kids. There is some resistance to serving severely handicapped kids when the level of progress is very small. Some of that is certainly out there.

"My guess is also that I think part of the reaction you see now from schools is . . . that it's hard to change a large bureaucratic system. When you come out with a major change agent, it's real hard. Schools are not known for being adaptive, flexible and novel in their responses. And here you have a law that demands they be those things."

McNulty said he thinks school officials' attitudes have improved over the years. As evidence, he cites the growing sophistication in the telephone calls he gets from local officials, asking for help in dealing with the law.

"It's changed from, 'Do I have to do it?' to real questions on sophisticated policy interpretation, [such as,] 'What happens if parents want to keep their child out of school and provide a home program, is that legal? What if I get two different assessments of one kid?'"

One parent offered this analysis: "The guidelines and the time frames they have to operate in do make them have to perform. And a lot of them, quite frankly, do not get support from the upper administration. There is a great deal of feeling on the upper administration's part that special education is a pain in the neck.

"Special education administrators are caught between parents and professionals pushing for placement on the one hand, and upper administrators on the other side. They get no support from either side. It has to be one of the most thankless jobs going. . . . Everyone is very pressed. In fairness to them, I think they have the children's best interest at heart."

# 9

# The New Mandate:
## To Serve The Youngest Handicapped Children

*"Make no mistake that today we send a message to the handicapped citizens of our nation that their needs are not going to be sacrificed at the altar of budget cuts or educational reforms."*
> — *Sen. Lowell Weicker, R-Conn.,*
> *after passage of the bill that*
> *was to become P.L. 99-457*

Probe an early intervention advocate and you'll get this visceral response: legislation to serve the youngest handicapped children was long overdue.

Probe an educator with responsibility for children of all ages and abilities and you'll get this one: we can't afford it.

Either way, with passage of the 1986 amendments to the Education of the Handicapped Act, P.L. 99-457, states will be serving infants, toddlers and preschoolers as they never have before.

The amendments provide strong financial incentives for states to extend special education and related services down to age 3 and establish a new grant program to help states serve handicapped infants and toddlers.

The concept of providing early intervention services to handicapped children has been before Congress, in one form or another, for two decades. In 1975, an early form of the bill that was to become P.L. 94-142 included a requirement to serve children starting at age 3. But, in a compromise that may have assured the bill's passage, Congress deleted that requirement, and the final law gave states discretion over serving preschoolers.

But, by 1986, the political climate had changed. "There has been a growing acceptance" outside the special education community of early intervention, said Frederick Weintraub, assistant executive director of the Council for Exceptional Children (CEC). For instance, he noted, the 1986 National Governors' Association report, "Time For Results: The Governors' 1991 Report on Education," called on states to develop new initiatives to help at-risk preschool children prepare for school.

Another crucial factor, said Weintraub, was the commitment from two key congressmen: Sen. Lowell Weicker, R-Conn., and Rep. Pat Williams, D-Mont., both strong advocates for handicapped children. Until 1986, neither lawmaker "had anything that they could say was their big contribution," said Weintraub. Before passage of P.L. 99-457, "all they could say was, 'I had good stewardship of the committee and preserved the work of 1975.' They both wanted to leave a mark."

Also critical to the bill's passage in 1986 was the growing movement in states toward enacting early childhood programs, said Barbara J. Smith, an early childhood consultant who is a member of the national executive board of CEC's Division for Early Childhood. Congress based its approval of the legislation, in part, on U.S. Education Department data that showed states were serving more than 75 percent, or 260,000, of the estimated 330,000 handicapped children ages 3 through 5 in the nation. Only seven states mandate services for handicapped children from birth, another 19 require them from ages 2, 3 or 4, and the rest mandate them from ages 5 or 6, according to the Education Department.

P.L. 99-457 reauthorizes the discretionary programs of the Education of the Handicapped Act for five years and sets up two major new programs:

1. A new state grant program for handicapped infants and toddlers from birth through age 2. States that want to participate must designate a lead agency, develop a statewide plan and agreements for interagency participation, require individualized family service plans for each child and his or her family, and guarantee full services within four years. P.L. 99-457 requires that services be provided to families at no cost except where federal or state law provides for a system of payments by families, including a schedule of sliding fees.

2. Strong incentives for states to serve handicapped children ages 3 through 5 by school year 1990-91. From fiscal year 1990 on, grants may be made only to states that assure the availability of a free appropriate public education for all handicapped children ages 3 through 5. The requirement will be delayed one year if Congress doesn't appropriate at least $656 million for fiscal years 1987, 1988 and 1989 combined, and $306 million for fiscal 1990. It increases funding for preschool children already served from about $100 per

child to $300 per child in fiscal 1987, $400 per child in 1988 and $500 per child in 1989, topping off at $1,000 in 1990. It also sets up a new funding mechanism — $3,800 per new child — for helping states serve children who previously were not receiving any services.

As with programs for school-age children, funding questions proliferate.

Don Sheldon, deputy executive director of the American Association of School Administrators, while quick to support the concept of early intervention, fears schools will be forced into "siphoning off funds from general education to provide for this new mandate."

Some districts, he said, may eliminate certain extracurricular activities; others may eliminate some elective programs; others may have no problem at all. "I don't know the effect on specific school districts, but having been there as a school superintendent, I understand the kind of trade-offs that can occur when there is a new mandate. The impact on programs can be very dramatic or can be minimal, depending on the resources of specific school districts."

### The Birth Through Two Program

Programs for infants and toddlers may take place in a child's home or in a school, child care center or other facility. Services may range in intensity from round-the-clock medical care to once-a-week sessions with a physical therapist.

The state grant program for handicapped infants and toddlers aims to help states provide early intervention services to children who are developmentally delayed or who have conditions that suggest a "high probability" of resulting in a delay. States also have the option of serving children who are at risk of "substantial" developmental delays if early intervention is not provided.

In recent years, research has shown that early intervention dramatically improves children's physical, cognitive and social abilities, minimizing the effects of existing and potential handicaps. "We're learning scientifically that starting early makes a significant difference in outcome," said Dr. T. Berry Brazelton, a leading early intervention researcher who is chief of the child development unit at Boston Children's Hospital.

Brazelton, who also is a professor of pediatrics at Harvard Medical School, noted another reason the issue has come to the fore is because medical science is able to save increasing numbers of low birthweight and other at-risk babies. To illustrate, in 1960, 28 percent of low birthweight babies were still alive at age 1, according to the National Center for Health Statistics. In 1980, the center said, more than 50 percent of these babies celebrated a first birthday.

And the number of babies that live continues to increase, according to Brazelton. "We're saving smaller and smaller babies. The kind of brains we're leaving them with are better and better. This makes it really worthwhile to get in and do something for them. We have babies with good brains but they may have social difficulties."

Basically, said Brazelton, early intervention can do two things: prevent many physical and psychological disorders, and mitigate their effects on the quality of life of the person involved.

For example, scientists have learned how to repair or make up for an impaired central nervous system. If the intervention starts early, some learning disabilities actually can be arrested, Brazelton said. And babies given the proper stimulation from birth can develop stronger self-images that can help them work through the limitations of a handicap as they get older, he said.

With such remarkable capability to improve children's potential, "it becomes more and more important that we be able to evaluate at-risk infants as early as possible with an eye to more sophisticated preventive and therapeutic approaches, before failure systems and the expectation to fail become established," wrote Brazelton.

In fact, researchers have moved way beyond the question of whether early intervention helps handicapped children. They are now grappling with the question of what kinds of programs best help handicapped children.

"Posing the overall question is a little bit foolish," said Phillip S. Strain, director of the Early Childhood Research Institute at the University of Pittsburgh. "You have to say, if you design a maximally effective program, one that's state of the art, what can you expect from that?"

The question then becomes, how do educators and others interested in setting up programs for infants and toddlers find a state-of-the-art program?

"To get that information, you have to look around and you have to do some detective work because not all of the outcomes you'd be interested in are available in any one particular study," said Strain. "But when you do that detective work, you see effects range very widely for kids. There are significant changes in children's cognitive skills, their social skills, their motor functioning."

Other studies show "significant changes" in terms of lessening stress on the child's parents, Strain said. And still others show a "reasonable portion" of seriously handicapped youngsters being educated in a regular classroom setting, he said.

But more research is needed. Researchers say an added benefit of the law will be that, by increasing the number of children served, it will provide a better research base for making future decisions about the kinds of programs that work best.

It's important to note that the school is not necessarily the agency intended to run infant and toddler programs. In fact, they may not even be the best ones to do it, said Brazelton. "The only reason to use schools is that they're the institution that reaches everyone. They're set up. I'm not really sure they're the right ones" because they're "limited" to education, while programs for infants and toddlers must be multidisciplinary. Any agency, as long as it is multidisciplinary, can handle it, he said.

The law clearly calls for an interagency program of services that coordinates the payments from federal, state, local and private sources, including public and private insurance coverage. To be eligible for a grant, the state must establish an interagency coordinating council and give responsibility for the program to a lead agency, which can be the state education agency or any other appropriate agency.

### Deciding Which Children Are Eligible

Because it is difficult to diagnose some handicaps properly in infants and toddlers, and because the resulting labels can be impossible to discard even if proven incorrect or unnecessary later in the child's life, P.L. 99-457 adds the term "developmental delay" as a way to serve children from birth through age 2 without labeling them. Each state, as part of its comprehensive system for serving infants and toddlers with disabilities, is to come up with its own definition of the term developmental delay.

Some educators fear the use of the term will open the floodgates, letting in children who may simply be slow learners and have no place in programs for handicapped children.

But early childhood specialists believe the use of the term is important for young children and they advocate extending its use through age 5. In fact, experts have debated for more than 20 years the merits of labeling any children, saying it can lead adults to lower their expectations for the children and for the children themselves to lower their self-images. For young children, the concern over mislabeling just adds to the arguments against labeling.

"Children under age 6 develop very unevenly," said CEC's Smith. "Their development fluctuates rapidly. They can show a lot of the same kinds of symptoms for various reasons. They can be showing delays in development . . . because they are mentally retarded, have cerebral palsy or are learning disabled." Their exact problems are not clear "because they are so young and responses are not so developed."

Smith is among those who believe "it's difficult to label 6- or 10-year-olds, but impossible to label some 3-year-olds," calling such attempts nothing more than "a shot in the dark."

Not only that, Smith said, but, bearing in mind that the label may be inaccurate or inapplicable down the road, "if you place a label on a child such as learning disabled, mentally retarded, it's sometimes difficult to get rid of the label. In fact, the child's delay may have been totally remediated but you can't get rid of the label."

While the law did not insert the term developmental delay in the 3 through 5 program, it did amend P.L. 94-142 to say 3- through 5-year-olds do not have to be labeled to be served. P.L. 94-142 requires states to count their children by category to be funded. Under the 1986 amendments, states just need to report the total number of 3- to 5-year-olds served, while still reporting the children age 6 and older by category.

The law also offers states the option of serving children who are "at risk of having substantial developmental delays if early intervention services are not provided." That includes children born into living conditions that would suggest that unless someone intervenes with them and their families, they will have problems.

States were given the discretion to serve environmentally at-risk children for two reasons, said Weintraub of CEC. First, some states — Maine, he said, is one example — "have decided to be rather creative and to try to put together early intervention models that are not solely" for children with acknowledged handicaps, and Congress did not want to penalize those states by excluding at-risk children. Second, it would have been too difficult politically to extend a mandate to the larger population, so what's left is a compromise that says environmentally at-risk children are included at state discretion, he said.

In Maine, the focus has been on the preschool years, but the state is moving toward serving the youngest children. And the state has a "significant interest and focus on the at-risk population, which we define very broadly," said David Stockford, state director of special education. The state is trying to look at the whole family situation, "including looking at the relationship between the infant and family members," he said.

Part of Maine's support for serving at-risk children, Stockford said, stems from its work with school-age children, many of whom would not have needed special education had they been served from an early age.

In addition, he said, Maine's Department of Human Services has been focusing on the issue of child abuse and neglect. "What you see are young people who exhibit significant problems that do interfere with their learning," he said. Instead of ignoring those problems and letting many of these children end up in institutions, the state has begun to "look very carefully" at expanding its programs for at-risk children.

It's unclear at this point how many states will follow Maine's example and how many will stick with a more conservative definition of eligibility. States that are economically sound and states expecting economic growth in the next five years, might be better able to address the broader needs of at-risk children than are other states in less favorable economic circumstances, noted Pascal Trohanis, director of the State Technical Assistance Resource Team (START) at the Frank Porter Graham Child Development Center at the University of North Carolina in Chapel Hill.

### The Three Through Five Program

The new preschool program poses a dual problem for states. They must fulfill an entitlement to serve all handicapped preschoolers by 1991 or risk losing a portion of their federal funding. They also must place these children in the least restrictive educational environment, but few options exist for integrating handicapped and nonhandicapped children in the classroom.

Until recently, the Education Department has not enforced classroom integration of handicapped preschoolers with their nonhandicapped peers, although it is required under P.L. 94-142. The federal government has judged preschool programs' compliance loosely because, unlike school-age programs, preschool programs for nonhandicapped children are not mandated by any state, a policy gap that severely limits the number of classrooms available for integration.

It is unclear whether the federal government will enforce the provision strictly. Least restrictive environment "was not the driving issue" in designing P.L. 99-457, according to Gray Garwood, staff director for the House Select Education Subcommittee during the development of the law.

Lisbeth Vincent, president of CEC's Division for Early Childhood, agreed convenience should not be the deciding factor. The handicapped preschooler's socialization needs must come first, said Vincent, who also is a professor of rehabilitation psychology and special education at the University of Wisconsin.

Because special education programs are administered by a variety of agencies operating under different standards, integration can be an administrative nightmare.

Integration is not very popular with schools, said Gloria Harbin, associate director of state policies for START in Chapel Hill. Schools "have to go through a lot of contortions to integrate children. Because it's difficult, people don't do it very often," she said.

Head Start programs have far more experience than the public schools in integrating and serving handicapped preschoolers. Since 1973 Head Start programs have had a federal mandate to reserve at least 10 percent of their enrollment for handicapped preschoolers. Because of Head Start's longstanding presence in the community, schools often view the programs as the most convenient vehicle for integration.

The degree of cooperation between Head Start and public schools differs from state to state and from community to community. Which program should serve the child, and, in the case of joint services, which program should pay for which services, are the questions that draw the most controversy.

The state education departments of New Jersey and Louisiana, for example, won't contract with Head Start to provide handicapped preschoolers with special education services. Both states say Head Start doesn't meet the standards of an approved education program and therefore is not eligible for state special education funds. "If a kid is in a day care surrounding, that's not an educational environment," said Jeffrey Osowski, New Jersey's special education director.

Neither will New Jersey integrate children into Head Start full time because it can't ensure program quality, said Osowski. Occasionally, however, a New Jersey public school will send a handicapped child to Head Start two days a week for a social experience. In these cases, the school pays for the child's related health services without paying Head Start tuition.

Another way to integrate is to bring nonhandicapped children into special education classrooms, an approach—termed reverse integration—that has been in practice since 1980 in New York's North Syracuse Central School District. The district places one or two nonhandicapped children, with their parents' permission, in classrooms with severely multiply handicapped preschoolers, according to Warren Grund, district assistant superintendent for special education. Like the handicapped students, the nonhandicapped children attend the program five days a week, from 9 a.m. to 2 p.m.

The program is not so much an educational as a socializing experience for the nonhandicapped children, said Grund, and their response to the experience is heartwarming. After a short while in the classroom, the nonhandicapped children try to teach the handicapped children. "The [nonhandicapped] kids just get in there. They're not afraid; they're sensitized to the situation" before they enter the class, he said.

From this experience, strong friendships develop between the handicapped and nonhandicapped children, Grund said. "These kids become advocates for the handicapped kids when they get into kindergarten and first grade."

A drawback of this integration model is that so few nonhandicapped children can be placed in the special education classrooms. Syracuse limits the number "to a level where the [nonhandicapped] kids are assets to the overall program and not detracting from teacher time available to each individual child," said Kathleen Esposito, principal of Main Street Elementary School, where the program is housed.

Another problem with using the reverse integration model for P.L. 99-457 programs is that federal law prohibits using special education funds to serve nonhandicapped children. Syracuse has avoided the issue, Grund said, because the program receives its support from the state.

Other communities also are using the reverse integration model, sometimes with support from state mental retardation agencies. One state special education director, who asked not to be identified, said her state was using this approach with public education funds, adding that no one ever has opposed the practice.

Another integration model would coordinate public school services with child care centers, Vincent said. Using one approach, a public school would offer a child care program space in its building at a below-market rent. In exchange, the child care center would free up five slots in the program for the school's handicapped children. The school would supply the center with support and supervisory staff, Vincent said.

Schools also could integrate handicapped children into community child care centers by placing special educators in the programs, she said. This approach has both benefits and drawbacks. Handicapped children probably would receive more education in a public school classroom using the reverse model, Vincent said. But a handicapped child placed in a community child care center would tend to develop friendships with nonhandicapped children that are likely to continue through the early elementary school grades. "That's critical for kids," she said.

California's state education department places some handicapped children in child care centers and serves children already enrolled in centers who are later identified as handicapped. Handicapped children attend the centers for part of the day, often accompanied by their special education aides or teachers.

The public schools pay for the accompanying staff and transportation to and from the centers, but parents are responsible for child care tuition, according to Nancy Obley-Kilborn, manager of the California education department's infant-preschool unit.

Integrating handicapped children into state-funded prekindergarten programs is another way to provide the least restrictive environment. As more states create and operate such programs in public schools, the possibilities expand. But because most of these programs are designed to serve low-income and disadvantaged preschoolers, states face the question of what constitutes pure integration.

About 20 states have started to develop networks of early childhood programs run by the public schools. And many of them have visions of eventually expanding their programs to serve all preschoolers.

But in the short term, most of these programs are set up to serve preschoolers who benefit most from developmental services — children who are poor or who are at risk of academic failure because they suffer from developmental delays, speak no English or come from difficult family situations.

In many of the states that offer public preschool programs, the schools are allowed, and sometimes encouraged, to contract with outside agencies to run the programs. Public schools can turn to Head Start programs, nonprofit child care centers or, in a few cases, private for-profit early childhood programs.

The idea of state-funded preschools is a relatively new one, becoming popular only in the 1980s. Most public preschool systems still are not widespread within their states and may not be available to coordinate with special education programs.

Some experts believe it is inappropriate to place handicapped children in at-risk preschool programs. Agreeing with this view is Edith Helmich, a research scientist for the Illinois state board of education.

"Putting a handicapped child in this situation might defeat both purposes," Helmich said. The disadvantaged children her program serves need the same amount of attention and individualization handicapped children would, she said. "In this program, [integration] really should not be happening." Illinois' at-risk program, started in 1985, operates in 100 of the state's 1,000 school districts.

Is the grouping of handicapped children with low-income and other disadvantaged children a true integration experience? "I've never seen any research to support that social interaction can only be effective if it's mixed across classes," said Garwood. "These low-income programs, they may have cheaper toys," but sharing among the children still goes on, he said.

Susan Baxter, Washington state's early childhood interagency coordinator, opposes integrating handicapped preschoolers with low-income children. "It further reinforces the caste system. We're sending a message to society about being different," she said.

Baxter said many parents of handicapped children favor integration because they want nonhandicapped children to form emotional bonds with their children and learn to see beyond their impairments. These nonhandicapped children later can become advocates for handicapped individuals when they mature and become our nation's decisionmakers, she said.

### Personnel Shortages

Nearly 90 percent of states in 1986 reported they lacked sufficient personnel to serve their handicapped children adequately from birth through age 2, while 80 percent said they could not provide full services to children ages 3 through 5, according to a study by the universities of Michigan and North Carolina. Most states expect the problem to continue at least until 1989.

Even states that mandated services for handicapped preschoolers before the 1986 Education of the Handicapped Act Amendments are struggling. To compensate for the lack of qualified personnel, they're using the "band-aid approach to dealing with shortages," said Judy Smith-Davis, an authority on training personnel to educate the handicapped and coauthor of the book *Personnel to Educate the Handicapped in America: A Status Report* (Institute for the Study of Exceptional Children and Youth, 1986).

Many states are issuing emergency or temporary teaching certificates to fill the void in school-based programs, placing teachers with no preschool special education training in early childhood classrooms and giving them a grace period in which to earn an appropriate certificate, said Smith-Davis, who also is editor of the quarterly special education publication, Counterpoint. In other states, rural districts are grouping children with varying disabilities and needs in one classroom to conserve personnel.

Universities could alleviate teacher shortages by creating more early childhood special education programs, but most institutions face budget problems and are reluctant to start programs in states where the personnel demand is weak. Most states allow generally certified teachers to conduct early childhood special education programs, thus discouraging universities from offering specialized early childhood training.

Unless states mandate programs to train early childhood special education personnel, "universities won't meet the demand," predicted John Melcher, an early childhood consultant with the Frank

Porter Graham Child Development Center in Chapel Hill and Wisconsin's special education director from 1956 to 1975.

An even worse problem exists with infant intervention programs. There is a dearth of infant services training programs in the country — far fewer than training programs that focus on 3- to 5-year-olds — because of the rarity of mandates for the youngest children.

States that already have gone through the process spent several years in transition — setting standards, outlining university curricula, issuing emergency teaching certificates and providing in-service training. States will have to rely on stopgap measures while they wait for a new generation of service providers to complete four to five years of early childhood training.

* * *

A key element to building a strong corps of qualified early childhood special education professionals is certification standards. But in devising these standards, states are faced with a difficult policy challenge. The standards must be tough enough to ensure preparedness, yet reasonable enough so people from various service delivery systems can meet them.

Seventeen states are ensuring classroom readiness by requiring teachers to earn preschool special education teaching certificates or by adding early childhood education requirements to general special education certificates, according to *Personnel to Educate the Handicapped in America*. But specialized certification has its drawbacks and is not the only avenue to personnel preparation.

Specialized certification requirements prolong a state's teacher shortage. States that require only general special education certification can pull from a large pool of special educators to fill their preschool programs. But it takes time to train teachers for an early childhood special education career, especially if a state decides to require a master's degree for certification.

If special certification were required, school administrators also would have less flexibility to transfer specialized teachers to fill personnel needs in other grades or academic areas.

The need for a specialized certificate, or even any teaching certificate, also might discourage professionals in the developmental disabilities field from working in school-based programs. Experts question the need for a trained developmental disabilities professional to complete core teaching courses before stepping into the classroom.

Specialized certification also may get in the way of integrating handicapped and nonhandicapped children. If states require preschool special education teachers to have a specialized certificate, "then they won't be able to put kids in Head Start and nursery school," where teachers must meet different standards, said START's Harbin.

For example, the California Department of Education will not subsidize a handicapped child served in a program in which no staff member has a general special education certificate.

States that developed early mandates to serve handicapped preschoolers are doing a poor job of integrating those children with their nonhandicapped peers, said Harbin. "Least restrictive environment is pretty much nonexistent at the preschool level." Head Start, even though it does not require its teachers to have education degrees, is one of the best models for serving handicapped children together with nonhandicapped students, she said.

Meanwhile, CEC is developing model special education training criteria as well as deciding what areas of specialization are needed, said Weintraub. CEC is trying to determine whether special requirements or certificates should be developed according to areas of disability or age.

CEC will determine the need for an early preschool special education certificate as well as the need for a certificate with special focus on serving the birth through age 2 population, Weintraub said.

Weintraub and Harbin both support a compromise plan in which teachers with general education backgrounds would be supervised by trained or specially certified early childhood special education teachers. This approach would facilitate integration of handicapped and nonhandicapped children, said Harbin.

* * *

In California, a team of professionals developing personnel standards for the state's preschool special education teachers are considering a similar model. The team hopes to establish a generic set of competencies "that all agencies will buy into," according to Linda Brekken, coordinator of the state education department's infant preschool special education research network.

Requiring a teaching certificate would alienate qualified professionals from other fields, such as occupational and physical therapists and psychologists, who would have to go back to school to earn general teaching credentials, Brekken said.

Instead, the standards should allow for the use of personnel without formal education training, she added. Urban areas such as Watts or East Los Angeles need people who know the language, culture and community of the children they serve.

Personnel without formal training also would be helpful in infant service programs, where staff members work very closely with families of handicapped babies. They could work under an infant services specialist while receiving in-service training to improve their skills, said Brekken.

Massachusetts is considering merging two certificates — early childhood education and early childhood special education — to facilitate integration at the preschool level.

The state has had an early childhood special education certificate since about 1979, said Carole Thomson, director of Massachusetts' Chapter 188 program, which in 1985 established a state-funded preschool program for disadvantaged children. In 1987 the state started developing early childhood education certification requirements for the Chapter 188 program.

The joint certificate would surmount the certification obstacle to integrating handicapped and disadvantaged preschoolers, according to Thomson. Chapter 188 teachers would be qualified to teach any handicapped preschooler placed in their classrooms.

The proposal is prompting a great deal of discussion around the state, said Thomson. Because the undergraduate joint certificate could be completed in the same amount of time as a single specialty certificate, colleges and universities question whether they will have time to prepare teachers adequately in both areas, she said.

Other universities "think it's not an issue," Thomson said. They suggest that regular education and special education faculty share the training task.

* * *

Greater problems exist for infant service personnel. States must devise training criteria for infant service personnel that develop skills different from those needed to serve handicapped preschoolers. To do this, they can look to the few model infant service training programs in the country that offer a multidisciplinary or transdisciplinary approach to learning. These programs blend the expertise of the medical, education and social welfare communities to provide a holistic approach to serving handicapped infants.

Two competencies are essential to infant intervention — medical knowledge and family assistance skills. Infant service personnel should be able to evaluate infants with overt physical disabilities very early. They also must be able to work not only with the baby, but also with a family still shocked at the arrival of a handicapped child.

* * *

Another shortage exists in the field of allied health professionals, a group that includes occupational and physical therapists and speech, language and hearing pathologists.

The new law accentuates the need for allied health professionals, changing the law's categorization of occupational and physical therapy and several other health-related services from a related to a primary service for infants and toddlers. This change will allow infants and toddlers in need of neurological therapy to receive it without having to show a need for special education.

In January 1986, 29 states already faced a shortage of physical therapists, with five reporting severe problems, according to *Personnel to Educate the Handicapped in America*. The study also showed 28 states suffered from a shortage of occupational therapists, with five of them in severe trouble.

\* \* \*

A key element of the new programs for the youngest children is the emphasis on state-level decisionmaking. The law leaves much discretion to states, a situation with both "pluses and minuses," said START's Trohanis.

On the plus side, Congress was interested in letting states create systems responsive to their particular needs, based on their history, their current array of services and resources, and the political context. The programs created "will be truly unique to each jurisdiction," he said. On the negative side, "The reality in this country is people do move, so if people are to be defined in one jurisdiction one way, a neighboring state another way, it could be problematic for families."

### The Other Side Of The Question: Older Children

Helping handicapped students make the transition from school to work or higher education has been a federal priority since 1983.

Making sure students get an unbroken chain of services from birth through adulthood has been the goal of Madeleine Will, the Education Department's assistant secretary for special education and rehabilitative services. In 1983, Congress established a program of grants to help smooth the way into the world for older students.

When Will became the nation's top special education policymaker a little more than two years ago, she spelled out that goal very clearly. Democrats and Republicans alike agree the Reagan administration appointee has used the power of her office to bring national attention to the plight of younger and older handicapped children.

The 1983 amendments followed intensive lobbying by Will, who many credit with bringing the issues to public attention.

But Will doesn't believe a federal mandate forcing states to educate older children is the next step.

"No, I think we are sending a message to states that through our formula program and our discretionary programs, that we place a high priority on services to children at . . . the later ages, the transition ages, and we have seen a tremendous response since the passage of 94-142," Will said.

The law requires states to serve children up to age 18, but lets them opt out of serving those 18 to 21.

Twenty-eight states serve handicapped youth through age 21 if they have not graduated from high school, according to ED data.

"So there is an interest and a very active role that the states are taking in developing these services. In terms of transition, I would be fearful of a mandate. What would we be mandating? They're pioneering right now, this is a whole new frontier. What are transition services, what are the roles to be played by professionals in the delivery of these services? There are many research questions unanswered. I think we need to allow the states to experiment," Will said.

The assistant secretary thus sees no need for a mandate "as long as we see a response from states, and we're continuing to see states increase services to youngsters at both ends of the age spectrum, we're seeing, increasingly, state legislation introduced and passed. We feel they're responding, they're doing what we've asked them to do."

One state in the forefront of transition services is Massachusetts, which in 1984 set up a Bureau of Transitional Planning to help disabled students move from school to adult social service agencies after they reach age 22. The program, formed under a law called Chapter 688, or, unofficially, the "Turning 22 Legislation," is said to be the first of its kind in the nation.

Transition plans for the students begin when they are 20 years old or two years before their graduation from high school. At that point, the transition planning bureau, which is in the state Office of Human Services, and the appropriate human service agency are alerted to the child's impending transfer.

In Arkansas, the state education department's Division of Special Education is funding a transition project designed to help mildly to moderately handicapped students move from public secondary special education classes to the workplace.

The project, run by the Western Arkansas Education Cooperative, is currently working to develop a model that can be put into place statewide in the 1986-87 school year, according to Cathy Williams, transition project supervisor.

Williams said the model will emphasize vocational assessment beginning in the eighth grade, prevocational and vocational training starting in the first year of high school and continuing through 12th grade, and actual work experience beginning in the 11th and 12th grades or the semester after the student has turned 16.

She stressed that the project has been a collaborative effort of three state agencies: special education, vocational education and vocational rehabilitation. "It has been extremely rewarding to see how one agency's resources can fill a void in another agency's services, usually without additional funding requirements," Williams said.

# Part Three
# Appendices

# Survey Talley

Surveys were sent to 3,000 *Education Daily* and *Education of the Handicapped* readers in August 1985, with a response deadline of Sept. 20, 1985. By that date, 748 responses had been returned. The responses were then tabulated by job title.

The totals for each question do not add to 748 because some repondents did not answer every question.

1. How would you describe the effect P.L. 94-142 has had on the education of handicapped children in the United States? (Circle one)

| | Federal Special Education Administrator | State Special Education Administrator | Regional Special Education Administrator | Local Special Education Administrator | Special Education Teacher | Superintendent | Principal | Parent | Advocate | Attorney | Other | Total | Percentage |
|---|---|---|---|---|---|---|---|---|---|---|---|---|---|
| A. Improved greatly | 3 | 34 | 69 | 330 | 4 | 10 | 11 | 3 | 19 | 3 | 59 | 545 | 72.9% |
| B. Improved somewhat | 0 | 6 | 29 | 109 | 2 | 2 | 3 | 1 | 9 | 5 | 16 | 182 | 24.3 |
| C. Little effect | 0 | 2 | 0 | 4 | 0 | 1 | 0 | 0 | 1 | 0 | 0 | 8 | 1.0 |
| D. Somewhat negative | 0 | 0 | 3 | 3 | 1 | 1 | 1 | 0 | 0 | 0 | 2 | 11 | 1.5 |
| E. Very negative | 0 | 0 | 2 | 0 | 0 | 0 | 0 | 0 | 0 | 0 | 0 | 2 | 0.3 |
| **Total** | **3** | **42** | **103** | **446** | **7** | **14** | **15** | **4** | **29** | **8** | **77** | **748** | **100%** |

2. How would you describe the effect P.L. 94-142 has had on the education of nonhandicapped children in the United States? (Circle one)

| | Federal Special Education Admin. | State Special Education Admin. | Regional Special Education Admin. | Local Special Education Admin. | Special Education Teacher | Superintendent | Principal | Parent | Advocate | Attorney | Other | Total | Percentage |
|---|---|---|---|---|---|---|---|---|---|---|---|---|---|
| A. Improved greatly | 0 | 3 | 2 | 31 | 0 | 1 | 0 | 0 | 4 | 0 | 7 | 48 | 6.5% |
| B. Improved somewhat | 0 | 13 | 33 | 169 | 3 | 1 | 3 | 1 | 14 | 3 | 24 | 264 | 35.5 |
| C. Little effect | 3 | 21 | 46 | 175 | 2 | 8 | 11 | 3 | 7 | 2 | 36 | 314 | 42.2 |
| D. Somewhat negative | 0 | 5 | 19 | 70 | 2 | 4 | 2 | 0 | 0 | 2 | 7 | 111 | 14.9 |
| E. Very negative | 0 | 0 | 1 | 3 | 1 | 0 | 0 | 0 | 0 | 1 | 1 | 7 | 0.9 |
| **Total** | **3** | **42** | **102** | **448** | **8** | **14** | **16** | **4** | **25** | **8** | **75** | **744** | **100%** |

119

3. How would you describe the effect P.L. 94-142 has had on the education of handicapped children in your jurisdiction? (Circle one)

| | Federal Special Education Admin. | State Special Education Admin. | Regional Special Education Admin. | Local Special Education Admin. | Special Education Teacher | Superintendent | Principal | Parent | Advocate | Attorney | Other | Total | Percentage |
|---|---|---|---|---|---|---|---|---|---|---|---|---|---|
| A. Improved greatly | 1 | 30 | 60 | 250 | 3 | 9 | 8 | 3 | 13 | 1 | 36 | 414 | 56.1% |
| B. Improved somewhat | 2 | 7 | 24 | 149 | 2 | 3 | 5 | 1 | 10 | 5 | 31 | 239 | 32.4 |
| C. Little effect | 0 | 1 | 11 | 35 | 3 | 1 | 3 | 0 | 0 | 0 | 5 | 60 | 8.1 |
| D. Somewhat negative | 0 | 2 | 4 | 8 | 0 | 1 | 1 | 0 | 0 | 0 | 4 | 20 | 2.7 |
| E. Very negative | 0 | 1 | 1 | 2 | 1 | 0 | 0 | 0 | 0 | 0 | 0 | 5 | 0.7 |
| Total | 3 | 41 | 100 | 444 | 9 | 14 | 17 | 4 | 23 | 7 | 76 | 738 | 100% |

4. How would you describe the effect P.L. 94-142 has had on the education of nonhandicapped children in your jurisdiction? (Circle one)

| | Federal Special Education Admin. | State Special Education Admin. | Regional Special Education Admin. | Local Special Education Admin. | Special Education Teacher | Superintendent | Principal | Parent | Advocate | Attorney | Other | Total | Percentage |
|---|---|---|---|---|---|---|---|---|---|---|---|---|---|
| A. Improved greatly | 0 | 2 | 0 | 32 | 0 | 1 | 0 | 0 | 4 | 0 | 7 | 46 | 6.3% |
| B. Improved somewhat | 0 | 19 | 39 | 148 | 4 | 2 | 4 | 2 | 10 | 1 | 24 | 253 | 35.1 |
| C. Little effect | 3 | 18 | 43 | 129 | 3 | 7 | 10 | 2 | 8 | 4 | 38 | 265 | 36.8 |
| D. Somewhat negative | 0 | 2 | 13 | 32 | 1 | 4 | 2 | 0 | 0 | 1 | 4 | 59 | 8.2 |
| E. Very negative | 0 | 0 | 1 | 94 | 1 | 0 | 0 | 0 | 0 | 1 | 1 | 98 | 13.6 |
| Total | 3 | 41 | 96 | 435 | 9 | 14 | 16 | 4 | 22 | 7 | 74 | 721 | 100% |

5. P.L. 94-142 was intended to ensure that all handicapped students are provided a free appropriate public education. Most experts estimate that nearly all handicapped children are now being served. Do you agree? (Circle one)

| | Federal Special Education Admin. | State Special Education Admin. | Regional Special Education Admin. | Local Special Education Admin. | Special Education Teacher | Superintendent | Principal | Parent | Advocate | Attorney | Other | Total | Percentage |
|---|---|---|---|---|---|---|---|---|---|---|---|---|---|
| A. Yes, nearly 100 percent are being served | 0 | 27 | 55 | 218 | 2 | 9 | 4 | 0 | 2 | 4 | 34 | 355 | 49.1% |
| B. More than 90 percent are being served | 3 | 12 | 30 | 164 | 3 | 5 | 5 | 3 | 12 | 3 | 24 | 264 | 36.5 |
| C. More than 75 percent are being served | 0 | 2 | 15 | 53 | 3 | 0 | 8 | 0 | 10 | 1 | 5 | 97 | 13.4 |
| D. Fewer than 50 percent are being served | 0 | 0 | 0 | 0 | 0 | 0 | 2 | 1 | 0 | 0 | 4 | 7 | 1.0 |
| Total | 3 | 41 | 100 | 435 | 8 | 14 | 19 | 4 | 24 | 8 | 67 | 723 | 100% |

**6. Is P.L. 94-142 placing a financial burden on your jurisdiction?**

| | Federal Special Education Admin. | State Special Education Admin. | Regional Special Education Admin. | Local Special Education Admin. | Special Education Teacher | Superintendent | Principal | Parent | Advocate | Attorney | Other | Total | Percentage |
|---|---|---|---|---|---|---|---|---|---|---|---|---|---|
| A. Yes | 2 | 32 | 71 | 311 | 7 | 14 | 9 | 1 | 14 | 6 | 39 | 506 | 73.2% |
| B. No | 1 | 8 | 26 | 109 | 3 | 0 | 6 | 2 | 4 | 0 | 26 | 185 | 26.8 |
| **Total** | **3** | **40** | **97** | **420** | **10** | **14** | **15** | **3** | **18** | **6** | **65** | **691** | **100%** |

**If yes, what is the solution? (Circle as many as apply)**

| | Federal Special Education Admin. | State Special Education Admin. | Regional Special Education Admin. | Local Special Education Admin. | Special Education Teacher | Superintendent | Principal | Parent | Advocate | Attorney | Other | Total | Percentage |
|---|---|---|---|---|---|---|---|---|---|---|---|---|---|
| A. More federal money | 1 | 27 | 56 | 248 | 3 | 10 | 8 | 0 | 11 | 5 | 38 | 407 | 42.5% |
| B. More state money | 1 | 22 | 52 | 237 | 2 | 9 | 5 | 3 | 10 | 3 | 36 | 380 | 39.7 |
| C. Raising local taxes | 2 | 8 | 10 | 50 | 0 | 1 | 2 | 0 | 4 | 2 | 20 | 99 | 10.3 |
| D. Reducing services to handicapped students | 0 | 1 | 8 | 43 | 2 | 1 | 1 | 1 | 0 | 1 | 2 | 60 | 6.3 |
| E. Reducing services to nonhandicapped students | 0 | 2 | 0 | 4 | 0 | 1 | 1 | 0 | 0 | 0 | 3 | 11 | 1.2 |
| **Total** | **4** | **60** | **126** | **582** | **7** | **22** | **17** | **4** | **25** | **11** | **99** | **957** | **100%** |

**7. How much of your special education money comes from federal sources? (Circle one)**

| | Federal Special Education Admin. | State Special Education Admin. | Regional Special Education Admin. | Local Special Education Admin. | Special Education Teacher | Superintendent | Principal | Parent | Advocate | Attorney | Other | Total | Percentage |
|---|---|---|---|---|---|---|---|---|---|---|---|---|---|
| A. 0 to 5 percent | N/A | 8 | 27 | 147 | 1 | 4 | 5 | 1 | 4 | 1 | 17 | 215 | 31.3% |
| B. 5 to 10 percent | N/A | 18 | 41 | 174 | 3 | 5 | 5 | 3 | 7 | 4 | 18 | 278 | 40.4 |
| C. 10 to 25 percent | N/A | 10 | 15 | 80 | 5 | 4 | 2 | 0 | 3 | 0 | 15 | 134 | 19.5 |
| D. More than 25 percent | N/A | 2 | 16 | 25 | 0 | 1 | 1 | 0 | 3 | 0 | 13 | 61 | 8.8 |
| **Total** | **N/A** | **38** | **99** | **426** | **9** | **14** | **13** | **4** | **17** | **5** | **63** | **688** | **100%** |

**8. How much of your special education money comes from state sources? (Circle one)**

| | Federal Special Education Admin. | State Special Education Admin. | Regional Special Education Admin. | Local Special Education Admin. | Special Education Teacher | Superintendent | Principal | Parent | Advocate | Attorney | Other | Total | Percentage |
|---|---|---|---|---|---|---|---|---|---|---|---|---|---|
| A. 0 to 10 percent | N/A | 2 | 17 | 49 | 0 | 2 | 0 | 0 | 2 | 0 | 8 | 80 | 11.6% |
| B. 10 to 25 percent | N/A | 3 | 22 | 79 | 0 | 4 | 2 | 1 | 2 | 0 | 4 | 117 | 16.9 |
| C. 25 to 50 percent | N/A | 10 | 22 | 117 | 3 | 4 | 3 | 0 | 3 | 1 | 25 | 188 | 27.2 |
| D. More than 50 percent | N/A | 27 | 38 | 182 | 5 | 4 | 7 | 3 | 11 | 3 | 26 | 306 | 44.3 |
| **Total** | **N/A** | **42** | **99** | **427** | **8** | **14** | **12** | **4** | **18** | **4** | **63** | **691** | **100%** |

**9. Many critics say federal PL. 94-142 dollars have encouraged schools to place nonhandicapped students in special education. Is overplacement happening in your jurisdiction?**

| | Federal Special Education Admin. | State Special Education Admin. | Regional Special Education Admin. | Local Special Education Admin. | Special Education Teacher | Superintendent | Principal | Parent | Advocate | Attorney | Other | Total | Percentage |
|---|---|---|---|---|---|---|---|---|---|---|---|---|---|
| A. Yes | 1 | 18 | 29 | 142 | 3 | 2 | 5 | 1 | 5 | 2 | 35 | 243 | 33.7% |
| B. No | 1 | 22 | 69 | 296 | 5 | 12 | 11 | 3 | 17 | 5 | 38 | 479 | 66.3 |
| **Total** | **2** | **40** | **98** | **438** | **8** | **14** | **16** | **4** | **22** | **7** | **73** | **722** | **100%** |

**Is overplacement happening in other jurisdictions that you know about?**

| | Federal Special Education Admin. | State Special Education Admin. | Regional Special Education Admin. | Local Special Education Admin. | Special Education Teacher | Superintendent | Principal | Parent | Advocate | Attorney | Other | Total | Percentage |
|---|---|---|---|---|---|---|---|---|---|---|---|---|---|
| A. Yes | 1 | 19 | 55 | 245 | 5 | 4 | 6 | 2 | 5 | 2 | 39 | 383 | 56.2% |
| B. No | 1 | 17 | 41 | 168 | 3 | 8 | 9 | 2 | 16 | 4 | 29 | 298 | 43.8 |
| **Total** | **2** | **36** | **96** | **413** | **8** | **12** | **15** | **4** | **21** | **6** | **68** | **681** | **100%** |

If you answer no to both parts of question 9, skip to question 12.

**10. In what category is overplacement the biggest problem? (Circle one)**

| | Federal Special Education Admin. | State Special Education Admin. | Regional Special Education Admin. | Local Special Education Admin. | Special Education Teacher | Superintendent | Principal | Parent | Advocate | Attorney | Other | Total | Percentage |
|---|---|---|---|---|---|---|---|---|---|---|---|---|---|
| A. Learning disabled | 2 | 22 | 57 | 234 | 5 | 3 | 8 | 3 | 5 | 2 | 13 | 384 | 85.4% |
| B. Emotionally disturbed | 0 | 1 | 10 | 24 | 0 | 1 | 0 | 0 | 4 | 0 | 6 | 46 | 10.2 |
| C. Mentally retarded | 0 | 0 | 1 | 4 | 0 | 0 | 0 | 1 | 2 | 1 | 2 | 11 | 2.4 |
| D. Speech impaired | 0 | 4 | 0 | 5 | 0 | 0 | 0 | 0 | 0 | 0 | 0 | 9 | 2.0 |
| Total | 2 | 27 | 68 | 267 | 5 | 4 | 8 | 4 | 11 | 3 | 51 | 450 | 100% |

**11. What causes overplacement in your area? (Circle as many as apply)**

| | Federal Special Education Admin. | State Special Education Admin. | Regional Special Education Admin. | Local Special Education Admin. | Special Education Teacher | Superintendent | Principal | Parent | Advocate | Attorney | Other | Total | Percentage |
|---|---|---|---|---|---|---|---|---|---|---|---|---|---|
| A. Improperly trained personnel | 0 | 9 | 18 | 54 | 1 | 2 | 3 | 1 | 5 | 1 | 13 | 107 | 30.1% |
| B. Higher financial reimbursement for handicapped students | 1 | 7 | 7 | 24 | 2 | 1 | 3 | 1 | 1 | 1 | 20 | 68 | 19.2 |
| C. Overburdened regular education teachers | 0 | 11 | 28 | 109 | 5 | 2 | 6 | 0 | 4 | 2 | 13 | 180 | 50.7 |
| Total | 1 | 27 | 53 | 187 | 8 | 5 | 12 | 2 | 10 | 4 | 46 | 355 | 100% |

**12. Have you or your agency been the target of a P.L. 94-142 lawsuit?**

| | Federal Special Education Admin. | State Special Education Admin. | Regional Special Education Admin. | Local Special Education Admin. | Special Education Teacher | Superintendent | Principal | Parent | Advocate | Attorney | Other | Total | Percentage |
|---|---|---|---|---|---|---|---|---|---|---|---|---|---|
| A. Yes | 0 | 28 | 23 | 115 | 1 | 6 | 1 | 0 | 2 | 4 | 12 | 192 | 27.8% |
| B. No | 4 | 14 | 74 | 297 | 6 | 8 | 14 | 3 | 17 | 1 | 61 | 499 | 72.2 |
| Total | 4 | 42 | 97 | 412 | 7 | 14 | 15 | 3 | 19 | 5 | 73 | 691 | 100% |

**If yes, could the problem have been solved without litigation, through: (Circle as many as apply)**

| | Federal Special Education Admin. | State Special Education Admin. | Regional Special Education Admin. | Local Special Education Admin. | Special Education Teacher | Superintendent | Principal | Parent | Advocate | Attorney | Other | Total | Percentage |
|---|---|---|---|---|---|---|---|---|---|---|---|---|---|
| A. Mediation | 0 | 13 | 11 | 41 | 0 | 2 | 1 | 0 | 1 | 0 | 5 | 74 | 52.9% |
| B. Better communication with parents | 0 | 10 | 12 | 34 | 0 | 3 | 0 | 0 | 3 | 0 | 4 | 66 | 47.1 |
| Total | 0 | 23 | 23 | 75 | 0 | 5 | 1 | 0 | 4 | 0 | 9 | 140 | 100% |

**13. For local officials: How much money, on average, does your district spend a year on litigation, excluding administrative hearings? (Circle one)**

| | Federal Special Education Admin. | State Special Education Admin. | Regional Special Education Admin. | Local Special Education Admin. | Special Education Teacher | Superintendent | Principal | Parent | Advocate | Attorney | Other | Total | Percentage |
|---|---|---|---|---|---|---|---|---|---|---|---|---|---|
| A. Less than $1,000 | N/A | N/A | 44 | 257 | 0 | 6 | 5 | 0 | 1 | 0 | 13 | 326 | 58.6% |
| B. $1,000 to $10,000 | N/A | N/A | 28 | 98 | 0 | 3 | 2 | 0 | 0 | 1 | 8 | 140 | 25.2 |
| C. $10,000 to $50,000 | N/A | N/A | 5 | 47 | 0 | 2 | 1 | 0 | 2 | 2 | 7 | 66 | 11.9 |
| D. $50,000 or more | N/A | N/A | 0 | 15 | 0 | 3 | 1 | 0 | 1 | 1 | 3 | 24 | 4.3 |
| Total | N/A | N/A | 77 | 417 | 0 | 14 | 9 | 0 | 4 | 4 | 31 | 556 | 100% |

**On administrative hearings alone? (Circle one)**

| | Federal Special Education Admin. | State Special Education Admin. | Regional Special Education Admin. | Local Special Education Admin. | Special Education Teacher | Superintendent | Principal | Parent | Advocate | Attorney | Other | Total | Percentage |
|---|---|---|---|---|---|---|---|---|---|---|---|---|---|
| A. Less than $1,000 | N/A | N/A | 40 | 225 | 0 | 7 | 4 | 0 | 1 | 0 | 13 | 290 | 57.0% |
| B. $1,000 to $10,000 | N/A | N/A | 27 | 113 | 0 | 2 | 3 | 0 | 0 | 3 | 10 | 158 | 31.0 |
| C. $10,000 to $50,000 | N/A | N/A | 7 | 33 | 0 | 3 | 0 | 0 | 2 | 1 | 3 | 49 | 9.6 |
| D. $50,000 or more | N/A | N/A | 1 | 5 | 0 | 0 | 0 | 0 | 1 | 0 | 5 | 12 | 2.4 |
| Total | N/A | N/A | 75 | 376 | 0 | 12 | 7 | 0 | 4 | 4 | 31 | 509 | 100% |

14. For state officials: How much money, on an average, does your state spend a year on litigation, excluding administrative hearings? (Circle one)

| | Federal Special Education Admin. | State Special Education Admin. | Regional Special Education Admin. | Local Special Education Admin. | Special Education Teacher | Superintendent | Principal | Parent | Advocate | Attorney | Other | Total | Percentage |
|---|---|---|---|---|---|---|---|---|---|---|---|---|---|
| a. Less than $10,000 | N/A | 19 | 5 | N/A | N/A | N/A | N/A | N/A | 1 | N/A | 5 | 30 | 40.5% |
| b. $10,000 to $50,000 | N/A | 20 | 2 | N/A | N/A | N/A | N/A | N/A | 0 | N/A | 1 | 23 | 31.1 |
| c. $50,000 to $100,000 | N/A | 8 | 0 | N/A | N/A | N/A | N/A | N/A | 1 | N/A | 5 | 14 | 18.9 |
| d. $100,000 or more | N/A | 4 | 1 | N/A | N/A | N/A | N/A | N/A | 1 | N/A | 1 | 7 | 9.5 |
| Total | N/A | 51 | 8 | N/A | N/A | N/A | N/A | N/A | 3 | N/A | 12 | 74 | 100% |

On administrative hearings alone? (Circle one)

| | Federal Special Education Admin. | State Special Education Admin. | Regional Special Education Admin. | Local Special Education Admin. | Special Education Teacher | Superintendent | Principal | Parent | Advocate | Attorney | Other | Total | Percentage |
|---|---|---|---|---|---|---|---|---|---|---|---|---|---|
| Less than $10,000 | N/A | 18 | 5 | N/A | N/A | N/A | N/A | N/A | 1 | N/A | 4 | 28 | 52.8% |
| $10,000 to $50,000 | N/A | 11 | 3 | N/A | N/A | N/A | N/A | N/A | 0 | N/A | 0 | 14 | 26.4 |
| $50,000 to $100,000 | N/A | 4 | 0 | N/A | N/A | N/A | N/A | N/A | 1 | N/A | 1 | 6 | 11.3 |
| $100,000 or more | N/A | 3 | 0 | N/A | N/A | N/A | N/A | N/A | 1 | N/A | 1 | 5 | 9.5 |
| Total | N/A | 36 | 8 | N/A | N/A | N/A | N/A | N/A | 3 | N/A | 6 | 53 | 100% |

15. Congress is trying to give parents the right to win attorneys' fees from the losing party in P.L. 94-142 cases. Do you support such litigation?

| | Federal Special Education Admin. | State Special Education Admin. | Regional Special Education Admin. | Local Special Education Admin. | Special Education Teacher | Superintendent | Principal | Parent | Advocate | Attorney | Other | Total | Percentage |
|---|---|---|---|---|---|---|---|---|---|---|---|---|---|
| Yes | 1 | 16 | 29 | 55 | 3 | 1 | 12 | 4 | 25 | 3 | 43 | 192 | 27.7% |
| No | 2 | 20 | 76 | 359 | 5 | 9 | 4 | 0 | 0 | 5 | 21 | 501 | 72.3 |
| Total | 3 | 36 | 105 | 414 | 8 | 10 | 16 | 4 | 25 | 8 | 64 | 693 | 100% |

16. Should the Education Department again try to deregulate P.L. 94-142?

| | Federal Special Education Admin. | State Special Education Admin. | Regional Special Education Admin. | Local Special Education Admin. | Special Education Teacher | Superintendent | Principal | Parent | Advocate | Attorney | Other | Total | Percentage |
|---|---|---|---|---|---|---|---|---|---|---|---|---|---|
| A. Yes | 0 | 16 | 32 | 181 | 4 | 4 | 4 | 0 | 1 | 3 | 18 | 262 | 36.4% |
| B. No | 3 | 24 | 68 | 251 | 4 | 6 | 12 | 4 | 25 | 5 | 58 | 457 | 63.6 |
| Total | 3 | 40 | 100 | 432 | 8 | 10 | 16 | 4 | 26 | 8 | 76 | 719 | 100% |

If yes, what areas should be looked at? (Circle as many as apply)

| | Federal Special Education Admin. | State Special Education Admin. | Regional Special Education Admin. | Local Special Education Admin. | Special Education Teacher | Superintendent | Principal | Parent | Advocate | Attorney | Other | Total | Percentage |
|---|---|---|---|---|---|---|---|---|---|---|---|---|---|
| A. Least restrictive environment | N/A | 5 | 16 | 54 | 2 | 2 | 3 | 0 | 1 | 2 | 15 | 100 | 17.7% |
| B. Related services | N/A | 18 | 30 | 156 | 2 | 5 | 3 | 0 | 1 | 2 | 16 | 233 | 41.2 |
| C. Due process | N/A | 4 | 17 | 94 | 2 | 0 | 3 | 0 | 1 | 3 | 11 | 135 | 23.8 |
| D. Discipline | N/A | 4 | 6 | 63 | 2 | 1 | 3 | 0 | 1 | 2 | 16 | 98 | 17.3 |
| Total | N/A | 31 | 69 | 367 | 8 | 8 | 12 | 0 | 4 | 9 | 58 | 566 | 100% |

# Education of the Handicapped Act

## Part A — General Provisions

### SHORT TITLE; STATEMENT OF FINDINGS AND PURPOSE

Sec. 601. (a) This title may be cited as the "Education of the Handicapped Act".

(b) The Congress finds that—

(1) there are more than eight million handicapped children in the United States today;

(2) the special educational needs of such children are not being fully met;

(3) more than half of the handicapped children in the United States do not receive appropriate educational services which would enable them to have full equality of opportunity;

(4) one million of the handicapped children in the United States are excluded entirely from the public school system and will not go through the educational process with their peers;

(5) there are many handicapped children throughout the United States participating in regular school programs whose handicaps prevent them from having a successful educational experience because their handicaps are undetected;

(6) because of the lack of adequate services within the public school system, families are often forced to find services outside the public school system, often at great distance from their residence and at their own expense;

(7) developments in the training of teachers and in diagnostic and instructional procedures and methods have advanced to the point that, given appropriate funding, State and local educational agencies can and will provide effective special education and related services to meet the needs of handicapped children;

(8) State and local educational agencies have a responsibility to provide education for all handicapped children, but present financial resources are inadequate to meet the special educational needs of handicapped children; and

(9) it is in the national interest that the Federal Government

127

assist State and local efforts to provide programs to meet the educational needs of handicapped children in order to assure equal protection of the law.

(c) It is the purpose of this Act to assure that all handicapped children have available to them, within the time periods specified in section 612(2)(b), a free appropriate public education which emphasizes special education and related services designed to meet their unique needs, to assure that the rights of handicapped children and their parents or guardians are protected, to assist States and localities to provide for the education of all handicapped children, and to assess and assure the effectiveness of efforts to educate handicapped children. *(20 USC 1401)*

## DEFINITIONS

Sec. 602. (a) As used in this title —

(1) The term "handicapped children" means mentally retarded, hard of hearing, deaf, speech or language impaired, visually handicapped, seriously emotionally disturbed, orthopedically impaired, or other health impaired children or children with specific learning disabilities who by reason thereof require special education and related services.

(2) (P.L. 98-199, sec. 2(2), repealed this paragraph which defined the term "Commissioner." That law further amended this Act by replacing all references to "Commissioner" or "Commissioner's" with "Secretary" or "Secretary's", respectively.)

(3) The term "Advisory Committee" means the National Advisory Committee on the Education of Handicapped Children.

(4) The term "construction", except where otherwise specified, means (A) erection of new or expansion of existing structures, and the acquisition and installation of equipment therefor; or (B) acquisition of existing structures not owned by any agency or institution making application for assistance under this title; or (C) remodeling or alteration (including the acquisition, installation, modernization, or replacement of equipment) of existing structures; or (D) acquisition of land in connection with the activities in clauses (A), (B), and (C); or (E) a combination of any two or more of the foregoing.

(5) The term "equipment" includes machinery, utilities, and built-in equipment and any necessary enclosures or structures to house them, and includes all other items necessary for the functioning of a particular facility as a facility for the provision of educational services, including items such as instructional equipment and necessary furniture, printed, published, and audio-visual instructional materials, telecommunications, sensory, and other technological aids and devices, and books, periodicals, documents, and other related materials.

(6) The term "State" means any of several States, the District of Columbia, the Commonwealth of Puerto Rico, the Virgin Islands, Guam, American Samoa, the Northern Marianna Islands, or the

Trust Territory of the Pacific Islands.

(7) The term "State educational agency" means the State board of education or other agency or officer primarily responsible for the State supervision of public elementary and secondary schools, or, if there is no such officer or agency, an officer or agency designated by the Governor or by State law.

(8) The term "local educational agency" means a public board of education or other public authority legally constituted within a State for either administrative control or direction of, or to perform a service function for public elementary or secondary schools in a city, county, township, school district, or other political subdivision of a State, or such combination of school districts or counties as are recognized in a State as an administrative agency for its public elementary or secondary schools. Such term also includes any other public institution or agency having administrative control and direction of a public elementary and secondary school.

(9) The term "elementary school" means a day or residential school which provides elementary education, as determined under State law.

(10) The term "secondary school" means a day or residential school which provides secondary education, as determined under State law, except that it does not include any education provided beyond grade 12.

(11) The term "institution of higher education" means an educational institution in any State which —

(A) admits as regular students only individuals having a certificate of graduation from a high school, or the recognized equivalent of such a certificate;

(B) is legally authorized within such State to provide a program of education beyond high school;

(C) provides an educational program for which it awards a bachelor's degree, or provides not less than a two-year program which is acceptable for full credit toward such a degree, or offers a two-year program in engineering, mathematics, or the physical or biological sciences which is designed to prepare the student to work as a technician and at a semiprofessional level in engineering, scientific, or other technological fields which require the understanding and application of basic engineering, scientific, or mathematical principles or knowledge;

(D) is a public or other nonprofit institution;

(E) is accredited by a nationally recognized accrediting agency or association listed by the Secretary pursuant to this paragraph or, if not so accredited, is an institution whose credits are accepted, on transfer, by not less than three institutions which are so accredited, for credit on the same basis as it transferred from an institution so accredited: *Provided, however,* That in the case of an institution offering a two-year program in engineering mathematics, or the physical or biological sciences which is designed to prepare the student to work as a technician and at a semiprofessional level in engineering, scientific, or technological fields which require the understanding and application of basic engineering, scientific, or mathematical principles of knowledge, if the Secretary determines that there is no nationally recognized accrediting agency or association qualified to accredit such institutions, he shall appoint an advisory committee, composed of persons specially qualified to evaluate training provided by such institutions to participate under this Act and shall also determine whether particular institutions meet such standards. For the purposes of this paragraph the Secretary shall publish a list of nationally recognized accrediting agencies or associations which he determines to be reliable authority as to the quality of education or training offered; and

(F) The term includes community colleges receiving funding from the Secretary of the Interior under Public Law 95-471. *(20 USC 1801 note)*

(12) The term "nonprofit" as applied to a school, agency, organization, or institution means a school, agency, organization, or institution owned and operated by one or more nonprofit corporations or associations no part of the net earnings of which inures, or may lawfully inure, to the benefit of any private shareholder or individual.

(13) The term "research and related purposes" means research, research training (including the payment of stipends and allowances), surveys, or demonstrations in the field of education of handicapped children, or the dissemination of information derived therefrom, including (but without limitation) experimental schools.

(14) The term "Secretary" means the Secretary of Education.

(15) The term "children with specific learning disabilities" means those children who have a disorder in one or more of the basic psychological processes involved in understanding or in using language, spoken or written, which disorder may manifest itself in imperfect ability to listen, think, speak, read, write, spell, or do mathematical calculations. Such disorders include such conditions as perceptual handicaps, brain injury, minimal brain disfunction, dyslexia, and developmental aphasia. Such term does not include children who have learning problems which are primarily the result of visual, hearing, or motor handicaps, of mental retardation, of emotional disturbance, or of environmental, cultural, or economic disadvantage.

(16) The term "special education" means specially designed instruction, at no cost to parents or guardians, to meet the unique needs of a handicapped child, including classroom instruction, instruction in physical education, home instruction, and instruction in hospitals and institutions.

(17) The term "related services" means transportation, and such

developmental, corrective, and other supportive services (including speech pathology and audiology, psychological services, physical and occupational therapy, recreation, and medical and counseling services, except that such medical services shall be for diagnostic and evaluation purposes only) as may be required to assist a handicapped child to benefit from special education, and includes the early identification and assessment of handicapping conditions in children.

(18) The term "free appropriate public education" means special education and related services which (A) have been provided at public expense, under public supervision and direction, and without charge, (B) meet the standards of the State educational agency, (C) include an appropriate preschool, elementary, or secondary school education in the State involved, and (D) are provided in conformity with the individualized education program required under section 614(a)(5).

(19) The term "individualized education program" means a written statement for each handicapped child developed in any meeting by a representative of the local educational agency or an intermediate educational unit who shall be qualified to provide, or supervise the provision of, specially designed instruction to meet the unique needs of handicapped children, the teacher, the parents or guardian of such child, and, whenever appropriate, such child, which statement shall include (A) a statement of the present levels of educational performance of such child, (B) a statement of annual goals, including short-term instructional objectives, (C) a statement of the specific educational services to be provided to such child, and the extent to which such child will be able to participate in regular educational programs, (D) the projected date for initiation and anticipated duration of such services, and (E) appropriate objective criteria and evaluation procedures and schedules for determining, on at least an annual basis, whether instructional objectives are being achieved.

(20) The term "excess costs" means those costs which are in excess of the average annual per student expenditure in a local educational agency during the preceding school year for an elementary or secondary school student, as may be appropriate, and which shall be computed after deducting (A) amounts received under this part or under title I or title VII of the Elementary and Secondary Education Act of 1965, and (B) any State or local funds expended for programs which would qualify for assistance under this part or under such titles.

(21) The term "native language" has the meaning given that term by section 703(a)(2) of the Bilingual Education Act (20 U.S.C. 880b-1(a)(2)).

(22) The term "intermediate educational unit" means any public authority, other than a local educational agency, which is under the general supervision of a State educational agency, which is

established by State law for the purpose of providing free public education on a regional basis, and which provides special education and related services to handicapped children within that State.

(b) For purposes of part C of this title, "handicapped youth" means any handicapped child (as defined in section 602(a)(1)) who —

(1) is twelve years of age or older; or

(2) is enrolled in the seventh or higher grade in school.

(23)(A) The term "public or private nonprofit agency or organization" includes an Indian tribe.

(B) The terms "Indian", "American Indian", and "Indian American" mean an individual who is a member of an Indian tribe.

(C) The term "Indian tribe" means any Federal or State Indian tribe, band, rancheria, pueblo, colony, or community, including any Alaskan native village or regional village corporation (as defined in or established under the Alaska Native Claims Settlement Act). *(20 USC 1401)*

### OFFICE OF SPECIAL EDUCATION PROGRAMS

SEC. 603. (a) There shall be, within the Office of Special Education and Rehabilitative Services in the Department of Education, an Office of Special Education Programs which shall be the principal agency in the Department for administering and carrying out this Act and other programs and activities concerning the education and training of the handicapped.

(b)(1) The Office established under subsection (a) shall be headed by a Deputy Assistant Secretary who shall be selected by the Secretary and shall report directly to the Assistant Secretary for Special Education and Rehabilitative Services. The position of Deputy Assistant Secretary shall be in grade GS-18 of the General Schedule under section 5104 of title 5, United States Code, and shall be a Senior Executive Service position for the purposes of section 3132(a)(2) of such title.

(2) In addition to such Deputy Assistant Secretary, there shall be established in such office not less than six positions for persons to assist the Deputy Assistant Secretary, including the position of Associate Deputy Assistant Secretary. Each such position shall be in grade GS-15 of the General Schedule under section 5104 of title 5, United States Code. *(20 USC 1402)*

### ACQUISITION OF EQUIPMENT AND CONSTRUCTION OF NECESSARY FACILITIES

SEC. 605. (a) In the case of any program authorized by this title, if the Secretary determines that such program will be improved by permitting the funds authorized for such program to be used for the acquisition of equipment and the construction of necessary facilities, he may authorize the use of such funds for such purposes.

(b) If within twenty years after the completion of any construction (except minor remodeling or alteration) for which funds have been paid pursuant to a grant or contract under this title the facility constructed ceases to be used for the purposes for which it was constructed, the United States, unless the Secretary determines that there is good cause for releasing the recipient of the funds from its obligation, shall be entitled to recover from the applicant or other owner of the facility an amount which bears the same ratio to the then value of the facility as the amount of such Federal funds bore to the cost of the portion of the facility financed with such funds. Such value shall be determined by agreement of the parties or by action brought in the United States district court for the district in which the facility is situated. *(20 USC 1404)*

### EMPLOYMENT OF HANDICAPPED INDIVIDUALS

SEC. 606. The Secretary shall assure that each recipient of assistance under this Act shall make positive efforts to employ and advance in employment qualified handicapped individuals in programs assisted under this Act. *(20 USC 1405)*

### GRANTS FOR THE REMOVAL OF ARCHITECTURAL BARRIERS

SEC. 607. (a) The Secretary is authorized to make grants and to enter into cooperative agreements with the Secretary of the Interior with State educational agencies to assist such agencies in making grants to local educational agencies or intermediate educational units to pay part or all of the cost of altering existing buildings and equipment in accordance with standards promulgated under the Act approved August 12, 1968 (Public Law 90-480), relating to architectural barriers.

(b) For the purposes of carrying out the provisions of this section, there are authorized to be appropriated such sums as may be necessary. *(20 USC 1406)*

### REQUIREMENTS FOR PRESCRIBING REGULATIONS

SEC. 608. (a) For purposes of complying with section 431(b) of the General Education Provisions Act with respect to regulations promulgated under part B of this Act, the thirty-day period under such section shall be ninety days.

(b) The Secretary may not implement, or publish in final form, any regulation prescribed pursuant to this Act which would procedurally or substantively lessen the protections provided to handicapped children under this Act, as embodied in regulations in effect on July 20, 1983 (particularly as such protections relate to parental consent to initial evaluation or initial placement in special education, least restrictive environment, related services, timelines, attendance of evaluation personnel at IEP meetings, or qualifications of personnel), except to the extent that such regulation reflects the clear and unequivocal intent of the Congress in legislation.

(c) The Secretary shall transmit a copy of any regulations promulgated under this Act to the National Advisory Committee on the Education of the Handicapped concurrently with publication in the Federal Register. *(20 USC 1407)*

### ELIGIBILITY FOR FINANCIAL ASSISTANCE

SEC. 609. Effective for fiscal years for which the Secretary may make grants under section 619(b)(1), no State or local educational agency or intermediate educational unit or other public institution or agency may receive a grant under parts C through G which relate exclusively to programs, projects, and activities pertaining to children aged three to five, inclusive, unless the State is eligible to receive a grant under section 619(b)(1).

## PART B — ASSISTANCE FOR EDUCATION OF ALL HANDICAPPED CHILDREN

### SETTLEMENTS AND ALLOCATIONS

SEC. 611. (a)(1) Except as provided in paragraph (3) and in section 619, the maximum amount of the grant to which a State is entitled under this part for any fiscal year shall be equal to —

(A) the number of handicapped children aged 3-5, inclusive, in a State who are receiving special education and related services as determined under paragraph (3) if the State is eligible for a grant under section 619 and the number of handicapped children aged 6-21, inclusive, in a State who are receiving special education and related services as so determined." *(20 USC 1419)*

multiplied by —

(B)(i) 5 per centum, for the fiscal year ending September 30, 1978, of the average per pupil expenditure in public elementary and secondary schools in the United States.

(ii) 10 per centum, for the fiscal year ending September 30, 1979, of the average per pupil expenditure in public elementary and secondary schools in the United States;

(iii) 20 per centum, for the fiscal year ending September 30, 1980, of the average per pupil expenditure in public elementary and secondary schools in the United States;

(iv) 30 per centum, for the fiscal year ending September 30, 1981, of the average per pupil expenditure in public elementary and secondary schools in the United States; and

(v) 40 per centum, for the fiscal year ending September 30, 1982, and for each fiscal year thereafter, of the average per pupil expenditure in public elementary and secondary schools in the United States;

except that no State shall receive an amount which is less than the amount which such State received under this part for the fiscal year ending September 30, 1977.

(2) For the purpose of this subsection and subsection (b) through subsection (e), the term "State" does not include Guam, American Samoa, the Virgin Islands, the Northern Mariana Islands, and the Trust Territory of the Pacific Islands.

(3) The number of handicapped children receiving special education and related services in any fiscal year shall be equal to the average of the number of such children receiving special education and related services on October 1 and February 1 of the fiscal year preceding the fiscal year for which the determination is made.

(4) For purposes of paragraph (1)(B), the term "average per pupil expenditure", in the United States, means the aggregate current expenditures, during the second fiscal year preceding the fiscal year for which the computation is made (or, if satisfactory data for such year are not available at the time of computation, then during the most recent preceding fiscal year for which satisfactory data are available) of all local educational agencies in the United States (which, for purposes of this subsection, means the fifty States and the District of Columbia), as the case may be, plus any direct expenditures by the State for operation of such agencies (without regard to the source of funds from which either of such expenditures are made), divided by the aggregate number of children in average daily attendance to whom such agencies provided free public education during such preceding year.

(5)(A) In determining the allotment of each State under paragraph (1), the Secretary may not count—

(i) handicapped children aged three to seventeen, inclusive, in such State under paragraph (1)(A) to the extent the number of such children is greater than 12 percent of the number of all children aged three to seventeen, inclusive, in such State and the State serves all handicapped children aged three to five, inclusive, in the State pursuant to State law or practice or the order of any court,

(ii) handicapped children aged five to seventeen, inclusive, in such State under paragraph (1)(A) to the extent the number of such children is greater than 12 percent of the number of all children aged five to seventeen, inclusive, in such State and the States does not serve all handicapped children aged three to five inclusive, in the State pursuant to State law or practice on the order of any court; and

(iii) handicapped children who are counted under section 121 of the Elementary and Secondary Education Act of 1965.

*(20 USC 2731)*

(B) For purposes of subparagraph (A), the number of children aged five to seventeen, inclusive, in any State shall be determined by the Secretary on the basis of the most recent satisfactory data available to him.

(b)(1) Of the funds received under subsection (a) by any State for the fiscal year ending September 30, 1978—

    (A) 50 per centum of such funds may be used by such State in accordance with the provisions of paragraph (2); and

    (B) 50 per centum of such funds shall be distributed by such State pursuant to subsection (d) to local educational agencies and intermediate educational units in such State, for use in accordance with the priorities established under section 612(3).

(2) Of the funds which any State may use under paragraph (1)(A) —

    (A) an amount which is equal to the greater of —

        (i) 5 per centum of the total amount of funds received under this part by such State; or

        (ii) $200,000;

may be used by such State for administrative costs related to carrying out sections 612 and 613;

    (B) the remainder shall be used by such State to provide support services and direct services in accordance with the priorities established under section 612(3).

(c)(1) Of the funds received under subsection (a) by any State for the fiscal year ending September 30, 1979, and for each fiscal year thereafter —

    (A) 25 per centum of such funds may be used by such State in accordance with the provisions of paragraph (2); and

    (B) except as provided in paragraph (4), 75 per centum of such funds shall be distributed by such State pursuant to subsection (d) to local educational agencies and intermediate educational units in such State, for use in accordance with priorities established under section 612(3).

(2)(A) Subject to the provisions of subparagraph (B), of the funds which any State may use under paragraph (1)(A) —

    (i) an amount which is equal to the greater of —

        (I) 5 per centum of the total amount of funds received under this part by such State; or

        (II) $300,000;

may be used by such State for administrative costs related to carrying out the provisions of sections 612 and 613; and

    (ii) the part remaining after use in accordance with clause (i) shall be used by the State (I) to provide support services and direct services in accordance with the priorities estabilshed under section 612(3), and (II) for the administrative costs of monitoring and complaint investigation but only to the extent that such costs exceed the costs of administration incurred during fiscal year 1985. *(20 USC 1412)*

    (B) The amount expended by any State from the funds available to such State under paragraph (1)(A) in any fiscal year for the provision of support services or for the provision of direct services shall be matched on a program basis by such State, from funds other than Federal funds, for the provision of support services or the provision of direct services for the fiscal year involved.

(3) The provisions of section 613(a)(9) shall not apply with respect to amounts available for use by any State under paragraph (2).

(4)(A) No funds shall be distributed by any State under this subsection in any fiscal year to any local educational agency or intermediate educational unit in such State if —

(i) such local educational agency or intermediate educational unit is entitled, under subsection (d), to less than $7,500 for such fiscal year; or

(ii) such local educational agency or intermediate educational unit has not submitted an application for such funds which meets the requirements of section 614.

(B) Whenever the provisions of subparagraph (A) apply, the State involved shall use such funds to assure the provision of a free appropriate education to handicapped children residing in the area served by such local educational agency or such intermediate educational unit. The provisions of paragraph (2)(B) shall not appy to the use of such funds.

(d) From the total amount of funds available to local educational agencies and intermediate educational units in any State under subsection (b)(1)(B) or subsection (c)(1)(B), as the case may be, each local educational agency or intermediate educational unit shall be entitled to an amount which bears the same ratio to the total amount available under subsection (b)(1)(B) or subsection (c)(1)(B), as the case may be, as the number of handicapped children aged three to twenty-one, inclusive, receiving special education and related services in such local educational agency or intermediate educational unit bears to the aggregate number of handicapped children aged three to twenty-one, inclusive, receiving special education and related services in all local educational agencies and intermediate educational units which apply to the State educational agency involved for funds under this part.

(e)(1) The jurisdictions to which this subsection applies are Guam, American Samoa, the Virgin Islands, the Northern Mariana islands, and the Trust Territory of the Pacific Islands.

(2) Each jurisdiction to which this subsection applies shall be entitled to a grant for the purposes set forth in section 601(c) in an amount equal to an amount determined by the Secretary in accordance with criteria based on respective needs, except that the aggregate of the amount to which such jurisdictions are so entitled for any fiscal year shall not exceed an amount equal to 1 per centum of the aggregate of the amounts available to all States under this part for that fiscal year. If the aggregate of the amounts, determined by the Secretary pursuant to the preceding sentence, to be so needed for any fiscal year exceeds an amount equal to such 1 per centum limitation, the entitlement of each such jurisdiction shall be reduced proportionately until such aggregate does not exceed such 1 per centum limitation.

(3) The amount expended for administration by each jurisdiction

under this subsection shall not exceed 5 per centum of the amount allotted to such jurisdiction for any fiscal year, or $35,000, whichever is greater.

(f)(1) The Secretary shall make payments to the Secretary of the Interior according to the need for assistance for the education of handicapped children on reservations serviced by elementary and secondary schools operated for Indian children by the Department of the Interior. The amount of such payment for any fiscal year shall be 1.25 percent of the aggregate amounts available to all States under this section for that fiscal year.

(2) The Secretary of the Interior may receive an allotment under paragraph (1) only after submitting to the Secretary an application which—

  (A) meets the applicable requirements of sections 612, 613, and 614(a), *(20 USC 1412)*

  (B) includes satisfactory assurance that all handicapped children aged 3 to 5, inclusive receive a free appropriate public education by or before the 1987-1988 school year, *(20 USC 1414)*

  (C) includes an assurance that there are public hearings, adequate notice of such hearings, and an opportunity for comment afforded to members of tribes, tribal governing bodies, and designated local school boards before adoption of the policies, programs, and procedures required under sections 612, 613, and 614(a), and

  (D) is approved by the Secretary.

  Section 616 shall appy to any such application.*(20 USC 1416)*

(g)(1) If the sums appropriated under subsection (h) for any fiscal year for making payments to States under subsection (a) are not sufficient to pay in full the total amounts which all States are entitled to receive under subsection (a) for such fiscal year, the maximum amounts which all States are entitled to receive under subsection (a) for such fiscal year shall be ratably reduced. In case additional funds become available for making such payments for any fiscal year during which the preceding sentence is applicable, such reduced amounts shall be increased on the same basis as they were reduced.

(2) In the case of any fiscal year in which the maximum amounts for which States are eligible have been reduced under the first sentence of paragraph (2), and in which additional funds have not been made available to pay in full the total of such maximum amounts under the last sentence of such paragraph, the State educational agency shall fix dates before which each local educational agency or intermediate educational unit shall report to the State educational agency or intermediate educational unit, under the provisons of subsection (d), which it estimates that it will expend in accordance with the provisions of this section. The amounts so available to any local educational agency or intermedite educational unit, or any amount which would be available to any other local educational agency or intermediate educational unit if it were to submit a program meeting

the requirements of this part, which the State educational agency determines will not be used for the period of its availability, shall be available for allocation to those local educational agencies or intermediate educational units, in the manner provided by this section, which the State educational agency determines will need and be able to use additional funds to carry out approved programs. *(20 USC 1411)*

(h) For grants under subsection (a) there are authorized to be appropriated such sums as may be necessary.

ELIGIBILITY

SEC. 612. In order to qualify for assistance under this part in any fiscal year, a State shall demonstrate to the Secretary that the following conditions are met:

(1) The State has in effect a policy that assures all handicapped children the right to a free appropriate public education.

(2) The State has developed a plan pursuant to section 613(b) in effect prior to the date of the enactment of the Education for All Handicapped Children Act of 1975 and submitted not later than August 21, 1975, which will be amended so as to comply with the provisions of this paragraph. Each such amended plan shall set forth in detail the policies and procedures which the State will undertake or has undertaken in order to assure that—

(A) there is established (i) a goal of providing full educational opportunity to all handicapped children, (ii) a detailed timetable for accomplishing such a goal, and (iii) a description of the kind and number of facilities, personnel, and services necessary throughout the State to meet such a goal;

(B) a free appropriate public education will be available for all handicapped children between the ages of three and eighteen within the State not later than September 1, 1978, and for all handicapped children between the ages of three and twenty-one within the State not later than Septmber 1, 1980, except that, with respect to handicapped children aged three to five and aged eighteen to twenty-one, inclusive, the requirements of this clause shall not be applied in any State if the application of such requirements would be inconsistent with State law or practice, or the order of any court, respecting public education within such age groups in the State;

(C) all children residing in the State who are handicapped, regardless of the severity of their handicap, and who are in need of special education and related services are identified, located, and evaluated, and that a practical method is developed and implemented to determine which children are currently receiving needed special education and related services and which are children are not currently receiving needed special education and related services;

(D) policies and procedures are established in accordance with detailed criteria prescribed under section 617(c); and

(E) the amendment to the plan submitted by the State required by this section shall be available to parents, guardians, and other members of the general public at least thirty days prior to the date of submission of the amendment to the Commission.

(3) The State has established priorities for providing a free appropriate public education to all handicapped children, which priorities shall meet the timetables set forth in clause (B) of paragraph (2) of this section, first with respect to handicapped children who are not receiving an education, and second with respect to handicapped children, within each disability, with the most severe handicaps who are receiving an inadequate education, and has made adequate progress in meeting the timetables set forth in clause (B) of paragraph (2) of this section.

(4) Each local educational agency in the State will maintain records of the individualized education program for each handicapped children, and such program shall be established, reviewed, and revised as provided in section 614(a)(5).

(5) The State has established (A) procedural safeguards as required by section 615, (B) procedures to assure that, to the maximum extent appropriate, handicapped children, including children in public or private institutions or other care facilities, are educated with children who are not handicapped, and that special classes, separate schooling, or other removal of handicapped children from the regular educational environment occurs only when the nature or severity of the handicap is such that education in regular classes with the use of supplementary aids and services cannot be achieved satisfactorily, and (C) procedures to assure that testing and evaluation materials and procedures utilized for the purposes of evaluation and placement of handicapped children will be selected and administered so as not to be racially or culturally discriminatory. Such materials or procedures shall be provided and administered in the child's native language or mode of communication, unless it clearly is not feasible to do so, and no single procedure shall be the sole criterion for determining an appropriate educational program for a child.

(6) The State educational agency shall be responsible for assuring that the requirements of this part are carried out and that all educational programs for handicapped children with the State including all such programs administered by any other State or local agency, will be under the general supervision of the persons responsible for educational programs for handicapped children in the State educational agency and shall meet educational standards of the State educational agency. This paragraph shall not be construed to limit the responsibility of agencies other than educational agencies in a State from providing or paying for some or all of the costs of a free appropriate public education to be provided handicapped children in the State.

(7) The State shall assure that (A) in carrying out the requirements

of this section procedures are established for consultation with individuals involved in or concerned with the education of handicapped children, including handicapped individuals and parents or guardians of handicapped children, and (B) there are public hearings, adequate notice of such hearings, and an opportunity for comment available to the general public prior to adoption of the policies, programs, and procedures required pursuant to the provisions of this section and section 613. *(20 USC 1412)*

STATE PLANS

Sec. 613. (a) Any State meeting the eligibility requirements set forth in section 612 and desiring to participate in the program under this part shall submit to the Secretary, through its State educational agency, a State plan at such time, in such manner, and containing or accompanied by such information, as he deems necessary. Each such plan shall —

(1) set forth policies and procedures designed to assure that funds paid to the State under this part will be expended in accordance with the provisions of this part, with particular attention given to the provisions of sections 611(b), 611(c), 611(d), 612(2), and 612(3);

(2) provide that programs and procedures will be established to assure that funds received by the State or any of its political subdivisions under any other Federal program, including section 121 of the Elementary and Secondary Education Act of 1965 (20 U.S.C. 241c-2), section 305(b)(8) of such Act (20 U.S.C. 844a(B)(8)) or its successor authority, and section 122(A)(4)(B) of the Vocational Education Act of 1963 (20 U.S.C. 1262(a)(4)(B)), under which there is specific authority for the provision of assistance for the education of handicapped children, will be utilized by the State, or any of its political subdivisions, only in a manner consistent with the goal of providing a free appropriate public education for all handicapped children, except that nothing in this clause shall be construed to limit the specific requirements of the laws governing such Federal programs;

(3) set forth, consistent with the purposes of this Act, a description of programs and procedures for (A) the development and implementation of a comprehensive system of personnel development which shall include the inservice training of general and special educational instructional and support personnel, detailed procedures to assure that all personnel necessary to carry out the purposes of this Act are appropriately and adequately prepared and trained, and effective procedures for acquiring and disseminating to teachers and administrators of programs for handicapped children significant information derived from educational research, demonstration, and similar projects, and (B) adopting, where appropriate, promising educational practices

and materials development through such projects:

(4) set forth policies and procedures to assure —

(A) that, to the extent consistent with the number and location of handicapped children in the State who are enrolled in private elementary and secondary schools, provision is made for the participation of such children in the program assisted or carried out under this part by providing for such children special education and related services; and

(B) that (i) handicapped children in private schools and facilities will be provided special education and related services (in conformance with an individualized educational program as required by this part) at no cost to their parents or guardian, if such children are placed in or referred to such schools or facilities by the State or appropriate local educational agency as the means of carrying out the requirements of this part or any other applicable law requiring the provision of special education and related services to all handicapped children within such State, and (ii) in all such instances the State educational agency shall determine whether such schools and facilities meet standards that apply to State and local educational agencies and that children so served have all the rights they would have if served by such agencies;

(5) set forth policies and procedures which assure that the State shall seek to recover any funds made available under this part for services to any child who is determined to be erroneously classified as eligible to be counted under section 611(a) or section 611(d):

(6) provide satisfactory assurance that the control of funds provided under this part, and title to property derived therefrom, shall be in a public agency for the uses and purposes provided in this part, and that a public agency will administer such funds and property;

(7) provide for (A) making such reports in such form and containing such information as the Secretary may require to carry out his functions under this part, and (B) keeping such records and affording such access thereto as the Secretary may find necessary to assure the correctness and verification of such reports and proper disbursement of Federal funds under this part;

(8) provide procedures to assure that final action with respect to any application submitted by a local educational agency or an intermediate educational unit shall not be taken without first affording the local educational agency or intermediate educational unit involved reasonable notice and opportunity for a hearing;

(9) provide satisfactory assurance that Federal funds made

available under this part (A) will not be commingled with State funds, and (B) will be so used as to supplement and increase the level of Federal, State, and local funds (including funds that are not under the direct control of State or local educational agencies) expended for special education and related services provided to handicapped children under this part and in no case to supplant such Federal, State, and local funds, except that, where the State provides clear and convincing evidence that all handicapped children have available to them a free appropriate public education, the Secretary may waive in part the requirement of this clause if he concurs with the evidence provided by the State;

(10) provide, consistent with procedures prescribed pursuant to section 617(a)(2), satisfactory assurance that such fiscal control and fund accounting procedures will be adopted as may be necessary to assure proper disbursement of, and accounting for, Federal funds paid under this part to the State, including any such funds paid by the State to local educational agencies and intermediate educational units;

(11) provide for procedures for evaluation at least annually of the effectiveness of programs in meeting the educational needs of handicapped children (including evaluation of individualized education programs), in accordance with such criteria that the Secretary shall prescribe pursuant to section 617;

(12) provide that the State has an advisory panel, appointed by the Governor or any other official authorized under State law to make such appointments, composed of individuals involved in or concerned with the education of handicapped children, including handicapped individuals, teachers, parents or guardians of handicapped children, State and local education officials, and administrators of programs for handicapped children, which (A) advises the State educational agency of unmet needs within the State in the education of handicapped children, (B) comments publicly on any rules or regulations proposed for issuance by the State regarding the education of handicapped children and the procedures for distribution of funds under this part, and (C) assists the State in developing and reporting such data and evaluations as may assist the Secretary in the performance of his responsibilities under section 618;

(13) set forth policies and procedures for developing and implementing interagency agreements between the State educational agency and other appropriate State and local agencies to (A) define the financial responsibility of each agency for providing handicapped children and youth with free appropriate education, and (B) resolve interagency disputes, including procedures under which local educational agencies may initiate proceedings under the agreement in order to secure reimbursement from other agencies or otherwise implement the

provisions of the agreement.

(14) policies and procedures relating to the establishment and maintenance of standards to ensure that personnel necessary to carry out the purposes of this part are appropriately and adequately prepared and trained, including —

(A) the establishment and maintenance of standards which are consistent with any State approved or recognized certification, licensing, registration, or other comparable requirements which apply to the area in which he or she is providing special education or related services, and

(B) to the extent such standards are not based on the highest requirements in the State applicable to a specific profession or discipline, the steps the State is taking to require the retraining or hiring of personnel that meet appropriate professional requirements in the State. *(20 USC 1413)*

(b) Whenever a State educational agency provides free appropriate public education for handicapped children, or provides direct services to such children, such State educational agency shall include, as part of the State plan required by subsection (a) of this section, such additional assurances not specified in such subsection (a) as are contained in section 614(a), except that funds available for the provision of such education or services may be expended without regard to the provisions relating to excess costs in section 614(a).

(c) The Secretary shall approve any State plan and any modification thereof which —

(1) is submitted by a State eligible in accordance with section 612; and

(2) meets the requirements of subsection (a) and subsection (b).

The Secretary shall disapprove any State plan which does not meet the requirements of the preceding sentence, but shall not finally disapprove a State plan except after reasonable notice and opportunity for a hearing to the State.

(d)(1) If, on the date of enactment of the Education of the Handicapped Act Amendments of 1983, a State educational agency is prohibited by law from providing for the participation in special programs of handicapped children enrolled in private elementary and secondary schools as required by subsection (a)(4), the Secretary shall waive such requirement, and shall arrange for the provision of service to such children through arrangements which shall be subject to the requirements of subsection (a)(4).

(2)(A) When the Secretary arranges for services pursuant to this subsection, the Secretary, after consultation with the appropriate public and private school officials, shall pay to the provider of such services an amount per child which may not exceed the Federal amount provided per child under this part to all handicapped children enrolled in the State for services for the fiscal year preceding the fiscal year for which the determination is made.

(B) Pending final resolution of any investigation or complaint that could result in a determination under this subsection, the Secretary may withhold from the allocation of the affected State educational agency the amount the Secretary estimates would be necessary to pay the cost of such services.

(C) Any determination by the Secretary under this section shall continue in effect until the Secretary determines that there will no longer be any failure or inability on the part of the State educational agency to meet the requirements of subsection (a)(4).

(3)(A) The Secretary shall not take any final action under this subsection until the State educational agency affected by such action has had an opportunity, for at least 45 days after receiving written notice thereof, to submit written objections and to appear before the Secretary or his designee to show cause why such action should not be taken.

(B) If a State educational agency is dissatisfied with the Secretary's final action after a proceeding under subparagraph (A) of this paragraph, it may, within 60 days after notice of such action, file with the United States court of appeals for the circuit in which such State is located a petition for review of that action. A copy of the petition shall be forthwith transmitted by the clerk of the court to the Secretary. The Secretary thereupon shall file in the court the record of the proceedings on which he based his action, as provided in section 2112 of title 28, United States Code.

(C) The findings of fact by the Secretary, if supported by substantial evidence, shall be conclusive; but the court, for good cause shown, may remand the cause to the Secretary to take further evidence, and the Secretary may thereupon make new or modified findings of fact and may modify his previous action, and shall file in the court the record of the further proceedings. Such new or modified findings of fact shall likewise be conclusive if supported by substantial evidence.

(D) Upon the filing of a petition under subparagraph (B), the court shall have jurisdiction to affirm the action of the Secretary or to set it aside, in whole or in part. The judgment of the court shall be subject to review by the Supreme Court of the United Sates upon certiorari or certification as provided in section 1254 of title 28, United States Code.

(e) This Act shall not be construed to permit a State to reduce medical and other assistance available or to alter eligibility under titles V and XIX of the Social Security Act with respect to the provision of a free appropriate public education for handicapped children within the State. *(42 USC 701)*

## APPLICATION

SEC. 614. (a) A local educational agency or an intermediate educational unit which desires to receive payments under section 611(d) for any fiscal year shall submit an application to the appropriate

State educational agency. Such application shall —

(1) provide satisfactory assurance that payments under this part will be used for excess costs directly attributable to programs which —

(A) provide that all children residing within the jurisdiction of the local educational agency or the intermediate educational unit who are handicapped, regardless of the severity of their handicap, and are in need of special education and related services will be identified, located, and evaluated, and provide for the inclusion of a practical method of determining which children are currently receiving needed special education and related services and which children are not currently receiving such education and services;

(B) establish policies and procedures in accordance with detailed criteria prescribed under section 617(c);

(C) establish a goal of providing full educational opportunities to all handicapped children, including —

(i) procedures for the implementation and use of the comprehensive system of personnel development established by the State educational agency under section 613(a)(3);

(ii) the provision of, and the establishment of priorities for providing, a free appropriate public education to all handicapped children, first with respect to handicapped children who are not receiving an education, and second with respect to handicapped children, within each disability, with the most severe handicaps who are receiving an inadequate education;

(iii) the participation and consultation of the parents or guardian of such children; and

(iv) to the maximum extent practicable and consistent with the provisions of section 612(5)(B), the provision of special services to enable such children to participate in regular educational programs;

(D) establish a detailed timetable for accomplishing the goal described in subclause (C); and

(E) provide a description of the kind and number of facilities, personnel, and services necessary to meet the goal described in subclause (C);

(2) provide satisfactory assurance that (A) the control of funds provided under this part, and title to property derived from such funds, shall be in a public agency for the uses and purposes provided in this part, and that a public agency will administer such funds and property, (B) Federal funds expended by local educational agencies and intermediate educational units for programs under this part (i) shall be used to pay only the excess costs directly attributable to the education of

handicapped children, and (ii) shall be used to supplement and, to the extent practicable, increase the level of State and local funds expended for the education of handicapped children, and in no case to supplant such State and local funds, and (C) State and local funds will be used in the jurisdiction of the local educational agency or intermediate educational unit to provide services in program areas which, taken as a whole, are at least comparable to services being provided in areas of such jurisdiction which are not receiving funds under this part;

(3)(A) provide for furnishing such information (which, in the case of reports relating to performance, is in accordance with specific performance criteria related to program objectives), as may be necessary to enable the State educational agency to perform its duties under this part, including information relating to the educational achievement of handicapped children participating in programs carried out under this part; and

(B) provide for keeping such records, and provide for affording such access to such records, as the State educational agency may find necessary to assure the correctness and vertification of such information furnished under subclause (A);

(4) provide for making the application and all pertinent documents related to such application available to parents, guardians, and other members of the general public, and provide that all evaluations and reports required under clause (3) shall be public information;

(5) provide assurances that the local educational agency or intermediate educational unit will establish, or revise, whichever is appropriate, an individualized education program for each handicapped child at the beginning of each school year and will then review and, if appropriate revise, its provisions periodically, but not less than annually;

(6) provide satisfactory assurance that policies and programs established and administered by the local educational agency or intermediate educational unit shall be consistent with the provisions of paragraph (1) through paragraph (7) of section 612 and section 613(a); and

(7) provide satisfactory assurance that the local educational agency or intermediate educational unit will establish and maintain procedural safeguards in accordance with the provisions of sections 612(5)(B), 612(5)(C), and 615.

(b)(1) A State educational agency shall approve any application submitted by a local educational agency or an intermediate educational unit under subsection (a) if the State educational agency determines that such application meets the requirements of subsection (a), except that no such application may be approved until the State plan submitted by such State educational agency under subsection (a) is approved by the Secretary under section 613(c). A State educational agency shall disapprove any application submitted by a local educational agency or an intermediate educational unit under subsection (a) if the State educational agency determines that such application does not meet the requirements of subsection (a).

(2)(A) Whenever a State educational agency, after reasonable notice and opportunity for a hearing, finds that a local educational agency or an intermediate educational unit, in the administration of an application approved by the State educational agency under paragraph (1), has failed to comply with any requirement set forth in such application, the State educational agency, after giving appropriate notice to the local educational agency or the intermediate educational unit, shall —

(i) make no further payments to such local educational agency or such intermediate educational unit under section 620 until the State educational agency is satisfied that there is no longer any failure to comply with the requirement involved; or

(ii) take such finding into account in its review of any application made by such local educational agency or such intermediate educational unit under subsection (a).

(B) The provisions of the last sentence of section 616(a) shall apply to any local educational agency or any intermediate educational unit receiving any notification from a State educational agency under this paragraph.

(3) In carrying out its functions under paragraph (1), each State educational agency shall consider any decision made pursuant to a hearing held under section 615 which is adverse to the local educational agency or intermediate educational unit involved in such decision.

(c)(1) A State educational agency may, for purposes of the consideration and approval of applications under this section, require local educational agencies to submit a consolidated application for payments if such State educational agency determines that any individual application submitted by any such local educational agency will be disapproved because such local educational agency is ineligible to receive payments because of the application of section 611(c)(4)(A)(i) or such local educational agency would be unable to establish and maintain programs of sufficient size and scope to effectively meet the educatinal needs of handicapped children.

(2)(A) In any case in which a consolidated application of local educational agencies is approved by a State educational agency under paragraph (1), the payments which such local educational agencies may receive shall be equal to the sum of payments to which each such local eduational agency would be entitled under section 611(d) if an individual application of any such local educational agency had been approved.

(B) The State educational agency shall prescribe rules and regulations with respect to consolidated applications submitted under this subsection which are consistent with the provisions of paragraph (1) through paragraph (7) of section 612 and section 613(a) and which provide participating local educational agencies with joint responsibilities for implementing programs receiving payments under this part.

(C) In any case in which an intermediate educational unit is required pursuant to State law to carry out the provisions of this part, the joint responsibilities given to local educational agencies under subparagraph (B) shall not apply to the administration and disbursement of any payments received by such intermediate educational unit. Such responsibilities shall be carried out exclusively by such intermediate educational unit.

(d) Whenever a State educational agency determines that a local educational agency —

(1) is unable or unwilling to establish and maintain programs of free appropriate public education which meet the requirements established in subsection (a);

(2) is unable or unwilling to be consolidated with other local educational agencies in order to establish and maintain such programs; or

(3) has one or more handicapped children who can best be served by a regional or State center designed to meet the needs of such children;

the State educational agency shall use the payments which would have been available to such local educational agency to provide special education and related services directly to handicapped childrn residing in the area served by such local educational agency. The State educational agency may provide such education and services in such manner, and at such locations (including regional or State centers), as it considers appropriate, except that the manner in which such education and services are provided shall be consistent with the requirements of this part.

(e) Whenever a State educational agency determines that a local educational agency is adequately providing a free appropriate public education to all handicapped children residing in the area served by such agency, the State educational agency may reallocate funds (or such portion of those funds as may not be required to provide such education and services) made available to such agency, pursuant to section 611(d), to such other local educational agencies within the State as are not adequately providing special education and related services to all handicapped children residing in the areas served by such other local educational agencies.

(f) Notwithstanding the provisions of subsection (a)(2)(B)(ii), any local educational agency which is required to carry out any program for the education of handicapped children pursuant to a State law shall be entitled to receive payments under section 611(d) for use in carrying out such program, except that such payments may not be used to reduce the level of expenditures for such program made by such local educational agency from State or local funds below the level of such expenditures for the fiscal year prior to the fiscal year for which such local educational agency seeks such payments. *(20 USC 1414)*

## PROCEDURAL SAFEGUARDS

SEC. 615. (a) Any State educational agency, any local educational agency, and any intermediate educational unit which receives assistance under this part shall establish and maintain procedures in accordance with subsection (b) through subsection (e) of this section to assure that handicapped children and their parents or guardians are guaranteed procedural safeguards with respect to the provision of free appropriate public education by such agencies and units.

(b)(1) The procedures required by this section shall include, but shall not be limited to —

(A) an opportunity for the parents or guardian of a handicapped child to examine all relevant records with respect to the identification, evaluation, and educational placement of the child, and the provision of a free appropriate public education to such child, and to obtain an independent educational evaluation of the child;

(B) procedures to protect the rights of the child whenever the parents or guardian of the child are not known, unavailable, or the child is a ward of the State, including the assignment of an individual (who shall not be an employee of the State educational agency, local educational agency, or intermediate educational unit involved in the education or care of the child) to act as a surrogate for the parents or guardian;

(C) written prior notice to the parents or guardian of the child whenever such agency or unit —

(i) proposes to initiate or change, or

(ii) refuses to initiate or change,

the identification, evaluation, or educational placement of the child or the provision of a free appropriate public education to the child;

(D) procedures designed to assure that the notice required by clause (C) fully inform the parents or guardian, in the parents' or guardian's native language, unless it clearly is not feasible to do so, of all procedures available pursuant to this section; and

(E) an opportunity to present complaints with respect to any matter relating to the identification, evaluation, or educational placement of the child, or the provision of a free appropriate public education to such child.

(2) Whenever a complaint has been received under paragraph (1) of this subsection, the parents or guardian shall have an opportunity for an impartial due process hearing which shall be conducted by the State educational agency or by the local educational agency or intermediate educational unit, as determined by State law or by the State educational agency. No hearing conducted pursuant to the requirements of this paragraph shall be conducted by an employee of such

agency or unit involved in the education or care of the child.

(c) If the hearing required in paragraph (2) of subsection (b) of this section is conducted by a local educational agency or an intermediate educational unit, any party aggrieved by the findings and decision rendered in such a hearing may appeal to the State educational agency which shall conduct an impartial review of such hearing. The officer conducting such review shall make an independent decision upon completion of such review.

(d) Any party to any hearing conducted pursuant to subsections (b) and (c) shall be accorded (1) the right to be accompanied and advised by counsel and by individuals with special knowledge or training with respect to the problems of handicapped children, (2) the right to present evidence and confront, cross-examine, and compel the attendance of witnesses, (3) the right to a written or electronic verbatim record of such hearing, and (4) the right to written findings of fact and decisions (which findings and decisions shall also be transmitted to the advisory panel established pursuant to section 613(a)(12)).

(e)(1) A decision made in a hearing conducted pursuant to paragraph (2) of subsection (b) shall be final, except that any party involved in such hearing may appeal such decision under the provisions of subsection (c) and paragraph (2) of this subsection. A decision made under subsection (c) shall be final, except that any party may bring an action under paragraph (2) of this subsection.

(2) Any party aggrieved by the findings and decision made under subsection (b) who does not have the right to an appeal under subsection (c), and any party aggrieved by the findings and decision under subsection (c), shall have the right to bring a civil action with respect to the complaint presented pursuant to this section, which action may be brought in any State court of competent jurisdiction or in a district court of the United States without regard to the amount in controversy. In any action brought under this paragraph the court shall receive the records of the administrative proceedings, shall hear additional evidence at the request of a party, and, basing its decision on the preponderance of the evidence, shall grant such relief as the court determines is appropriate.

(3) During the pendency of any proceedings conducted pursuant to this section, unless the State or local educational agency and the parents or guardian otherwise agree, the child shall remain in the then current educational placement of such child, or, if applying for initial admission to a public school, shall, with the consent of the parents or guardian, be placed in the public school program until all such proceedings have been completed.

(4) The district courts of the United States shall have jurisdiction of actions brought under this subsection without regard to the amount in controversy. *(20 USC 1415)*

## WITHHOLDING AND JUDICIAL REVIEW

SEC. 616. (a) Whenever the Secretary, after reasonable notice and opportunity for hearing to the State educational agency involved (and to any local educational agency or intermediate educational unit affected by any failure described in clause (2)), finds —

(1) that there has been a failure to comply substantially with any provision of section 612 or section 613, or

(2) that in the administration of the State plan there is a failure to comply with any provision of this part or with any requirements set forth in the application of a local educational agency or intermediate educational unit approved by the State educational agency pursuant to the State plan,

the Secretary (A) shall, after notifying the State educational agency, withhold any further payments to the State under this part, and (B) may, after notifying the State educational agency, withhold futher payments to the State under the Federal programs specified in section 613(a)(2) within his jurisdiction, to the extent that funds under such programs are available for the provision of assistance for the education of handicapped children. If the Secretary withholds further payments under clause (A) or clause (B) he may determine that such withholding will be limited to programs or projects under the State plan, or portions thereof, affected by the failure, or that the State educational agency shall not make further payments under this part to specified local educational agencies or intermediate educational units affected by the failure. Until the Secretary is satisfied that there is no longer any failure to comply with the provisions of this part, as specified in clause (1) or clause (2), no further payment shall be made to the State under this part or under the Federal programs specified in section 613(a)(2) within his jurisdiction to the extent that funds under such programs are available for the provision of assistance for the education of handicapped children, or payments by the State educational agency under this part shall be limited to local educational agencies and intermediate educational units whose actions did not cause or were not involved in the failure, as the case may be. Any State educational agency, local educational agency, or intermediate educational unit in receipt of a notice pursuant to the first sentence of this subsection shall, by means of a public notice, take such measures as may be necessary to bring the pendency of an action pursuant to this subsection to the attention of the public within the jurisdiction of such agency or unit.

(b)(1) If any State is dissatisfied with the Secretary's final action with respect to its State plan submitted under section 613, such State may, within sixty days after notice of such action, file with the United States court of appeals for the circuit in which such State is located a petition for review of that action. A copy of the petition shall be forthwith transmitted by the clerk of the court to the Secretary. The Secretary thereupon shall file in the court the record of the proceedings on which he based his action, as provided in section 2112 of title 28, United States Code.

(2) The findings of fact by the Secretary, if supported by substantial

evidence, shall be conclusive, but the court, for good cause shown, may remand the cause to the Secretary to take further evidence, and the Secretary may thereupon make new or modified findings of fact and may modify his previous action, and shall file in the court the record of the further proceedings. Such new or modified findings of fact shall likewise be conclusive if supported by substantial evidence.

(3) Upon the filing of such petition, the court shall have jurisdiction to affirm the action of the Secretary or to set it aside, in whole or in part. The judgment of the court shall be subject to review by the Supreme Court of the United States upon certiorari or certification as provided in section 1254 of title 28, United States Code. *(20 USC 1416)*

### ADMINISTRATION

SEC. 617. (a)(1) In carrying out his duties under this part, the Secretary shall —

(A) cooperate with, and furnish all technical assistance necessary, directly or by grant or contract, to the States in matters relating to the education of handicapped children and the execution of the provisions of this part;

(B) provide such short-term training programs and institutes as are necessary;

(C) disseminate information, and otherwise promote the education of all handicapped children within the States; and

(D) assure that each State shall, within one year after the date of the enactment of the Education for All Handicapped Children Act of 1975, provide certification of the actual number of handicapped children receiving special education and related services in each State.

(2) As soon as practicable after the date of the enactment of the Education for All Handicapped Children Act of 1975, the Secretary shall, by regulation, prescribe a uniform financial report to be utilized by State educational agencies in submitting plans under this part in order to assure equity among the States.

(b) In carrying out the provisions of this part, the Secretary (and the Secretary, in carrying out the provisions of subsection (c)) shall issue, not later than January 1, 1977, amend, and revoke such rules and regulations as may be necessary. No other less formal method of implementing such provisions is authorized.

(c) The Secretary shall take appropriate action, in accordance with the provisions of section 438 of the General Education Provisions Act, to assure the protection of the confidentiality of any personally identifiable data, information, and records collected or maintained by the Secretary and by State and local educational agencies pursuant to the provisions of this part.

(d) The Secretary is authorized to hire qualified personnel necessary to conduct data collection and evaluation activities required by subsections (b), (c) and (d) of section 618 and to carry out his duties under subsection (a)(1) of this subsection without regard to the provisions of title 5, United States Code, relating to appointments in the competitive service and without regard to chapter 51 and subchapter III of chapter 53 of such title relating to classification and general schedule pay rates except that no more than twenty such personnel shall be employed at any time. *(20 USC 1417)*

EVALUATION

SEC. 618. (a) The Secretary shall directly or by grant, contract, or cooperative agreement, collect data and conduct studies, investigations, and evaluations —

(1) to assess progress in the implementation of this Act, the impact, and the effectiveness of State and local efforts and efforts by the Secretary of Interior to provide free appropriate public education to all handicapped children and youth and early intervention services to handicapped infants and toddlers, and

(2) to provide —

(A) Congress with information relevant to policymaking, and

(B) Federal, State, and local agencies and the Secretary of Interior with information relevant to program management, administration, and effectiveness with respect to such education and early intervention services.

(b) In carrying out subsection (a), the Secretary, on at least an annual basis, shall obtain data concerning programs and projects assisted under this Act and under other Federal laws relating to handicapped infants, toddlers, children, and youth, and such additional information, from State and local educational agencies, the Secretary of Interior, and other appropriate sources, as is necessary for the implementation of this Act including —

(1) the number of handicapped infants, toddlers, children, and youth in each State receiving a free appropriate public education or early intervention services (A) in age groups 0-2 and 3-5, and (B) in age groups 6-11, 12-17, and 18-21 by disability category,

(2) the number of handicapped children and youth in each State who are participating in regular educational programs (consistent with the requirements of sections 612(5)(B) and 614(a)(1)(C)(iv) by disability category, and the number of handicapped children and youth in separate classes, separate schools or facilities, or public or private residential facilities or who have been otherwise removed from the regular education environment, *(20 USC 1412, 1414)*

(3) the number of handicapped children and youth exiting the educational system each year through program completion or otherwise (A) in age group 3-5, and (B) in age groups 6-11,

12-17, and 18-21 by disability category and anticipated services for the next year,

(4) the amount of Federal, State, and local funds expended in each State specifically for special education and related services and for early intervention services (which may be based upon a sampling of data from State agencies including State and local educational agencies),

(5) the number and type of personnel that are employed in the provision of special education and related services to handicapped children and youth and early intervention services to handicapped infants and toddlers by disability category served, and the estimated number and type of additional personnel by disability category needed to adequately carry out the policy established by this Act, and

(6) a description of the special education and related services and early intervention services needed to fully implement this Act throughout each State, including estimates of the number of handicapped infants and toddlers in the 0-2 age group and estimates of the number of handicapped children and youth (A) in age group 3-5 and (B) in age groups 6-11, 12-17, and 18-21 and by disability category.

(c) The Secretary shall, by grant, contract, or cooperative agreement, provide for evaluation studies to determine the impact of this Act. Each such evaluation shall include recommendations for improvement of the programs under this Act. The Secretary shall, not later than July 1 of each year, submit to the appropriate committees of each House of the Congress and publish in the Federal Register proposed evaluation priorities for review and comment.

(d)(1) The Secretary may enter into cooperative agreements with State educational agencies and other State agencies to carry out studies to assess the impact and effectiveness of programs assisted under this Act.

(2) An agreement under paragraph (1) shall —

(A) provide for the payment of not to exceed 60 percent of the total cost of studies conducted by a participating State agency to assess the impact and effectiveness of programs assisted under this Act, and

(B) be developed in consultation with the State Advisory Panel established under this Act, the local educational agencies, and others involved in or concerned with the education of handicapped children and youth and the provision of early intervention services to handicapped infants and toddlers.

(3) The Secretary shall provide technical assistance to participating State agencies in the implementation of the study design, analysis, and reporting procedures.

(4) In addition, the Secretary shall disseminate information from such studies to State agencies, regional resources centers, and clearinghouses established by this Act, and, as appropriate, to others

involved in, or concerned with, the education of handicapped children and youth and the provision of early intervention services to handicapped infants and toddlers.

(e)(1) At least one study shall be a longitudinal study of a sample of handicapped students, encompassing the full range of handicapping conditions, examining their educational progress while in special education and their occupational, educational and independent living status after graduating from secondary school or otherwise leaving special education.

(2) At least one study shall focus on obtaining and compiling current information available, through State educational agencies and local educational agencies and other service providers, regarding State and local expenditures for educational services for handicapped students (including special education and related services) and shall gather information needed in order to calculate a range of per pupil expenditures by handicapping condition.

(f)(1) Not later than 120 days after the close of each fiscal year, the Secretary shall publish and disseminate an annual report on the progress being made toward the provision of a free appropriate public education to all handicapped children and youth and early intervention services for handicapped infants and toddlers. The annual report shall be transmitted to the appropriate committees of each House of Congress and published and disseminated in sufficient quantities to the education community at large and to other interested parties.

(2) The Secretary shall include in each annual report under paragraph (1) —

(A) a compilation and analysis of data gathered under subsection (b)

(B) an index and summary of each evaluation activity and results of studies conducted under subsection (c),

(C) a description of findings and determinations resulting from monitoring reviews of State implementation of part B of this Act, *(20 USC 1411)*

(D) an analysis and evaluation of the participation of handicapped children and youth in vocational education programs and services,

(E) an analysis and evaluation of the effectiveness of procedures undertaken by each State educational agency, local educational agency, and intermediate educational unit to ensure that handicapped children and youth receive special education and related services in the least restrictive environment commensurate with their needs and to improve programs of instruction for handicapped children and youth in day or residential facilities, and

(F) any recommendation for change in the provisions of this Act or any other Federal law providing support for the education of handicapped children and youth.

(3) In the annual report under paragraph (1) for fiscal year 1985 which is published in 1986 and for every third year thereafter, the Secretary shall include in the annual report —

(A) an index of all current projects funded under parts C through G of this title, and *(20 USC 1421-1454)*

(B) data reported under sections 621, 622, 623, 627, 634, 641 and 661. *(20 USC 1421-1454)*

(4) In the annual report under paragraph (1) for fiscal year 1988 which is published in 1989, the Secretary shall include special sections addressing the provision of a free appropriate public education to handicapped infants, toddlers, children, and youth in rural areas and to handicapped migrants, handicapped Indians (particularly programs operated under section 611(f)), handicapped Native Hawaiian, and other native Pacific basin children and youth, handicapped infants, toddlers, children and youth of limited English proficiency. *(20 USC 1426, 1434)*

(5) Beginning in 1986, in consultation with the National Council for the Handicapped and the Bureau of Indian Affairs Advisory Committee for Exceptional Children, a description of the status of early intervention services for handicapped infants and toddlers from birth through age two, inclusive, and special education and related services to handicapped children from 3 through 5 years of age (including those receiving services through Head Start, Developmental Disabilities Programs, Crippled Children's Services, Mental Health/Mental Retardation Agency, and State child-development centers and private agencies under contract with local schools).

(g) There are authorized to be appropriated $3,800,000 for fiscal year 1987, $4,000,000 for fiscal year 1988, and $4,200,000 for fiscal year 1989 to carry out this section.

PRE-SCHOOL GRANTS

SEC. 619. (a)(1) For fiscal years 1987 through 1989 (or fiscal year 1990 if the Secretary makes a grant under this paragraph for such fiscal year) the Secretary shall make a grant to any State which —

(A) has met the eligibility requirements of section 612, *(20 USC 1412)*

(B) has a State plan approved under section 613, and *(20 USC 1413)*

(C) provides special education and related services to handicapped children aged three to five, inclusive.

(2)(A) For fiscal year 1987 the amount of a grant to a State under paragraph (1) may not exceed —

(i) $300 per handicapped child aged three to five, inclusive, who received special education and related services in such State as determined under section 611(a)(3), or *(20 USC 1411)*

(ii) if the amount appropriated under subsection (e) exceeds the product of $300 and the total number of handicapped children aged three to five, inclusive, who received special education and related services as determined under section 611(a)(3) —

(I) $300 per handicapped child aged three to five, inclusive, who received special education and related services in such State as determined under section 611(a)(3), plus

(II) an amount equal to the portion of the appropriation available after allocating funds to all States under subclause (1) (the excess appropriation) divided by the estimated increase, from the preceding fiscal year, in the number of handicapped children aged three to five, inclusive, who will be receiving special education and related services in all States multiplied by the estimated number of such children in such State.

(B) For fiscal year 1988, funds shall be distributed in accordance with clause (i) or (ii) of paragraph (2)(A), except that the amount specified therein shall be $400 instead of $300.

(C) For fiscal year 1989, funds shall be distributed in accordance with clause (i) or (ii) of paragraph (2)(A), except that the amount specified therein shall be $500 instead of $300.

(D) If the Secretary makes a grant under paragraph (1) for fiscal year 1990, the amount of a grant to a State under such paragraph may not exceed $1,000 per handicapped child aged three to five, inclusive, who received special education and related services in such State as determined under section 611(a)(3). *(20 USC 1411)*

(E) If the actual number of additional children served in a fiscal year differs from the estimate made under clause (ii)(II) of the applicable subparagraph, subparagraph (A)(ii)(II), the Secretary shall adjust (upwards or downwards) a State's allotment in the subsequent fiscal year.

(F)(i) The amount of a grant under subparagraph (A), (B), or (C) to any State for a fiscal year may not exceed $3,800 per estimated handicapped child aged three to five, inclusive, who will be receiving or handicapped child aged three to five, inclusive, who is receiving special education and related services in such State.

(ii) If the amount appropriated under subsection (e) for any fiscal year exceeds the amount of grants which may be made to the States for such fiscal year, the excess amount appropriated shall remain available for obligation under this section for 2 succeeding fiscal years.

(3) To receive a grant under paragraph (1) a State shall make an application to the Secretary at such time, in such manner, and containing or accompanied by such information as the Secretary may reasonably require.

(b)(1) For fiscal year 1990 (or fiscal year 1991 if required by paragraph (2)) and fiscal years thereafter the Secretary shall make a grant to any State which —

(A) has met the eligibility requirements of section 612, and

(B) has a State plan approved under section 613 which

includes policies and procedures that assure the availability under the State law and practice of such State of a free appropriate public education for all handicapped children aged three to five, inclusive.

(2) The Secretary may make a grant under paragraph (1) only for fiscal 1990 and fiscal years thereafter, except that if —

(A) the aggregate amount that was appropriated under subsection (e) for fiscal years 1987, 1988, and 1989 was less than $656,000,000, and

(B) the amount appropriated for fiscal year 1990 under subsection (e) is less than $306,000,000,

the Secretary may not make a grant under paragraph (1) until fiscal year 1991 and shall make a grant under subsection (a)(1) for fiscal year 1990.

(3) The amount of any grant to any State under paragraph (1) for any fiscal year may not exceed $1,000 for each handicapped child in such State aged three to five, inclusive.

(4) To receive a grant under paragraph (1) a State shall make an application to the Secretary at such time, in such manner and containing or accompanied by such information as the Secretary may reasonably require.

(c)(1) For fiscal year 1987, a State which receives a grant under subsection (a)(1) shall —

(A) distribute at least 70 percent of such grant to local educational agencies and intermediate educational units in such State in accordance with paragraph (3), except that in applying such section only handicapped children aged three to five, inclusive, shall be considered.

(B) use not more than 25 percent of such grant for the planning and development of a comprehensive delivery system for which a grant could have been made under section 623(b) in effect through fiscal year 1987 and for direct and support services for handicapped children, and

(C) use not more than 5 percent of such grant for administrative expenses related to the grant.

(2) For fiscal years beginning after fiscal year 1987, a State which receives a grant under subsection (a)(1) or (b)(1) shall —

(A) distribute at least 75 percent of such grant to local educational agencies and intermediate educational units in such State in accordance with paragraph (3), except that in applying such section only handicapped children aged three to five, inclusive, shall be considered,

(B) use not more than 20 percent of such grant for the planning and development of a comprehensive delivery system for which a grant could have been made under section 623(b) in effect through fiscal year 1987 and for direct and support services for handicapped children, and

(C) use not more than 5 percent of such grant for administrative expenses related to the grant.

(3) From the amount of funds available to local educational agencies and intermediate educational units in any State under this section, each local educational agency or intermediate educational unit shall be entitled to —

(A) an amount which bears the same ratio to the amount available under subsection (a)(2)(A)(i) or subsection (a)(2)(A)(ii)(I), as the case may be, as the number of handicapped children aged three to five, inclusive, who received special education and related services, as determined under section 611(a)(3) in such local educational agency or intermediate educational unit bears to the aggregate number of handicapped children aged three to five, inclusive, who received special education and related services in all local educational agencies and intermediate educational units in the State entitled to funds under this section, and *(20 USC 1411)*

(B) to the extent funds are available under subsection (a)(2)(A)(ii)(II), an amount which bears the same ratio to the amount available under subsection (a)(2)(A)(ii)(II) as the estimated number of additional handicapped children aged three to five, inclusive, who will be receiving special education and related services in such local educational agency or intermediate educational unit bears to the aggregate number of handicapped children aged three to five, inclusive, who will be receiving special education and related services in all local educational agencies and intermediate educational units in the State entitled to funds under this section.

(d) If the sums appropriated under subsection (e) for any fiscal year for making payments to States under subsection (a)(1) or (b)(1) are not sufficient to pay in full the maximum amounts which all States may receive under such subsection for such fiscal year, the maximum amounts which all States may receive under such sub section for such fiscal year shall be ratably reduced by first ratably reducing amounts computed under the excess appropriation provision of subsection (a)(2)(A)(ii)(II). If additional funds become available for making such payments for any fiscal year during which the preceding sentence is applicable, the reduced maximum amounts shall be increased on the same basis as they were reduced.

(e) For grants under subsections (a)(1) and (b)(1) there are authorized to be appropriated such sums as may be necessary.

PAYMENTS

SEC. 620. (a) The Secretary shall make payments to each State in amounts which the State educational agency of such State is eligible to receive under this part. Any State educational agency receiving payments under this subsection shall distribute payments to the local educational agencies and intermediate educational units of such State in amounts which such agencies and units are eligible to receive under this part after the State educational agency has approved applications of such agencies or units for payments in accordance with section 614(b).

(b) Payments under this part may be made in advance or by way of reimbursement and in such installments as the Secretary may determine necessary. *(20 USC 1420)*

## PART C — CENTERS AND SERVICES TO MEET SPECIAL NEEDS OF THE HANDICAPPED

### REGIONAL RESOURCE AND FEDERAL CENTERS

SEC. 621. (a) The Secretary may make grants to, or enter into contracts or cooperative agreements with, institutions of higher education, public agencies, private nonprofit organizations, State educational agencies, or combinations of such agencies or institutions (which combinations may include one or more local educational agencies) within particular regions of the United States, to pay all or part of the cost of the establishment and operation of regional resource centers. Each regional resource center shall provide consultation, technical assistance, and training to State educational agencies and through such State educational agencies to local educational agencies and to other appropriate State agencies providing early intervention services. The services provided by a regional resource center shall be consistent with the priority needs identified by the States served by the center and the findings of the Secretary in monitoring reports prepared by the Secretary under section 617 of the Act. Each regional resource center established or operated under this section shall — *(20 USC 1417)*

(1) assist in identifying and solving persistent problems in providing quality special education and related services for handicapped children and early intervention services to handicapped infants and toddlers and their families,

(2) assist in developing, identifying, and replicating successful programs and practices which will improve special education and related services to handicapped children and youth and their families and early intervention services to handicapped infants and toddlers and their families,

(3) gather and disseminate information to all State educational agencies within the region and coordinate activities with other centers assisted under this subsection and other relevant projects conducted by the Department of Education,

(4) assist in the improvement of information dissemination to and training activities for professionals and parents of handicapped infants, toddlers, children, and youth, and

(5) provide information to and training for agencies, institutions, and organizations, regarding techniques and approaches for submitting applications for grants, contracts, and cooperative agreements under this part and parts D through G. *(20 USC 1422-1454)*

(b) In determining whether to approve an application for a project under subsection (a), the Secretary shall consider the need for such a center in the region to be served by the applicant and the capability of the applicant to fulfill the responsibilities under subsection (a).

(c) Each regional resource center shall report a summary of materials produced or developed and the summaries reported shall be included in the annual report to Congress required under section 618. *(20 USC 1418)*

(d) The Secretary may establish one coordinating technical assistance center focusing on national priorities established by the Secretary to assist the regional resource centers in the delivery of technical assistance, consistent with such national priorities.

(e) Before using funds made available in any fiscal year to carry out this section for purposes of subsection (d), not less than the amount made available for this section in the previous fiscal year shall be made available for regional resource centers under subsection (a) and in no case shall more than $500,000 be made available for the center under subsection (d). *(20 USC 1421)*

### SERVICES FOR DEAF-BLIND CHILDREN AND YOUTH

SEC. 622. (a)(1) The Secretary is authorized to make grants to, or to enter into cooperative agreements or contracts with, public or nonprofit private agencies, institutions, or organizations to assist State edcuational agencies to —

(A) assure deaf-blind children and youth provision of special education and related services as well as vocational and transitional services; and

(B) make available to deaf-blind youth upon attaining the age of twenty-two, programs and services to facilitate their transition from educational to other services; and

(2) A grant, cooperative agreement, or contract pursuant to paragraph (1)(A) may be made only for programs providing (A) technical assistance to agencies, institutions, or organizations providing educational services to deaf-blind children or youth; (B) preservice or inservice training to paraprofessionals, professionals, and related services personnel preparing to serve, or serving, deaf-blind children or youth; (C) replication of successful innovative approaches to providing educational or related services to deaf-blind children and youth; and (D) facilitation of parental involvement in the education of their deaf-blind children and youth. Such programs may include —

(i) the diagnosis and educational evaluai on of children and youth at risk of being certified deaf-blind;

(ii) programs of adjustment, education, and orientation for deaf-blind children and youth; and

(iii) consultative, counseling, and training services for the families of deaf-blind children and youth.

(3) A grant, cooperative agreement, or contract pursuant to

paragraph (1)(B) may be made only for programs providing (A) technical assistance to agencies, institutions, and organizations serving, or proposing to serve, deaf-blind individuals who have attained age twenty-two years; (B) training or inservice training to paraprofessionals or professionals serving, or preparing to serve, such individuals; and (C) assistance in the development or replication of successful innovative approaches to providing rehabilitative, semisupervised, or independent living programs.

(4) In carrying out this subsection, the Secretary shall take into consideration the need for a center for deaf-blind children and youth in light of the general availability and quality of existing services for such children and youth in the part of the country involved.

(b) The Secretary is also authorized to enter into a limited number of cooperative agreements or contracts to establish and support regional programs for the provision of technical assistance in the education of deaf-blind children and youth.

(c)(1) Programs supported under this section shall report annually to the Secretary on (A) the numbers of deaf-blind children and youth served by age, severity, and nature of deaf-blindness; (B) the number of paraprofessionals, professionals, and family members directly served by each activity; and (C) the types of services provided.

(2) The Secretary shall examine the number of deaf-blind children and youth (A) reported under subparagraph (c)(1)(A) and by the States; (B) served by the programs under part B of this Act and subpart 2 of part B, title I, of the Elementary and Secondary Education Act of 1965 (as modified by chapter 1 of the Education Consolidation and Improvement Act of 1981); and (C) the Deaf-Blind Registry of each State. The Secretary shall revise the count of deaf-blind children and youth to reflect the most accurate count.

(3) The Secretary shall summarize these data for submission in the annual report required under section 618.

(d) The Secretary shall disseminate materials and information concerning effective practices in working with deaf-blind children and youth.

(e) The Secretary is authorized to make grants to, or enter into contracts or cooperative agreements with, public or nonprofit private agencies, institutions, or organizations for the development and operation of extended school year demonstration programs for severely handicapped children and youth, including deaf-blind children and youth.

(f) The Secretary may make grants to, or enter into contracts or cooperative agreements with, the entities under section 624(a) for the purposes in such section. *(20 USC 1422)*

### EARLY EDUCATION FOR HANDICAPPED CHILDREN

SEC. 623. (a)(1) The Secretary may arrange by contract, grant, or cooperative agreement with appropriate public agencies and private nonprofit organizations, for the development and operation of experimental, demonstration, and outreach preschool and early intervention programs for handicapped children which the Secretary determines show promise of promoting a comprehensive and strengthened approach to the special problems of such children. Such programs shall include activities and services designed to (1) facilitate the intellectual, emotional, physical, mental, social, speech, language development, and self-help skills of such children, (2) encourage the participation of the parents of such children in the development and operation of any such program, and (3) acquaint the community to be served by any such program with the problems and potentialities of such children, (4) offer training about exemplary models and practices to State and local personnel who provide services to handicapped children from birth through eight, and (5) support the adaption of exemplary models and practices in States and local communities.

(2) Programs authorized by paragraph (1) shall be coordinated with similar programs in the schools operated or supported by State or local educational agencies of the community to be served and with similar programs operated by other public agencies in such community.

(3) As much as is feasible, programs assisted under paragraph (1) shall be geographically dispersed throughout the Nation in urban as well as rural areas.

(4)(A) Except as provided in subparagraph (B), no arrangement under paragraph (1) shall provide for the payment of more than 90 percent of the total annual costs of development, operation, and evaluation of any program. Non-Federal contributions may be in cash or in kind, fairly evaluated, including plant, equipment, and services.

(B) The Secretary may waive the requirement of subparagraph (A) in the case of an arrangement entered into under paragraph (1) with governing bodies of Indian tribes located on Federal or State reservations and with consortia of such bodies.

(b) The Secretary shall arrange by contract, grant, or cooperative agreement with appropriate public agencies and private nonprofit organizations for the establishment of a technical assistance development system to assist entities operating experimental, demonstration, and outreach programs and to assist State agencies to expand and improve services provided to handicapped children.

(c) The Secretary shall arrange by contract, grant, or cooperative agreement with appropriate public agencies and public nonprofit organizations for the establishment of early childhood research institutes to carry on sustained research to generate and disseminate new information on preschool and early intervention for handicapped children and their families.

(d) The Secretary may make grants to, enter into contracts or cooperative agreements under this section with, such organizations or institutions, as are determined by the Secretary to be appropriate, for research to identify and meet the full range of special needs of handicapped children and for training of personnel for programs specifically designed for handicapped children.

(e) At least one year before the termination of a grant, contract, or cooperative agreement made or entered into under subsections (b) and (c), the Secretary shall publish in the Federal Register a notice of intent to accept application for such a grant, contract, or cooperative agreement contingent on the appropriation of sufficient funds by Congress.

(f) For purposes of this section the term "handicapped children" includes children from birth through eight years of age. *(20 USC 1423)*

PROGRAMS FOR SEVERELY HANDICAPPED CHILDREN

SEC. 624. (a) The Secretary may make grants to, or enter into contracts or cooperative agreements with, such organizations or institutions, as are determined by the Secretary to be appropriate, to address the needs of severely handicapped children and youth, for—

(1) research to identify and meet the full range of special needs of such handicapped children and youth,

(2) the development or demonstration of new, or improvements in, existing, methods, approaches, or techniques which would contribute to the adjustment and education of such handicapped children and youth,

(3) training of personnel for programs specifically designed for such children, and

(4) dissemination of materials and information about practices found effective in working with such children and youth.

(b) In making grants and contracts under subsection (a), the Secretary shall ensure that the activities funded under such grants and contracts will be coordinated with similar activities funded from grants and contracts under other sections of this Act.

(c) To the extent feasible, programs, authorized by subsection (a) shall be geographically dispersed throughout the nation in urban and rural areas. *(20 USC 1424)*

POSTSECONDARY EDUCATION

SEC. 625. (a)(1) The Secretary may make grants to, or enter into contracts with, State educational agencies, institutions of higher education, junior and community colleges, vocational and technical institutions, and other appropriate nonprofit educational agencies for the development, operation, and dissemination of specifically designed model programs of postsecondary, vocational, technical, continuing, or adult education for handicapped individuals.

(2) In making grants or contracts on a competitive basis under paragraph (1), the Secretary shall give priority consideration to 4 regional centers for the deaf and to model programs for individuals with handicapping conditions other than deafness—

(A) for developing and adapting programs of postsecondary, vocational, technical, continuing, or adult education to meet the special needs of handicapped individuals, and

(B) for programs that coordinate, facilitate, and encourage education of handicapped individuals with their nonhandicapped peers.

(3) Persons operating programs for handicapped persons under a grant or contract under paragraph (1) must coordinate their efforts with and disseminate information about their activities to the clearinghouse on postsecondary programs established under section 633(b). *(20 USC 1433)*

(4) At least one year before the termination of a grant or contract with any of the 4 regional centers for the deaf, the Secretary shall publish in the Federal Register a notice of intent to accept application for such grant or contract, contingent on the appropriation of sufficient funds by Congress.

(5) To the extent feasible, programs authorized by paragraph (1) shall be geographically dispensed throughout the nation in urban and rural areas.

(6) Of the sums made available for programs under paragraph (1), not less than $2,000,000 shall first be available for the 4 regional centers for the deaf.

(b) For the purposes of subsection (a) the term "handicapped individuals" means individuals who are mentally retarded, hard of hearing, deaf, speech or language impaired, visually handicapped, seriously emotionally disturbed, orthopedically impaired, other health impaired individuals, or individuals with specific learning disabilities who by reason thereof require special education and related services.

### SECONDARY EDUCATION AND TRANSITIONAL SERVICES FOR HANDICAPPED YOUTH

SEC. 626. (a) The Secretary may make grants to, or enter into contracts with, institutions of higher education, State educational agencies, local educational agencies, or other appropriate public and private nonprofit institutions or agencies (including the State job training coordinating councils and service delivery area administrative entities established under the Job Training Partnership Act (Public Law 97-300)) to — *(29 USC 1501 note)*

(1) strengthen and coordinate special education and related services for handicapped youth currently in school or who recently left school to assist them in the transition of postsecondary education, vocational training, competitive employment (including supported employment), continuing education, or adult services,

(2) stimulate the improvements and development of programs for secondary special education, and

(3) stimulate the improvement of the vocational and life

skills of handicapped students to enable them to be better prepared for transition to adult life and services.

To the extent feasible, such programs shall be geographically dispersed through the Nation in urban and rural areas.

(b) Projects assisted under subsection (a) may include —

(1) developing strategies and techniques for transition to independent living, vocational training, vocational rehabilitation, postsecondary education, and competitive employment (including supported employment) for handicapped youth,

(2) establishing demonstration models for services, programs, and individualized education programs, which emphasize vocational training, transitional services, and placement for handicapped youth,

(3) conducting demographic studies which provide information on the numbers, age levels, types of handicapping conditions, and services required for handicapped youth in need of transitional programs,

(4) specially designed vocational programs to increase the potential for competitive employment for handicapped youth,

(5) research and development projects for exemplary service delivery models and the replication and dissemination of successful models,

(6) initiating cooperative models between educational agencies and adult service agencies, including vocational rehabilitation, mental health, mental retardation, public employment, and employers, which facilitate the planning and developing of transitional services for handicapped youth to postsecondary education and vocational training, employment, continuing education, and adult services,

(7) developing appropriate procedures for evaluating vocational training, placement, and transitional services for handicapped youth,

(8) conducting studies which provide information on the numbers, age levels, types of handicapping conditions and reasons why handicapped youth drop out of school,

(9) developing special education curriculum and instructional techniques that will improve handicapped students' acquisition of the skills necessary for transition to adult life and services, and

(10) specifically designed physical education and therapeutic recreation programs to increase the potential of handicapped youths for community participation.

(c) For purposes of paragraphs (1) and (2) of subsection (b), if an applicant is not an educational agency, such applicant shall coordinate with the State educational agency.

(d) Applications for assistance under subsection (a) other than for the purpose of conducting studies or evaluations shall —

(1) describe the procedures to be used for disseminating

relevant findings and data to regional resource centers, clearinghouses, and other interested persons, agencies, or organizations,

(2) describe the procedures that will be used for coordinating services among agencies for which handicapped youth are or will be eligible, and

(3) to the extent appropriate, provide for the direct participation of handicapped students and the parents of handicapped students in the planning, development, and implementation of such projects.

(e) The Secretary is authorized to make grants to, or to enter into contracts or cooperative agreements with, such organizations or institutions as are determined by the Secretary to be appropriate for the development or demonstration of new or improvements in existing methods, approaches, or techniques which will contribute to the adjustment and education of handicapped children and youth and the dissemination of materials and information concerning practices found effective in working with such children and youth.

(f) The Secretary, as appropriate, shall coordinate programs described under subsection (a) with projects developed under section 311 of the Rehabilitation Act of 1973 (29 U.S.C. 777a). *(20 USC 1425)*

### PROGRAM EVALUATIONS

SEC. 627. The Secretary shall conduct, either directly or by contract, a thorough and continuing evaluation of the effectiveness of each program assisted under this part. Results of the evaluations shall be analyzed and submitted to the appropriate committees of each House of Congress together with the annual report under section 618. *(20 USC 1426)*

### AUTHORIZATION OF APPROPRIATIONS

SEC. 628. (a) There are authorized to be appropriated to carry out section 621, $6,700,000 for fiscal year 1987, $7,100,000 for fiscal year 1988, and $7,500,000 for fiscal year 1989.

(b) There are authorized to be appropriated to carry out section 622, $15,900,000 for fiscal year 1987, $16,800,000 for fiscal year 1988, and $17,800,000 for fiscal year 1989.

(c) There are authorized to be appropriated to carry out section 623, $24,470,000 for fiscal year 1987, $25,870,000 for fiscal year 1988, and $27,410,000 for fiscal year 1989.

(d) There are authorized to be appropriated to carry out section 624, $5,300,000 for fiscal year 1987, $5,600,000 for fiscal year 1988, and $5,900,000 for fiscal year 1989.

(e) There are authorized to be appropriated to carry out section 625, $5,900,000 for fiscal year 1987, $6,200,000 for fiscal year 1988, and $6,600,000 for fiscal year 1989.

(f) There are authorized to be appropriated to carry out section 626, $7,300,000 for fiscal year 1987, $7,700,000 for fiscal year

1988, and $8,100,000 for fiscal year 1989. *(20 USC 1427)*

## PART D — TRAINING PERSONNEL FOR THE EDUCATION OF THE HANDICAPPED

### GRANTS FOR PERSONNEL TRAINING

SEC. 631. (a)(1) The Secretary may make grants, which may include scholarships with necessary stipends and allowances, to institutions of higher education (including the university-affiliated facilities program under the Rehabilitation Act of 1973 and satellite network of the developmental disabilities program) and other appropriate nonprofit agencies to assist them in training personnel for careers in special education and early intervention, including — *(29 USC 701 note)*

(A) special education teaching, including speech-language pathology and audiology, and adaptive physical education,

(B) related services to handicapped children and youth in educational settings,

(C) special education supervision and administration,

(D) special education research, and

(E) training of special education personnel and other personnel providing special services and pre-school and early intervention services for handicapped children.

(2)(A) In making grants under paragraph (1), the Secretary shall base the determination of such grants on information relating to the present and projected need for the personnel to be trained based on identified State, regional, or national shortages, and the capacity of the institution or agency to train qualified personnel, and other information considered appropriate by the Secretary.

(B) The Secretary shall ensure that grants are only made under paragraph (1) to applicant agencies and institutions that meet State and professionally recognized standards for the preparation of special education and related services personnel unless the grant is for the purpose of assisting the applicant agency or institution to meet such standards.

(3) Grants under paragraph (1) may be used by institutions to assist in covering the cost of courses of training or study for such personnel and for establishing and maintaining fellowships or traineeships with such stipends and allowances as may be determined by the Secretary.

(4) The Secretary in carrying out paragraph (1) may reserve a sum not to exceed 5 percent of the amount available for paragraph (1) in each fiscal year for contracts to prepare personnel in areas where shortages exist when a response to that need has not been adequately addressed by the grant process.

(b) The Secretary may make grants to institutions of higher education and other appropriate nonprofit agencies to conduct special projects to develop and demonstrate new approaches (including the application of new technology) for the preservice training purposes set forth in subsection (a), for regular educators, for the training of teachers to work in community and school settings with handicapped secondary school students, and for the inservice training of special education personnel, including classroom aides, related services personnel, and regular education personnel who serve handicapped children and personnel providing early intervention services.

(c)(1) The Secretary may make grants through a separate competition to private nonprofit organizations for the purpose of providing training and information to parents of handicapped children and persons who work with parents to enable such individuals to participate more effectively with professionals in meeting the educational needs of handicapped children. Such grants shall be designed to meet the unique training and information needs of parents of handicapped children living in the area to be served by the grant, particularly those who are members of groups that have been traditionally underrepresented.

(2) In order to receive a grant under paragraph (1) a private nonprofit organization shall —

(A) be governed by a board of directors on which a majority of the members are parents of handicapped children and which includes members who are professionals in the field of special education and related services who serve handicapped children and youth, or if the nonprofit private organization does not have such a board, such organization shall have a membership which represents the interests of individuals with handicapping conditions, and shall establish a special governing committee on which a majority of the members are parents of handicapped children and which includes members who are professionals in the fields of special education and related services to operate the training and information program under paragraph (1).

(B) serve the parents of children with the full range of handicapping conditions under such grant program, and

(C) demonstrate the capacity and expertise to conduct effectively the training and information activities for which a grant may be made under paragraph (1).

(3) The board of directors or special governing committee of a private nonprofit organization receiving a grant under paragraph (1) shall meet at least once in each calendar quarter to review the parent training and information activities for which the grant is made, and each such committee shall advise the governing board directly of its views and recommendations. Whenever a private nonprofit organization requests the renewal of a grant under paragraph (1) for a fiscal year, the board of directors or the special governing committee shall submit to the Secretary a written review of the parent training and information program conducted by that private nonprofit organization during the preceding fiscal year.

(4) The Secretary shall ensure that grants under paragraph (1) will —

(A) be distributed geographically to the greatest extent possible throughout all the States and give priority to grants which involve unserved areas, and

(B) be targeted to parents of handicapped children in both urban and rural areas or on a State or regional basis.

(5) Parent training and information programs assisted under paragraph (1) shall assist parents to —

(A) better understand the nature and needs of the handicapping conditions of children,

(B) provide followup support for handicapped children's educational programs,

(C) communicate more effectively with special and regular educators, administrators, related services personnel, and other relevant professionals,

(D) participate in educational decisionmaking processes including the development of a handicapped child's individualized educational program,

(E) obtain information about the programs, services, and resources available to handicapped children and the degree to which the programs, services, and resources are appropriate, and

(F) understand the provisions for the education of handicapped children as specified under part B of this Act.
*(20 USC 1411)*

(6) Parent training and information programs may, at a grant recipient's discretion, include State or local educational personnel where such participation will further an objective of the program assisted by the grant.

(7) Each private nonprofit organization operating a program receiving a grant under paragraph (1) shall consult with appropriate agencies which serve or assist handicapped children and youth and are located in the jurisdictions served by the program.

(8) The Secretary shall provide technical assistance, by grant or contract, for establishing, developing, and coordinating parent training and information programs.

#### GRANTS TO STATE EDUCATIONAL AGENCIES AND INSTITUTIONS FOR TRAINEESHIPS

SEC. 632. The Secretary shall make grants to each State educational agency and may make grants to institutions of higher education to assist in establishing and maintaining preservice and inservice programs to prepare personnel to meet the needs of handicapped infants, toddlers, children, and youth or supervisors of such persons, consistent with the personnel needs identified in the State's comprehensive system of personnel development under section 613. *(20 USC 1432)*

#### CLEARINGHOUSES

SEC. 633. (a) The Secretary is authorized to make a grant to or enter into a contract with a public agency or a nonprofit private organization or institution for a national clearinghouse on the education of the handicapped and to make grants or contracts with a public agency or a nonprofit private organization or institution for other support projects which may be deemed necessary by the Secretary to disseminate information and provide technical assistance on a national basis to parents, professionals, and other interested parties concerning —

(1) programs relating to the education of the handicapped under this Act and under other Federal laws, and

(2) participation in such programs, including referral of individuals to appropriate national, State, and local agencies and organizations for further assistance.

(b) In addition to the clearinghouse established under subsection (a), the Secretary shall make a grant or enter into a contract for a national clearinghouse on postsecondary education for handicapped individuals for the purpose of providing information on available services and programs in postsecondary education for the handicapped.

(c) The Secretary shall make a grant or enter into a contract for a national clearinghouse designed to encourage students to seek careers and professional personnel to seek employment in the various fields relating to the education of handicapped children and youth through the following:

(1) Collection and dissemination of information on current and future national, regional, and State needs for special education and related services personnel.

(2) Dissemination to high school counselors and others concerning current career opportunities in special education, location of programs, and various forms of financial assistance (such as scholarships, stipends, and allowances).

(3) Identification of training programs available around the country.

(4) Establishment of a network among local and State educational agencies and institutions of higher education concerning the supply of graduates and available openings.

(5) Technical assistance to institutions seeking to meet State and professionally recognized standards. *(20 USC 1433)*

(d)(1) In awarding the grants and contracts under this section, the Secretary shall give particular attention to any demonstrated experience at the national level relevant to performance of the functions established in the section, and ability to conduct such projects, communicate with the intended consumers of information, and maintain the necessary communication with other agencies and organizations.

(2) The Secretary is authorized to make contracts with profit-making organizations under this section only when necessary for materials or media access. *(20 USC 1433)*

REPORTS TO THE SECRETARY

SEC. 634. (a) Not more than sixty days after the end of any fiscal year, each recipient of a grant or contract under this part during such fiscal year shall prepare and submit a report to the Secretary. Each such report shall be in such form and detail as the Secretary determines to be appropriate, and shall include —

(1) the number of individuals trained under the grant or contract, by category of training and level of training; and

(2) the number of individuals trained under the grant or contract receiving degrees and certification, by category and level of training.

(b) A summary of the date required by this section shall be included in the annual report of the Secretary under section 618 of this Act. *(20 USC 1434)*

AUTHORIZATION OF APPROPRIATIONS

SEC. 635. (a) There are authorized to be appropriated to carry out this part (other than section 633) $70,400,000 for fiscal year 1987, $74,500,000 for fiscal year 1988, and $79,000,000 for fiscal year 1989. There are authorized to be appropriated to carry out section 633, $1,200,000 for fiscal year 1987, $1,900,000 for fiscal year 1988, and $2,000,000 for fiscal year 1989.

(b) Of the funds appropriated pursuant to subsection (a) for any fiscal year, the Secretary shall reserve not less than 65 per centum for activities described in subparagraphs (A) through (E) of section 631(a)(1).

(c) Of the funds appropriated under subsection (a) for any fiscal year, the Secretary shall reserve 10 percent for activities under section 631(c).

## PART E — RESEARCH IN THE EDUCATION OF THE HANDICAPPED

RESEARCH AND DEMONSTRATION PROJECTS IN EDUCATION OF HANDICAPPED CHILDREN

SEC. 641 (a) The Secretary may make grants to, or enter into contracts or cooperative agreements with, State and local educational agencies, institutions of higher education, and other public agencies and nonprofit private organizations for research and related activities to assist special education personnel, related services personnel, early intervention personnel, and other appropriate persons, including parents, in improving the special education and related services and early intervention services for handicapped infants, toddlers, children, and youth. Research and related activities shall be designed to increase knowledge and understanding of handicapping conditions, and teaching, learning, and education-related developmental practices and services for handicapped infants, toddlers, children and youth. Research and related activities assisted under this section shall include the following:

(1) The development of new and improved techniques and devices for teaching handicapped infants, toddlers, children and youth.

(2) The development of curricula which meet the unique educational and developmental needs for handicapped infants, toddlers, children and youth.

(3) The application of new technologies and knowledge for the purpose of improving the instruction of handicapped infants, toddlers, children and youth.

(4) The development of program models and exemplary practices areas of special education and early intervention.

(5) The dissemination of information on research and related activities conducted under this part to regional resource centers and interested individuals and organizations.

(6) The development of instruments, including tests, inventories, and scales for measuring progress of handicapped infants, toddlers, children and youth across a number of developmental domains.

(b) In carrying out subsection (a), the Secretary shall consider the special education or early intervention experience of applicants under such subsection.

(c) The Secretary shall publish proposed research priorities in the Federal Register every 2 years, not later than July 1, and shall allow a period of 60 days for public comments and suggestions. After analyzing and considering the public comments, the Secretary shall publish final research priorities in the Federal Register not later than 30 days after the close of the comment period.

(d) The Secretary shall provide an index (including the title of each research project and the name and address of the researching organization) of all research projects conducted in the prior fiscal year in the annual report described under section 618. The Secretary shall make reports of research projects available to the education community at large and to other interested parties.

(e) The Secretary shall coordinate the research priorities established under subsection (c) with research priorities established by the National Institute of Handicapped Research and shall provide information concerning research priorities established under such subsection to the National Council on the Handicapped, and to the Bureau of Indian Affairs Advisory Committee for Exceptional Children. *(20 USC 1441)*

RESEARCH AND DEMONSTRATION PROJECTS IN PHYSICAL EDUCATION AND RECREATION FOR HANDICAPPED CHILDREN

SEC. 642. The Secretary is authorized to make grants to States, State or local educational agencies, institutions of higher education, and other public or nonprofit private educational or research agencies and organizations, and to make contracts with States, State or local educational agencies, institutions of higher education, and other public or private educational or research, agencies and organizations, for research and related purposes relating to physical education or recreation for handicapped children, and to conduct research, surveys, or demonstrations relating to physical education or recreation for handicapped children. *(20 USC 1442)*

## PANELS OF EXPERTS

SEC. 643. (a) The Secretary shall convene, in accordance with subsection (b), panels of experts who are competent to evaluate proposals for projects under parts C through G. The panels shall be composed of — *(20 USC 1421-1454)*

(1) individuals from the field of special education for the handicapped and other relevant disciplines who have significant expertise and experience in the content areas and age levels addressed in the proposals, and

(2) handicapped individuals and parents of handicapped individuals when appropriate.

(b)(1) The Secretary shall convene panels under subsection (a) for any application which includes a total funding request exceeding $60,000 and may convene or otherwise appoint panels for applications which include funding requests that are less than such amount.

(2) Such panels shall include a majority of non-Federal members. Such non-Federal members shall be provided travel and per diem not to exceed the rate provided to other educational consultants used by the Department and shall be provided consultant fees at such a rate.

(c) The Secretary may use funds available under parts C through G to pay expenses and fees of non-Federal members under subsection (b). *(20 USC 1421-1454)*

## AUTHORIZATION OF APPROPRIATIONS

SEC. 644. For purposes of carrying out this part, there are authorized to be appropriated $18,000,000 for fiscal year 1987, $19,000,000 for fiscal year 1988, and $20,100,000 for fiscal year 1989. *(20 USC 1444)*

## PART F — INSTRUCTIONAL MEDIA FOR THE HANDICAPPED

### PURPOSE

SEC. 651. (a) The purposes of this part are to promote —

(1) the general welfare of deaf persons by (A) bringing to such persons understanding and appreciation of those films which play such an important part in the general and cultural advancement of hearing persons, (B) providing through these films enriched educational and cultural experiences through which deaf persons can be brought into better touch with the

realities of their environment, and (C) providing a wholesome and rewarding experience which deaf persons may share together; and

(2) the educational advancement of handicapped persons by (A) carrying on research in the use of educational media for the handicapped, (B) producing and distributing educational media for the use of handicapped persons, their parents, their actual or potential employers, and other persons directly involved in work for the advancement of the handicapped, and (C) training persons in the use of educational media for the instruction of the handicapped. *(20 USC 1451)*

### CAPTIONED FILMS AND EDUCATIONAL MEDIA FOR HANDICAPPED PERSONS

SEC. 652. (a) The Secretary shall establish a loan service of captioned films and educational media for the purpose of making such materials available, in accordance with regulations, in the United States for nonprofit purposes to handicapped persons, parents of handicapped persons, and other persons directly involved in activities for the advancement of the handicapped, including for the purpose of addressing problems of illiteracy among the handicapped.

(b) The Secretary is authorized to —

(1) acquire films (or rights thereto) and other educational media by purchase, lease, or gift;

(2) acquire by lease or purchase equipment necessary to the administration of this part;

(3) provide by grant or contract, for the captioning of films;

(4) provide, by grant or contract, for the distribution of captioned films and other educational media and equipment through State schools for the handicapped, public libraries, and such other agencies as the Secretary may deem appropriate to serve as local or regional centers for such distribution;

(5) provide, by grant or contract, for the conduct of research in the use of educational and training films and other educational media for the handicapped, for the production and distribution of educational and training films and other educational media for the handicapped and the training of persons in the use of such films and media, including the payment to those persons of such stipends (including allowances for travel and other expenses of such persons and their dependents) as he may determine, which shall be consistent with prevailing practices under comparable federally supported programs;

(6) utilize the facilities and services of other governmental agencies; and

(7) accept gifts, contributions, and voluntary and uncompensated services of individuals and organizations; and

(8) provide by grant or contract for educational media and materials for the deaf.

(c) The Secretary may make grants to or enter into contracts or cooperative agreements with the national Theatre of the Deaf, Inc. for the purpose of providing theatrical experiences to —

    (1) enrich the lives of deaf children and adults,

    (2) increase public awareness and understanding of deafness and of the artistic and intellectual achievements of deaf people, and

    (3) promote the integration of hearing and deaf people through shared cultural experiences. *(20 USC 1452)*

### AUTHORIZATION

SEC. 653. For the purposes of carrying out this part, there are authorized to be appropriated $15,000,000 for fiscal year 1987, $15,750,000 for fiscal year 1988, and $16,540,000 for fiscal year 1989. *(20 USC 1454)*

## PART G — TECHNOLOGY, EDUCATIONAL MEDIA AND MATERIALS FOR THE HANDICAPPED

### FINANCIAL ASSISTANCE

SEC. 661. The Secretary may make grants or enter into contracts or cooperative agreements with institutions of higher education, State and local educational agencies, or other appropriate agencies and organizations for the purpose of advancing the use of new technology, media, and materials in the education of handicapped students and the provision of early intervention to handicapped infants and toddlers. In carrying out this subsection, the Secretary may fund projects or centers for the purposes of — *(20 USC 1461)*

    (1) determining how technology, media, and materials are being used in the education of the handicapped and how they can be used more effectively,

    (2) designing and adapting new technology, media, and materials to improve the education of handicapped students,

    (3) assisting the public and private sectors in the development and marketing of new technology, media, and materials for the education of the handicapped, and

    (4) disseminating information on the availability and use of new technology, media, and materials for the education of the handicapped.

### AUTHORIZATION OF APPROPRIATIONS

SEC. 662. For the purposes of carrying out this part, there are authorized to be appropriated $10,000,000 for fiscal year 1987, $10,500,000 for fiscal year 1988, and $11,025,000 for fiscal year 1989. *(20 USC 1462)*

## PART H — HANDICAPPED INFANTS AND TODDLERS

### FINDINGS AND POLICY

SEC. 671. (a) FINDINGS. — The Congress finds that there is an urgent and substantial need — *(20 USC 1471)*

(1) to enhance the development of handicapped infants and toddlers and to minimize their potential for developmental delay,

(2) to reduce the educational costs to our society, including our Nation's schools, by minimizing the need for special education and related services after handicapped infants and toddlers reach school age,

(3) to minimize the likelihood of institutionalization of handicapped individuals and maximize the potential for their independent living in society, and

(4) to enhance the capacity of families to meet the special needs of their infants and toddlers with handicaps.

(b) POLICY. — It is therefore the policy of the United States to provide financial assistance to States —

(1) to develop and implement a statewide, comprehensive, coordinated, multidisciplinary, interagency program of early intervention services for handicapped infants and toddlers and their families,

(2) to facilitate the coordination of payment for early intervention services from Federal, State, local, and private sources (including public and private insurance coverage), and

(3) to enhance its capacity to provide quality early intervention services and expand and improve existing early intervention services being provided to handicapped infants, toddlers, and their families.

### DEFINITIONS

SEC. 672. As used in this part — *(20 USC 1472)*

(1) The term "handicapped infants and toddlers" means individuals from birth to age 2, inclusive, who need early intervention services because they —

(A) are experiencing developmental delays, as measured by appropriate diagnostic instruments and procedures in one or more of the following areas: Cognitive development, physical development, language and speech development, psychosocial development, or self-help skills, or

(B) have a diagnosed physical or mental condition which has a high probability of resulting in developmental delay. Such term may also include, at a State's discretion, individuals from birth to age 2, inclusive, who are at risk of having substantial developmental delays if early intervention services are not provided.

(2) "Early intervention services" are developmental services which —

(A) are provided under public supervision,

(B) are provided at no cost except where Federal or State law provides for a system of payments by families, including a schedule of sliding fees,

(C) are designed to meet a handicapped infant's or toddler's developmental needs in any one or more of the following areas:

    (i) physical development,

    (ii) cognitive development,

    (iii) language and speech development,

    (iv) psycho-social development, or

    (v) self-help skills,

(D) meet the standards of the State, including the requirements of this part,

(E) include —

    (i) family training, counseling, and home visits,

    (ii) special instruction,

    (iii) speech pathology and audiology,

    (iv) occupational therapy,

    (v) physical therapy,

    (vi) psychological services,

    (vii) case management services,

    (viii) medical services only for diagnostic or evaluation purposes,

    (ix) early identification, screening, and assessment services, and

    (x) health services necessary to enable the infant or toddler to benefit from the other early intervention services,

(F) are provided by qualified personnel, including —

    (i) special educators,

    (ii) speech and language pathologists and audiologists,

    (iii) occupational therapists,

    (iv) physical therapists,

    (v) psychologists,

    (vi) social workers,

    (vii) nurses, and

    (viii) nutritionists, and

(G) are provided in conformity with an individualized family service plan adopted in accordance with section 677.

(3) The term "developmental delay" has the meaning given such term by a State under section 676(b)(1).

(4) The term "Council" means the State Interagency Coordinating Council established under section 682.

## GENERAL AUTHORITY

SEC. 673. The Secretary shall, in accordance with this part, make grants to States (from their allocations under section 684) to assist each State to develop a statewide, comprehensive, coordinated, multidisciplinary, interagency system to provide early intervention services for handicapped infants and toddlers and their families. *(20 USC 1473)*

## GENERAL ELIGIBILITY

SEC. 674. In order to be eligible for a grant under section 673 for any fiscal year, a State shall demonstrate to the Secretary (in its application under section 678) that the State has established a State Interagency Coordinating Council which meets the requirements of section 682. *(20 USC 1474)*

## CONTINUING ELIGIBILITY

SEC. 675. (a) FIRST TWO YEARS. — In order to be eligible for a grant under section 673 for the first or second year of a State's participation under this part, a State shall include in its application under section 678 for that year assurances that funds received under section 673 shall be used to assist the State to plan, develop, and implement the statewide system required by section 676. *(20 USC 1475)*

(b) THIRD AND FOURTH YEAR. — (1) In order to be eligible for a grant under section 673 for the third or fourth year of a State's participation under this part, a State shall include in its application under Section 678 for that year information and assurances demonstrating to the satisfaction of the Secretary that —

(A) the State has adopted a policy which incorporates all of the components of a statewide system in accordance with section 676 or obtained a waiver from the Secretary under paragraph (2),

(B) funds shall be used to plan, develop, and implement the statewide system required by section 676, and

(C) such statewide system will be in effect no later than the beginning of the fourth year of the State's participation under section 673, except that with respect to section 676(b)(4), a State need only conduct multidisciplinary assessments, develop individualized family service plans, and make available case management services.

(2) Notwithstanding paragraph (1), the Secretary may permit a State to continue to receive assistance under section 673 during such third year even if the State has not adopted the policy required by paragraph (1)(A) before receiving assistance if the State demonstrates in its application —

(A) that the State has made a good faith effort to adopt such a policy,

(B) the reasons why it was unable to meet the timeline and the steps remaining before such a policy will be adopted, and

(C) an assurance that the policy will be adopted and go into effect before the fourth year of such assistance.

(c) FIFTH AND SUCCEEDING YEARS. — In order to be eligible for a grant under section 673 for a fifth and any succeeding year of a State's participation under this part, a State shall include in its application under section 678 for that year information and assurances demonstrating to the satisfaction of the Secretary that the State has in effect the statewide system required by section 676 and a description of services to be provided under section 676(b)(2).

(d) EXCEPTION. — Notwithstanding subsections (a) and (b), a State which has in effect a State law, enacted before September 1, 1986, that requires the provision of free appropriate public education to handicapped children from birth through age 2, inclusive, shall be eligible for a grant under section 673 for the first through fourth years of a State's participation under this part.

REQUIREMENTS FOR STATEWIDE SYSTEM

SEC. 676. (a) IN GENERAL. — A statewide system of coordinated, comprehensive, multidisciplinary, interagency programs providing appropriate early intervention services to all handicapped infants and toddlers and their families shall include the minimum components under subsection (b). *(20 USC 1476)*

(b) MINIMUM COMPONENTS. — The statewide system required by subsection (a) shall include, at a minimum —

(1) a definition of the term "developmentally delayed" that will be used by the State in carrying out programs under this part,

(2) timetables for ensuring that appropriate early intervention services will be available to all handicapped infants and toddlers in the State before the beginning of the fifth year of a State's participation under this part,

(3) a timely, comprehensive, multidisciplinary evaluation of the functioning of each handicapped infant and toddler in the State and the needs of the families to appropriately assist in the development of the handicapped infant or toddler,

(4) for each handicapped infant and toddler in the State, an individualized family service plan in accordance with section 677, including case management services in accordance with such service plan,

(5) a comprehensive child find system, consistent with part B, including a system for making referrals to service providers that includes timelines and provides for the participation by primary referral sources,

(6) a public awareness program focusing on early identification of handicapped infants and toddlers,

(7) a central directory which includes early intervention services, resources, and experts available in the State and research and demonstration projects being conducted in the State,

(8) a comprehensive system of personnel development,

(9) a single line of responsibility in a lead agency designated or established by the Governor for carrying out —

(A) the general administration, supervision, and monitoring of programs and activities receiving assistance under section 673 to ensure compliance with this part,

(B) the identification and coordination of all available resources within the State from Federal, State, local and private sources,

(C) the assignment of financial responsibility to the appropriate agency,

(D) the development of procedures to ensure that services are provided to handicapped infants and toddlers and their families in a timely manner pending the resolution of any disputes among public agencies or service providers,

(E) the resolution of intra- and interagency disputes, and

(F) the entry into formal interagency agreements that define the financial responsibility of each agency for paying for early intervention services (consistent with State law) and procedures for resolving disputes and that include all additional components necessary to ensure meaningful cooperation and coordination,

(10) a policy pertaining to the contracting or making of other arrangements with service providers to provide early intervention services in the State, consistent with the provisions of this part, including the contents of the application used and the conditions of the contract or other arrangements,

(11) a procedure for securing timely reimbursement of funds used under this part in accordance with section 681(a),

(12) procedural safeguards with respect to programs under this part as required by section 680, and

(13) policies and procedures relating to the establishment and maintenance of standards to ensure that personnel necessary to carry out this part are appropriately and adequately prepared and trained, including —

(A) the establishment and maintenance of standards which are consistent with any State approved or recognized certification, licensing, registration, or other comparable requirements which apply to the area in which such personnel are providing early intervention services, and

(B) to the extent such standards are not based on the highest requirements in the State applicable to a specific profession or discipline, the steps the State is taking to require the retraining or hiring of personnel that meet appropriate professional requirements in the State, and

(14) a system for compiling data on the numbers of handicapped infants and toddlers and their families in the State in need of appropriate early intervention services (which may be based on a sampling of data), the numbers of such infants and

toddlers and their families served, the types of services provided (which may be based on a sampling of data), and other information required by the Secretary.

INDIVIDUALIZED FAMILY SERVICE PLAN

SEC. 677. (a) ASSESSMENT AND PROGRAM DEVELOPMENT. — Each handicapped infant or toddler and the infant or toddler's family will receive — *(20 USC 1477)*

(1) a multidisciplinary assessment to unique needs and the identification of services appropriate to meet such needs, and

(2) a written individualized family service plan developed by a multidisciplinary team, including the parent or guardian, as required by subsection (d).

(b) PERIODIC REVIEW. — The individualized family service plan shall be evaluated once a year and the family shall be provided a review of the plan at 6 month-intervals (or more often where appropriate based on infant and toddler and family needs).

(c) PROMPTNESS AFTER ASSESSMENT. — The individualized family service plan shall be developed within a reasonable time after the assessment required by subsection (a)(1) is completed. With the parent's consent, early intervention services may commence prior to the completion of such assessment.

(d) CONTENT OF PLAN. — The individualized family service plan shall be in writing and contain —

(1) a statement of the infant's or toddler's present levels of physical development, cognitive development, language and speech development, psycho-social development, and self-help skills, based on acceptable objective criteria,

(2) a statement of the family's strengths and needs relating to enhancing the development of the family's handicapped infant or toddler,

(3) a statement of the major outcomes expected to be achieved for the infant and toddler and the family, and the criteria, procedures, and timelines used to determine the degree to which progress toward achieving the outcomes are being made and whether modifications or revisions of the outcomes or services are necessary,

(4) a statement of specific early intervention services necessary to meet the unique needs of the infant or toddler and the family, including the frequency, intensity, and the method of delivering services,

(5) the projected dates for initiation of services and the anticipated duration of such services,

(6) the name of the case manager from the profession most immediately relevant to the infant's and toddler's or family's needs who will be responsible for the implementation of the plan and coordination with other agencies and persons, and

(7) the steps to be taken supporting the transition of the

handicapped toddler to services provided under part B to the extent such services are considered appropriate. *(20 USC 1411)*

STATE APPLICATION AND ASSURANCES

Sec. 678. (a) Application. — Any State desiring to receive a grant under section 673 for any year shall submit an application to the Secretary at such time and in such manner as the Secretary may reasonably require by regulation. Such an application shall contain — *(20 USC 1478)*

(1) a designation of the lead agency in the State that will be responsible for the administration of funds provided under section 673,

(2) information demonstrating eligibility of the State under section 674,

(3) the information or assurances required to demonstrate eligibility of the State for the particular year of participation under section 675, and

(4)(A) information demonstrating that the State has provided (i) public hearings, (ii) adequate notice of such hearings, and (iii) an opportunity for comment to the general public before the submission of such application and before the adoption by the State of the policies described in such application, and (B) a summary of the public comments and the State's responses,

(5) a description of the uses for which funds will be expended in accordance with this part and for the fifth and succeeding fiscal years a description of the services to be provided,

(6) a description of the procedure used to ensure an equitable distribution of resources made available under this part among all geographic areas within the State, and

(7) such other information and assurances as the Secretary may reasonably require by regulation.

(b) Statement of Assurances. — Any State desiring to receive a grant under section 673 shall file with the Secretary a statement at such time and in such manner as the Secretary may reasonably require by regulation. Such statement shall —

(1) assure that funds paid to the State under section 673 will be expended in accordance with this part,

(2) contain assurances that the State will comply with the requirements of section 681,

(3) provide satisfactory assurance that the control of funds provided under section 673, and title to property derived therefrom, shall be in a public agency for the uses and purposes provided in this part and that a public agency will administer such funds and property.

(4) provide for (A) making such reports in such form and containing such information as the Secretary may require to carry out the Secretary's functions under this part, and (B) keeping such records and affording such access thereto as the

Secretary may find necessary to assure the correctness and verification of such reports and proper disbursement of Federal funds under this part,

(5) provide satisfactory assurance that Federal funds made available under section 673 (A) will not be commingled with State funds, and (B) will be so used as to supplement and increase the level of State and local funds expended for handicapped infants and toddlers and their families and in no case to supplant such State and local funds,

(6) provide satisfactory assurance that such fiscal control and fund accounting procedures will be adopted as may be necessary to assure proper disbursement of, and accounting for, Federal funds paid under section 673 to the State, and

(7) such other information and assurances as the Secretary may reasonably require by regulation.

(c) APPROVAL OF APPLICATION AND ASSURANCES REQUIRED. — No state may receive a grant under section 673 unless the Secretary has approved the application and statement of assurances of that state. The Secretary shall not disapprove such an application or statement of assurances unless the Secretary determines, after notice and opportunity for a hearing, that the application or statement of assurances fails to comply with the requirements of this section.

## USES OF FUNDS

SEC. 679. In addition to using funds provided under section 673 to plan, develop, and implement the statewide system required by section 676, a State may use such funds — *(20 USC 1479)*

(1) for direct services for handicapped infants and toddlers that are not otherwise provided from other public or private sources, and

(2) to expand and improve on services for handicapped infants and toddlers that are otherwise available.

## PROCEDURAL SAFEGUARDS

SEC. 680. The procedural safeguards required to be included in a statewide system under section 676(b)(12) shall provide, at a minimum, the following: *(20 USC 1480)*

(1) The timely administrative resolution of complaints by parents. Any party aggrieved by the findings and decision regarding an administrative complaint shall have the right to bring a civil action with respect to the complaint, which action may be brought in any State court of competent jurisdiction or in a district court of the United States without regard to the amount in controversy. In any action brought under this paragraph, the court shall receive the records of the administrative proceedings, shall hear additional evidence at the request of a party, and, basing its decision on the preponderance of the evidence, shall grant such relief as the court determines is appropriate.

(2) The right to confidentiality of personally identifiable information.

(3) The opportunity for parents and a guardian to examine records relating to assessment, screening, eligibility determinations, and the development and implementation of the individualized family service plan.

(4) Procedures to protect the rights of the handicapped infant and toddlers whenever the parents or guardian of the child are not known or unavailable or the child is a ward of the State, including the assignment of an individual (who shall not be an employee of the State agency providing services) to act as a surrogate for the parents or guardian.

(5) Written prior notice to the parents or guardian of the handicapped infant or toddler whenever the State agency or service provider proposes to initiate or change or refuses to initiate or change the identification, evaluation, placement, or the provision of appropriate early intervention services to the handicapped infant or toddler.

(6) Procedures designed to assure that the notice required by paragraph (5) fully informs the parents or guardian, in the parents' or guardian's native language, unless it clearly is not feasible to do so, of all procedures available pursuant to this section.

(7) During the pendency of any proceeding or action involving a complaint, unless the State agency and the parents or guardian otherwise agree, the child shall continue to receive the appropriate early intervention services currently being provided or if applying for initial services shall receive the services not in dispute.

### PAYOR OF LAST RESORT

SEC. 681. (a) NONSUBSTITUTION. — Funds provided under section 673 may not be used to satisfy a financial commitment for services which would have been paid for from another public or private source but for the enactment of this part, except that whenever considered necessary to prevent the delay in the receipt of appropriate early intervention services by the infant or toddler or family in a timely fashion, funds provided under section 673 may be used to pay the provider of services pending reimbursement from the agency which has ultimate responsibility for the payment. *(20 USC 1481)*

(b) REDUCTION OF OTHER BENEFITS. — Nothing in this part shall be construed to permit the State to reduce medical or other assistance available or to alter eligibility under title V of the Social Security Act (relating to maternal and child health) or title XIX of the Social Security Act (relating to medicaid for handicapped infants and toddlers) within the State. *(42 USC 701, 42 USC 1396)*

### STATE INTERAGENCY COORDINATING COUNCIL

SEC. 682. (a) ESTABLISHMENT. — (1) Any State which desires to receive financial assistance under section 673 shall establish a State Interagency Coordinating Council composed of 15 members. *(20 USC 1482)*

(2) The council and the chairperson of the Council shall be appointed by the Governor. In making appointments to the Council, the Governor shall ensure that the membership of the Council reasonably represents the population of the State.

(b) COMPOSITION. — The council shall be composed of —

(1) at least 3 parents of handicapped infants or toddlers or handicapped children aged 3 through 6, inclusive,

(2) at least 3 public or private providers of early intervention services,

(3) at least one representative from the State legislature,

(4) at least one person involved in personnel preparation, and

(5) other members representing each of the appropriate agencies involved in the provision of or payment for early intervention services to handicapped infants and toddlers and their families and others selected by the Governor.

(c) MEETINGS. — The Council shall meet at least quarterly and in such places as it deems necessary. The meetings shall be publicly announced, and, to the extent appropriate, open and accessible to the general public.

(d) MANAGEMENT AUTHORITY. — Subject to the approval of the Governor, the Council may prepare and approve a budget using funds under this part to hire staff, and obtain the services of such professional, technical, and clerical personnel as may be necessary to carry out its functions under this part.

(e) FUNCTIONS OF COUNCIL. — The Council shall —

(1) advise and assist the lead agency designated or established under section 676(b)(9) in the performance of the responsibilities set out in such section, particularly the identification of the sources of fiscal and other support for services for early intervention programs, assignment of financial responibility to the appropriate agency, and the promotion of the interagency agreements,

(2) advise and assist the lead agency in the preparation of applications and amendments thereto, and

(3) prepare and submit an annual report to the Governor and to the Secretary on the status of early intervention programs for handicapped infants and toddlers and their families operated within the State.

(f) CONFLICT OF INTEREST. — No member of the Council shall cast a vote on any matter which would provide direct financial benefit to that member or otherwise give the appearance of a conflict of interest under State law.

(g) USE OF EXISTING COUNCILS. — To the extent that a State has established a Council before September 1, 1986, that is comparable to the Council described in this section, such Council shall be considered to be in compliance with this section. Within 4 years after the date the State accepts funds under section 673, such State shall establish a council that complies in full with this section.

## FEDERAL ADMINISTRATION

SEC. 683. Sections 616, 617 and 620 shall, to the extent not inconsistent with this part, apply to the program authorized by this part, except that — *(20 USC 1483)*

(1) any reference to a State educational agency shall be deemed to be a reference to the State agency established or designated under section 676(b)(9), *(20 USC 1416, 1417, 1420)*

(2) any reference to the education of handicapped children and the education of all handicapped children and the provision of free public education to all handicapped children shall be deemed to be a reference to the provision of services to handicapped infants and toddlers in accordance with this part, and

(3) any reference to local educational agencies and intermediate educational agencies shall be deemed to be a reference to local service providers under this part.

## ALLOCATION OF FUNDS

SEC. 684. (a) From the sums appropriated to carry out this part for any fiscal year, the Secretary may reserve 1 percent for payments to Guam, American Samoa, the Virgin Islands, the Republic of the Marshall Islands, the Federated State of Micronesia, the Republic of Palau, and the Commonwealth of the Northern Mariana Islands in accordance with their respective needs. *(20 USC 1484)*

(b)(1) The Secretary shall make payments to the Secretary of the Interior according to the need for such assistance for the provision of early intervention services to handicapped infants and toddlers and their families on reservations serviced by the elementary and secondary schools operated for Indians by the Department of the Interior. The amount of such payment for any fiscal year shall be 1.25 percent of the aggregate of the amount available to all States under this part for that fiscal year. *(20 USC 1484)*

(2) The Secretary of the Interior may receive an allotment under paragraph (1) only after submitting to the Secretary an application which meets the requirements of section 678 and which is approved by the Secretary. Section 616 shall apply to any such applications. *(20 USC 1416)*

(c)(1) For each of the fiscal years 1987 through 1991 from the funds remaining after the reservation and payments under subsections (a) and (b), the Secretary shall allot to each State an amount which bears the same ratio to the amount of such remainder as the number of infants and toddlers in the State bears to the number of infants and toddlers in all States, except that no State shall receive less than 0.15 percent of such remainder.

(2) For the purpose of paragraph (1) —

(A) the terms "infants" and "toddlers" mean children from birth to age 2, inclusive, and

(B) the term "State" does not include the jurisdictions described in subsection (a).

(d) If any State elects not to receive its allotment under subsection (c)(1), the Secretary shall reallot, among the remaining States, amounts from such State in accordance with such subsection.

AUTHORIZATION OF APPROPRIATIONS

SEC. 685. There are authorized to be appropriated to carry out this part $50,000,000 for fiscal year 1987, $75,000,000 for fiscal year 1988, and such sums as may be necessary for each of the 3 succeeding fiscal years. *(20 USC 1485)*

(b) STUDY OF SERVICES; COORDINATION OF ACTIONS. — (1) The Secretary of Education and the Secretary of Health and Human Services shall conduct a joint study of Federal funding sources and services for early intervention programs currently available and shall jointly act to facilitate interagency coordination of Federal resources for such programs and to ensure that funding available to handicapped infants, toddlers, children, and youth from Federal programs, other than programs under the Education of the Handicapped Act, is not being withdrawn or reduced. *(20 USC 1485 note)*

(2) Not later than 18 months after the date of the enactment of this Act, the Secretary of Education and the Secretary of Health and Human Services shall submit a joint report to the Congress describing the findings of the study conducted under paragraph (1) and describing the joint action taken under that paragraph. *(20 USC 1400)*

## Education Department Handicapped Child Count, 1976-77 to 1986-87

| | 1986-87 | | 1976-77 | |
|---|---|---|---|---|
| | Children Served | Allocation | Children Served | Allocation |
| Alabama | 90,225 | $25,128,396 | 52,796 | $3,776,498 |
| Alaska | 8,941 | 2,490,141 | 5,498 | 490,567 |
| Arizona | 50,637 | 14,102,816 | 35,473 | 2,537,384 |
| Arkansas | 43,881 | 12,221,215 | 24,710 | 1,829,462 |
| California | 376,103 | 104,747,742 | 326,206 | 23,333,515 |
| Colorado | 43,592 | 12,140,726 | 39,781 | 2,845,535 |
| Connecticut | 62,058 | 17,283,657 | 54,834 | 3,922,276 |
| Delaware | 11,527 | 3,210,363 | 10,880 | 778,246 |
| District of Columbia | 3,020 | 841,095 | 6,341 | 668,848 |
| Florida | 163,380 | 45,502,658 | 111,541 | 7,978,528 |
| Georgia | 90,263 | 25,138,979 | 82,857 | 5,926,761 |
| Hawaii | 11,415 | 3,179,170 | 9,017 | 836,262 |
| Idaho | 18,807 | 5,237,902 | 12,526 | 895,985 |
| Illinois | 205,940 | 57,355,964 | 208,472 | 14,912,002 |
| Indiana | 96,262 | 26,809,749 | 81,639 | 5,839,638 |
| Iowa | 55,935 | 15,578,352 | 46,041 | 3,293,313 |
| Kansas | 39,299 | 10,944,534 | 35,804 | 2,561,060 |
| Kentucky | 70,392 | 19,602,795 | 54,396 | 3,890,946 |
| Louisiana | 71,925 | 19,991,314 | 81,928 | 5,860,310 |
| Maine | 26,532 | 7,389,378 | 19,993 | 1,430,099 |
| Maryland | 87,146 | 24,270,869 | 71,416 | 5,108,386 |
| Massachusetts | 126,448 | 35,216,796 | 118,024 | 8,442,257 |
| Michigan | 150,041 | 41,787,638 | 140,848 | 10,074,857 |
| Minnesota | 81,067 | 22,577,818 | 68,996 | 4,935,284 |
| Mississippi | 51,929 | 14,462,370 | 27,638 | 2,317,010 |
| Missouri | 96,962 | 27,004,705 | 89,448 | 6,398,215 |
| Montana | 14,785 | 4,117,743 | 8,094 | 735,291 |
| Nebraska | 30,182 | 8,405,932 | 24,749 | 1,770,296 |
| Nevada | 13,567 | 3,778,520 | 8,256 | 599,425 |
| New Hampshire | 14,896 | 4,148,657 | 8,674 | 760,460 |
| New Jersey | 165,237 | 46,019,848 | 137,524 | 9,837,092 |
| New Mexico | 29,143 | 8,116,562 | 14,464 | 1,128,789 |
| New York | 249,180 | 69,398,655 | 220,635 | 15,782,022 |
| North Carolina | 109,477 | 30,490,234 | 91,143 | 6,519,459 |
| North Dakota | 11,251 | 3,133,495 | 8,472 | 671,532 |
| Ohio | 190,447 | 53,041,038 | 154,520 | 11,052,816 |
| Oklahoma | 63,635 | 17,722,865 | 39,825 | 2,848,682 |
| Oregon | 41,304 | 11,503,500 | 32,758 | 2,343,180 |
| Pennsylvania | 182,319 | 50,777,323 | 193,018 | 13,806,578 |
| Rhode Island | 18,529 | 5,160,477 | 14,636 | 1,046,913 |
| South Carolina | 71,058 | 19,794,130 | 69,448 | 4,967,615 |
| South Dakota | 13,082 | 3,643,443 | 9,192 | 698,770 |
| Tennessee | 94,091 | 26,205,108 | 81,262 | 5,812,671 |
| Texas | 282,184 | 78,590,538 | 217,002 | 15,522,153 |
| Utah | 39,985 | 11,136,148 | 28,758 | 2,057,060 |
| Vermont | 8,186 | 2,279,868 | 4,084 | 539,113 |
| Virginia | 100,866 | 28,092,001 | 74,048 | 5,296,653 |
| Washington | 64,699 | 18,019,197 | 68,044 | 4,867,187 |
| West Virginia | 44,840 | 12,488,305 | 29,055 | 2,078,304 |
| Wisconsin | 73,488 | 20,467,005 | 54,089 | 4,348,328 |
| Wyoming | 9,322 | 2,596,253 | 5,512 | 470,988 |
| **Total** | **4,121,356** | **$1,163,282,000** | **3,414,365** | **$246,444,621** |

*Note: 1986-87 totals include figures for U.S. territories and the Indian Affairs Bureau.*

*Source: U.S. Education Department*

191

## Federal Education For The Handicapped Appropriations, 1976-1987

| | 1976 | 1977 | 1978 | 1979 |
|---|---|---|---|---|
| | *(dollars in thousands)* | | | |
| **State Assistance (EHA)** | | | | |
| State grant program (Part B) | $100,000 | $315,000[1] | $535,000 | $804,000 |
| Preschool incentive grants (Part B) | --- | 12,500 | 15,000 | 17,500 |
| Early intervention grants (Part H) | --- | --- | --- | --- |
| **Subtotal, State Assistance** | **$100,000** | **$327,500** | **$550,000** | **$821,500** |
| **Special Purpose Funds** | | | | |
| Deaf-blind centers (Part C) | 16,000 | 16,000 | 16,000 | 16,000 |
| Severely handicapped projects (Part C) | 3,250 | 5,000 | 5,000 | 5,000 |
| Specific learning disabilities (Part C) | 5,000 | 9,000 | --- | --- |
| Early childhood education (Part C) | 22,000 | 22,000 | 22,000 | 22,000 |
| Postsecondary programs (Part C) | 2,000 | 2,000 | 2,400 | 2,400 |
| Innovation and development (Part E) | 11,000 | 11,000 | 20,000 | 20,000 |
| Media services and captioned films (Part F and G) | 16,250 | 19,000 | 19,000 | 19,000 |
| Special education technology (Part G) | --- | --- | --- | --- |
| Regional resource centers (Part C) | 10,000 | 9,750 | 9,750 | 9,750 |
| Recruitment and information (Part D) | 500 | 1,000 | 1,000 | 1,000 |
| Special education personnel development (Part D) | 40,375 | 45,375 | 45,375 | 57,687 |
| Special studies (Part B) | --- | 1,735 | 2,300 | 2,300 |
| Transitional services | --- | --- | --- | --- |
| **Subtotal, Special Purpose Funds** | **$126,375** | **$141,860** | **$142,825** | **$155,137** |
| **Total, Education for the Handicapped** | **$226,375** | **$469,360** | **$692,825** | **$976,637** |

### Federal Education For The Handicapped Appropriations, 1976-1987 (Cont.)

| | 1980 | 1981 | 1982 | 1983 |
|---|---|---|---|---|
| | *(dollars in thousands)* | | | |
| **State Assistance (EHA)** | | | | |
| State grant program (Part B) | $874,500 | $874,500 | $931,008 | $970,000 |
| Preschool incentive grants (Part B) | 25,000 | 25,000 | 24,000 | 25,000 |
| Early intervention grants (Part H) | --- | --- | --- | --- |
| **Subtotal, State Assistance** | **$899,500** | **$899,500** | **$995,008** | **$995,000** |
| **Special Purpose Funds** | | | | |
| Deaf-blind centers (Part C) | 16,000 | 16,000 | 15,360 | 15,360 |
| Severely handicapped projects (Part C) | 5,000 | 4,375 | 2,880 | 2,880 |
| Specific learning disabilities (Part C) | --- | --- | --- | --- |
| Early childhood education (Part C) | 20,000 | 17,500 | 16,800 | 16,800 |
| Postsecondary programs (Part C) | 2,400 | 2,950 | 2,832 | 2,832 |
| Innovation and development (Part E) | 20,000 | 15,000 | 10,800 | 12,000 |
| Media services and captioned films (Part F and G) | 119,000 | 17,000 | 11,520 | 12,000 |
| Special education technology (Part G) | --- | --- | --- | --- |
| Regional resource centers (Part C) | 9,750 | 7,656 | 2,880 | 2,880 |
| Recruitment and information (Part D) | 1,000 | 750 | 720 | 720 |
| Special education personnel development (Part D) | 55,375 | 43,500 | 49,300 | 49,300 |
| Special studies (Part B) | 1,000 | 1,000 | 480 | 480 |
| Transitional services | --- | --- | --- | --- |
| **Subtotal, Special Purpose Funds** | **$149,525** | **$125,731** | **$113,572** | **$115,252** |
| **Total, Education for the Handicapped** | **$1,049,025** | **$1,025,231** | **$1,068,580** | **$1,110,252** |

## Federal Education For The Handicapped Appropriations, 1976-1987 (Cont.)

|  | 1984 | 1985 | 1986 | 1987 |
|---|---|---|---|---|
|  | *(dollars in thousands)* | | | |
| **State Assistance** | | | | |
| State grant program | | | | |
| (Part B) | $1,068,875 | $1,135,145 | $1,163,282 | $1,338,000 |
| Preschool incentive | | | | |
| grants (Part B) | 26,330 | 29,000 | 28,710 | 180,000 |
| Early intervention grants | | | | |
| (Part H) | --- | --- | --- | 50,000 |
| **Subtotal, State Assistance** | **$1,095,205** | **$1,164,145** | **$1,191,992** | **$1,568,000** |
| **Special Purpose Funds** | | | | |
| Deaf-blind centers | | | | |
| (Part C) | 15,000 | 15,000 | 14,119 | 15,000 |
| Severely handicapped | | | | |
| projects (Part C) | 4,000 | 4,300 | 4,785 | 5,300 |
| Specific learning disabilities | | | | |
| (Part C) | --- | --- | --- | --- |
| Early childhood education | | | | |
| (Part C) | 21,100 | 22,500 | 22,968 | 24,470 |
| Postsecondary programs | | | | |
| (Part C) | 5,000 | 5,300 | 5,264 | 5,900 |
| Innovation and development | 15,000 | 16,000 | 16,080 | 18,000 |
| (Part E) | | | | |
| Media services and captioned films | | | | |
| (Part F and G) | 14,000 | 16,500 | 16,676 | 13,804[2] |
| Special education technology | | | | |
| (Part G) | --- | --- | --- | 4,696[2] |
| Regional resource centers | | | | |
| (Part C) | 5,700 | 6,000 | 6,029 | 6,700 |
| Recruitment and information | | | | |
| (Part D) | 1,000 | 1,025 | 1,062 | 1,200 |
| Special education personnel | | | | |
| development (Part D) | 55,540 | 61,00 | 61,154 | 67,730 |
| Special studies | | | | |
| (Part B) | 3,100 | 3,170 | 3,301 | 3,800 |
| Transitional services | 6,000 | 6,330 | 6,316 | 7,300 |
| **Subtotal, Special** | | | | |
| **Purpose Funds** | **$145,440** | **$157,125** | **$157,754** | **$173,900** |
| **Total, Education for the** | | | | |
| **Handicapped** | **$1,240,645** | **$1,321,270** | **$1,349,746** | **$1,741,900** |

[1]*$63 million in state assistance was unused in 1977 because of a low child count. The surplus was carried over to 1978.*

[2]*Reflects proposed reprogramming of $1.196 million from media and captioning services to special education technology.*

*Source: U.S. Education Department*

# State Resource Directory

## ALABAMA

*State Director:*
Anne Ramsey
Coordinator
Student Instructional Services
State Department of Education
1020 Monticello Court
Montgomery, Ala. 36117
(205)261-5099

*Regional Resource Center Parent Representative:*
Ann James
6607 Hollis Dr.
Montgomery, Ala. 36117
(205)272-3392

*Federally Funded Parent Training Grant:*
Carol Blades
President
Special Education Action Committee
P.O. Box 81112
Mobile, Ala. 36689
(205)633-9588

## ALASKA

*State Director:*
William Mulnix
Administrator
Office of Special Services
Alaska Department of Education
P.O. Box F
Juneau, Alaska 99811
(907)465-2970

*Regional Resource Center Parent Representatives:*
Connie Ellingson
901 Lake Box 1214
Sitka, Alaska 99835
(907)747-8064

Sherrel Hodge
P.O. Box 82
Central, Alaska 99730
(907)520-5114

*State Parent Group:*
Marsha Buck
SE RRC
218 Front St.
Juneau, Alaska 99801
(907)586-6806

## AMERICAN SAMOA

*State Director:*
Jane French
Director of Special Education
Department of Education
Pago Pago, American Samoa 96799
(684)633-1323

## ARIZONA

*State Director:*
Diane Peterson
Deputy Associate Superintendent
Special Education Section
Department of Education
1535 W. Jefferson
Phoenix, Ariz. 85007
(602)255-3183

*Regional Resource Center Parent Representative:*
Barbara Gear
6817 N. 57th Place
Paradise Valley, Ariz. 86253
(602)263-8484 or 998-0533

*Federally Funded Parent Training Grant:*
Mary Slaughter
Pilot Parents
121 East Voltaire Ave.
Phoenix, Ariz. 85022
(602)863-4048

## ARKANSAS

*State Director:*
Diane Sydoriak
Associate Director of Special
   Education
Arkansas Department of Education
Education Bldg., Room 105-C
S4 Capitol Mall
Little Rock, Ark. 72201
(501)371-2161

*Regional Resource Center Parent Representative:*
Patsy Fordyce
7 McKinley Circle
Little Rock, Ark. 72207
(501)376-3420 (o) or
   (501)666-6021 (h)

*Federally Funded Parent Training Grants:*
Paul Kelly
Arkansas Coalition for the
   Handicapped
519 E. Fifth St.
Little Rock, Ark. 72202
(501)376-0378

Barbara Semrau
Focus, Inc.
2917 King St., Suite C
Little Rock, Ark. 72202
(501)935-2750

## BUREAU OF INDIAN AFFAIRS

Charles Cordova
Bureau of Exceptional Education
   Chief
Office of Indian Education
   Programs
Bureau of Indian Affairs
18th and C Sts. NW, Room 4642
Washington, D.C. 20245
(202)343-4071

## CALIFORNIA

*State Director:*
Shirley Thornton
Associate Superintendent/Director
Specialized Programs Branch
Special Education Division
P.O. Box 944272
Sacramento, Calif. 94244
(916)323-4768

*Regional Resource Center Parent Representative:*
Beverly Doyle
3740 Bolsa Court
Sacramento, Calif. 95864
(916)921-0521

*Federally Funded Parent Training Grant:*
Joan Tellefsen
Team of Advocates for Special Kids
Task Parent Training Projects
1800 E. La Veta Ave.
Orange, Calif. 92666
(714)771-6542

*State Parent Groups:*
Prudy Stephens
Special Education Parent Facilitator
   Program
Whittier School
3401 Clairemont Dr., Room 7A
San Diego, Calif. 92117

COPE
Joanne Travers
UCP of California
P.O. Box 1475
Upland, Calif. 91785

Parents Helping Parents, Inc.
Florence Payadue
535 Race St., Suite 220
San Jose, Calif. 95126
(408)288-5010

Jean Styris
Special Education Community
 Advisory Committee Network
1610 Franrose Lane
Concord, Calif. 94519
(415)827-3863

## COLORADO

*State Director:*
Brian McNulty
Executive Director of the Special
 Education Services Unit
Colorado Department of Education
201 E. Colfax Ave.
Denver, Colo. 80203
(303)866-6694

*Regional Resource Center Parent
 Representative:*
Carol Wait
4511 S. Bannock
Englewood, Colo. 80110
(303)781-8368

*Federally Funded Parent Training
 Grant:*
Barbara Buswell
Parents Encouraging Parents, Inc.
1320 N. Wahsatch
Colorado Springs, Colo. 80903
(303)635-9017

*State Parent Group:*
Effective Parents Program (ARC)
Attn: Eula Boelke
930 Ute Ave.
Grand Junction, Colo. 81501
(303)243-4689

## CONNECTICUT

*State Director:*
Tom Gillung
Bureau of Special Education and
 Pupil Personnel Services Chief
Connecticut Department of
 Education
P.O. Box 2219
Hartford, Conn. 06102
(203)566-3561

*Regional Resource Center Parent
 Representative:*
Evan Woolacott
Combustion Engineering, Inc.
P.O. Box 500
100 Prospect Hill Road
Windsor, Conn. 06095
(203)688-1922, Ext. 3319

*Federally Funded Parent Training
 Grant:*
Nancy Prescott
Connecticut Parent Advocacy
 Center
c/o Mohegan Community College
Norwich, Conn. 06360
(203)886-5250

## DELAWARE

*State Director:*
Carl Haltom
State Director
Exceptional Children/Special
 Programs Division
Department of Public Instruction
P.O. Box 1402
Dover, Del. 19903
(302)736-5471

*Regional Resource Center Parent
 Representative:*
Nancy Horstmann
4800 Washington St. Ext.
Wilmington, Del. 19809
(302)762-1099

*Federally Funded Parent Training Grant:*
Patricia Gail Herbert
Parent Information Center of
  Delaware, Inc.
193 West Park Place
West Park Community Center
Newark, Del. 19711
(302)366-0152

## DISTRICT OF COLUMBIA

*State Director:*
Doris Woodson
Assistant Superintendent
Division of Special Eduation and
  Pupil Personnel Services
D.C. Public Schools
Webster Administration Bldg.
10th and H Sts. NW
Washington, D.C. 20001
(202)724-4018

*Regional Resource Center Parent Representative:*
Trecy Breece
4406 S. Dakota Ave. NE
Washington, D.C. 20017
(202)576-6090 (o) or
  (202)635-7386 (h)

*Federally Funded Parent Training Grant:*
Marsha Parker
Parents Reaching Out Service, Inc.
D.C. General Hospital
Department of Pediatrics
West Wing, 4th Floor
1900 Massachusetts Ave. SE
Washington, D.C. 20003
(202)727-3866

## FLORIDA

*State Director:*
Wendy Cullar
Bureau of Education for
  Exceptional Students Chief
Florida Department of Education
Knott Bldg.
Tallahassee, Fla. 32301
(904)488-1570

*Regional Resource Center Parent Representatives:*
Jackie Sipple
Association for Children with
  Learning Disabilities
2881 Coral Way
Punta Gorda, Fla. 33950
(813)639-3912

Walter Schoenig
2428 Fairbanks Dr.
Clearwater, Fla. 33546
(813)536-3477

*Federally Funded Parent Training Grant:*
Nadine Johnson
Parent Education Network
  Florida, Inc.
2215 E. Henry Ave.
Tampa, Fla. 33610
(813)239-1179

## GEORGIA

*State Director:*
Joan Jordan
Program for Exceptional Children
  Director
Georgia Department of Education
1970 Twin Towers East
205 Butler St.
Atlanta, Ga. 30334
(404)656-2425

*Regional Resource Center
  Representative:*
Joyce Long
531 Sugar Hill Dr. NW
Marietta, Ga. 30060
(404)426-3206 (o) or
  (404)422-1905 (h)

*Federally Funded Parent Training
  Grant:*
Mildred Hill
PEP Project Director
Association for Retarded Citizens
  of Georgia
1851 Ram Runway, Suite 102
College Park, Ga. 30337
(404)761-3150

*State Parent Group:*
Parent to Parent National
University of Georgia
850 College Station Road
Athens, Ga. 30610

## GUAM

*State Director:*
Steve Spencer
Acting Associate Superintendent
  of Special Education
Department of Education
P.O. Box DE
Agana, Guam 96910
(671)472-8901

## HAWAII

*State Director:*
Miles Kawatachi
Special Needs Branch Director
State Department of Education
3430 Leahi Ave.
Honolulu, Hawaii 96815
(808)737-3720

*Regional Resource Center Parent
  Representative:*
Marceline Freitas
854 Hao St.
Honolulu, Hawaii 96821
(808)471-3964

*State Parent Groups:*
Evalee Sinclair
Executive Director
Hawaii Association for Children and
  Adults with Learning Disabilities
200 N. Vinyard Blvd., Room 402
Honolulu, Hawaii 96813
(808)536-9684

Judy McGuire
Commission on the Handicapped
Old Federal Bldg.
335 Merchand St., Room 215
Honolulu, Hawaii 96813
(808)471-3964

## IDAHO

*State Director:*
Martha Noffsinger
Special Education Supervisor
State Department of Education
650 W. State St.
Boise, Idaho 83720
(208)334-3940

*Regional Resource Center Parent
  Representative:*
Sue Lundgren
Star Route 2, Box 481
Kooskia, Idaho 83539
(208)962-0062

*State Parent Group:*
Billie Paetel
1300 Chicadee
Boise, Idaho 83709
(208)322-8006

## ILLINOIS

*State Director:*
Joseph Fisher
Assistant Superintendent
Illinois State Board of Education
Mail Code E-216
100 N. First St.
Springfield, Ill. 62777
(217)782-6601

*Regional Resource Center Parent
  Representative:*
Sally Hoerr
Illinois Alliance for Exceptional
  Children and Adults
515 W. Giles Lane
Peoria, Ill. 61614
(309)691-0256

*Federally Funded Parent Training
  Grants:*
Donald Moore
Designs for Change
220 S. State St.
Chicago, Ill. 60604
(312)922-0317

Charlotte DesJardins
Coordinating Council for
  Handicapped Children
220 S. State St., Room 212
Chicago, Ill. 60604
(312)939-3513

Advocate for Families of the
  Handicapped
224 W. Hickory Road
Lombard, Ill. 60148
(312)627-0603

Marjorie Lee
President
Special Education Parents Alliance
305 22nd St., Suite K-164
Glen Ellyn, Ill. 60137
(312)790-3060

## INDIANA

*State Director:*
Gilbert Bliton
Division of Special Education
  Director
Indiana Department of Education
Room 229, State House
Indianapolis, Ind. 46204
(317)927-0216

*Regional Resource Center Parent
  Representative and Federally
  Funded Parent Training Grant:*
Richard Burden
Task Force on Education of the
  Handicapped
812 E. Jefferson Blvd.
South Bend, Ind. 46617
(219)234-7101

*State Parent Group:*
Pat Koerber
Parentele
5538 N. Pennsylvania St.
Indianapolis, Ind. 46220
(317)259-1654

## IOWA

*State Director:*
J. Frank Vance
Special Education Director
Division of Special Education
Iowa Department of Public
  Instruction
Grimes State Office Bldg.
Des Moines, Iowa 50319
(515)281-3176

*Regional Resource Center Parent
  Representative:*
Deborah Samson
1721 Sixth St.
Nevada, Iowa 50201
(515)382-6082

*Federally Funded Parent Training
  Grant:*
Iowa Pilot Parents
Carla Lawson
1602 10th St. North
P.O. Box 1151
Fort Dodge, Iowa 50501
(515)576-5870

*State Parent Group:*
Bill Landers
Parent-Educator Partnership
4401 Sixth St. SW
Cedar Rapids, Iowa 52404
(319)399-6700 or (800)332-8488

## KANSAS

*State Director:*
James Marshall
Director of Special Education
Kansas State Department of
Education
120 E. Tenth St.
Topeka, Kan. 66612
(913)296-4945

*Regional Resource Center Parent
Representative:*
Marianne Ravenstein
RR #2, Box 42
Jetmore, Kan. 67854
(316)357-8361 (o) or
(316)357-6564 (h)

*Federally Funded Parent Training
Grant:*
Patricia Gerdel
Families Together, Inc.
410 Yorkshire
Topeka, Kan. 66606
(613)273-0763

## KENTUCKY

*State Director:*
Vivian Link
Associate Superintendent
Kentucky Department of Education
Office of Education for Exceptional
Children
Room 820, Capitol Plaza Tower
Frankfort, Ky. 40601
(502)564-4970

*Regional Resource Center Parent
Representative:*
Gail Lincoln
Route 2, Box 214
Morehead, Ky. 40351
(606)784-7586 (o) or
(606)783-1858 (h)

*State Parent Group:*
Denzil Edge
Department of Special Education
Parent Education and Resource
Center
University of Louisville
Louisville, Ky. 40292

## LOUISIANA

*State Director:*
Elizabeth Borel
Louisiana Department of Education
Special Educational Services
P.O. Box 94064, 9th Floor
Baton Rouge, La. 70804
(504)342-3633

*Regional Resource Center Parent
Representative:*
Pat Bontempo
616 Oakwood Dr.
Gretna, La. 70053
(504)361-3377

*Federally Funded Parent Training
Grant:*
Glennie Wray
UCP of Greater New Orleans
Harahan, La. 70183
(504)733-6851

*State Parent Group:*
National Federation of the Blind
Parents Group
Dr. Joseph Feinendes
2509 Fox Creek Dr.
P.O. Box 2067
Ruston, La. 71210

## MAINE

*State Director:*
David Noble Stockford
Division of Special Education
Director
Maine Department of Education and
Cultural Services
Station #23
Augusta, Maine 04333
(207)289-5953

*Regional Resource Center Parent
Representative:*
Debora Tuck
11 Salmond St.
Belfast, Maine 04915
(207)338-4314

*Federally Funded Parent Training
Grant:*
Caroline Hyde
Maine Parent Federation, Inc.
P.O. Box 2067
Augusta, Maine 04330
(207)688-4726

## MARYLAND

*State Director:*
Martha Fields
Assistant State Superintendent
Division of Special Education
Maryland State Department of
Education
200 W. Baltimore St.
Baltimore, Md. 21201
(301)659-2489

*Regional Resource Center Parent
Representative:*
Queen Stafford
3612 Eversley St.
Baltimore, Md. 21229
(301)566-3777 (o) or
(301)362-8571 (h)

*State Parent Group:*
Cory Moore
Montgomery County ARC
11600 Nebel St.
Rockville, Md. 20852
(301)984-5792

## MASSACHUSETTS

*State Director:*
Roger Brown
Associate Commissioner
Division of Special Education
Massachusetts Department of
Education
1385 Hancock St., 3rd Floor
Quincy, Mass. 02169
(617)770-7468

*Regional Resource Center Parent
Representative:*
Patricia Blake
P.O. Box 186
Green Harbor, Mass. 02041

*Federally Funded Parent Training
Grant:*
Martha Ziegler
Federation for Children with Special
Needs
312 Stuart St.
Boston, Mass 02116
(617)482-2915

*State Parent Groups:*
ART Project
Barbara Cutler
36 Pleasant St.
Watertown, Mass. 02172
(617)923-0797

Addie Comegy
TASH
P.O. Box 491
Wenham, Mass. 01984
(617)468-1484

VIA Inc.
Betty Hoorihan
460 Quincy Ave.
Quincy, Mass. 02169
(617)770-4000

## MICHIGAN

*State Director:*
Edward Birch
Special Education Services Director
Michigan Department of Education
P.O. Box 30008
Lansing, Mich. 48909
(517)373-9433

*Regional Resource Center Parent*
*Representatives and Federally*
*Funded Parent Training Grants:*
Eileen Cassidy
Citizens Alliance to Uphold
Special Education
313 W. Washington Square
Third Floor
Lansing, Mich. 48933
(517)485-4084

United Cerebral Palsy
C. Richard Heiser
7770 Second St.
Detroit, Mich. 48202
(313)871-8177

## MINNESOTA

*State Director:*
Norena Hale
Special Education Section Manager
Department of Education
812 Capitol Square Bldg.
550 Cedar St.
St. Paul, Minn. 55101
(612)296-1793

*Regional Resource Center Parent*
*Representative:*
Paula Goldberg
Codirector
PACER Center
4826 Chicago Ave. South
Minneapolis, Minn. 55417
(612)827-2966

## MISSISSIPPI

*State Director:*
Walter Moore
Bureau of Special Services Director
State Department of Education
P.O. Box 771
Jackson, Miss. 39205
(601)359-3498

*Regional Resource Center Parent*
*Representative:*
Martha Lenoir
Parent Representative
1150 Arnold
Greenville, Miss. 38701
(601)332-1818

*Federally Funded Parent Training*
*Grant:*
Anne Presley
President
Association of Developmental
Organizations of Mississippi, Inc.
6055 Highway 18 S, Suite A
Jackson, Miss. 39209
(601)922-3210

## MISSOURI

*State Director:*
John Heskett
Coordinator of Special Education
Department of Elementary and
Secondary Education
P.O. Box 480
Jefferson City, Mo. 65102
(314)751-4909

*Regional Resource Center Parent*
*Representative:*
Madeline Wendland
1018 Bedford Lane
Ballwin, Mo. 63011
(314)227-1391

## MONTANA

*State Director:*
Gail Gray
Director of Special Education
Office of Public Instruction
State Capitol, Room 106
Helena, Mont. 59620
(406)444-4429

*Regional Resource Center Parent Representative:*
Rusty Koch
4315 Murphy Ave.
Billings, Mont. 59101
(406)248-6487

*Federally Funded Parent Training Grant*
Katharin Kelker
Parents, Let's Unite for Kids
2210 Fairview Place
Billings, Mont. 59101
(406)657-2055

## NEBRASKA

*State Director:*
Gary Sherman
Director of Special Education
Nebraska Department of Education
P.O. Box 94987
Lincoln, Neb. 68509
(402)471-2471

*Regional Resource Center Parent Representative:*
Michael Remus
Box 278
Osmond, Neb. 68765
(402)887-5041

*State Parent Groups:*
Dee Everitt
National President
Association for Retarded Citizens of the United States
4325 Meredeth
Lincoln, Neb. 68506

Brenda Sutton
Pilot Parents
3610 Dodge St.
Omaha, Neb. 68131
(402)346-5220

## NEVADA

*State Director:*
Jane Early
Special Education Director
Nevada Department of Education
400 W. King, Capitol Complex
Carson City, Nev. 89710
(702)885-3140

*Regional Resource Center Parent Representative:*
Eugene Maretin
5124 Casco Way
Las Vegas, Nev. 89107
(702)386-4685 (o) or
(702)870-8221 (h)

*Federally Funded Parent Training Grant:*
Vince Triggs
Director
Nevada Association for the Handicapped
P.O. Box 28458
Las Vegas, Nev. 89126
(702)870-7050

## NEW HAMPSHIRE

*State Director:*
Robert Kennedy
Special Education Bureau Director
New Hampshire Department of Education
101 Pleasant St.
Concord, N.H. 03301
(603)271-3741

*Regional Resource Center Parent
Representative and Federally
Funded Parent Training Grant:*
Judith Raskin
Parent Information Center
P.O. Box 1422
Concord, N.H. 03301
(603)224-7005

## NEW JERSEY

*State Director:*
Jeffrey Osowski
Division of Special Education
Director
New Jersey Department of
Education
P.O. Box CN 500
225 W. State St.
Trenton, N.J. 08625
(609)633-6833

*Regional Resource Center Parent
Representative:*
Esther Van Luvanee
3 Maywood Court
Fairlawn, N.J. 07410
(201)444-8882 (o) or
(201)791-2848 (h)

*Federally Funded Parent Training
Grants:*
Mary Callahan
Involve New Jersey, Inc.
199 Pancoast Ave.
Moorestown, N.J. 08057

Jose Morales
Puerto Rican Congress of
New Jersey
515 S. Broad St.
Trenton, N.J. 08611
(609)989-8888

## NEW MEXICO

*State Director:*
Elie Gutierrez
State Director of Special Education
State Department of Education
State Educational Bldg.
Santa Fe, N.M. 87501
(505)827-6541

*Regional Resource Center Parent
Representative:*
Sharon Benson
7409 Carriveau NE
Albuquerque, N.M. 87110
(505)884-5059

*Federally Funded Parent Training
Grants:*
James Jackson
Protection and Advocacy System
2201 San Pedro NE
Bldg. 4, Suite 140
Albuquerque, N.M. 87110
(505)888-0111

Southwest Communication
Res., Inc.
Norman Segel
P.O. Box 788
Bernalillo, N.M. 87004
(505)867-3396

*State Parent Group:*
New Mexico P.R.O.
1127 University Blvd. NE
Albuquerque, N.M. 87102

## NEW YORK

*State Director:*
Lawrence Gloeckler
Assistant Commissioner
New York State Education
Department
Office of Education of Children
with Handicapped Conditions
Rm. 1073, Education Bldg. Annex
Albany, N.Y. 12234
(518)474-5548

*Regional Resource Center Parent
Representative:*
Arlene Penfield
328 Lake St.
Rouses Point, N.Y. 12979
(581)297-5331

*Federally Funded Parent Training
Grants:*
Jane Stern
Advocates for Children of
New York, Inc.
24-16 Bridge Plaza South
Long Island City, N.Y. 11101
(212)729-8866

Charlotte Vogelsang
Parent Network
92 Lancaster Ave.
Buffalo, N.Y. 14222
(716)882-0168

Parents Information Group
Exceptional Child
Susan Watson
#73 700 Audubon Pkwy.
Syracuse, N.Y. 13224

*State Parent Groups:*
New York State ARC
Marilyn Wessel, Parent Advocacy
Coordinator
393 Delaware Ave.
Delmor, N.Y. 12054
(518)439-8311

Pat Lilac
Association for Children and Adults
with Learning Disabilities
New York Chapter
155 Washington Ave.
Albany, N.Y. 12210
(518)436-4633

Esther Spindel
Association for the Learning
Disabled
64-33 215th St.
Bayside, N.Y. 11364

Betty Pendler
Member, New York State
Association for Retarded
Children
267 W. 70th St.
New York, N.Y. 10023

## NORTH CAROLINA

*State Director:*
E. Lowell Harris
Division for Exceptional Children
Director
North Carolina State Department
of Public Instruction
Room 442, Education Bldg.
116 W. Edenton
Raleigh, N.C. 27603
(919)733-3921

*Regional Resource Center Parent
Representative:*
Thea Monroe
2912 Debra Dr.
Raleigh, N.C. 27612
(919)782-4620

*Federally Funded Parent Training
Grants:*
Carl Dunst
Family, Infant and Preschool
Program Director
Western Carolina Center
300 Enola Road
Morganton, N.C. 28655
(704)433-2661

Connie Hawkins
Exceptional Children's Advisory
Council Parent Training, Inc.
P.O. Box 16
Davidson, N.C. 29036
(704)892-1321

*State Parent Group:*
Parents' Educational Advocacy
Center
Governor's Council for Persons
with Disabilities
116 W. Jones St.
Raleigh, N.C. 27611
(919)733-9250

## NORTH DAKOTA

*State Director:*
Gary Gronberg
Director of Special Education
Department of Public Instruction
State Capitol
Bismarck, N.D. 58505
(701)224-2277

*Regional Resource Center Parent
Representative:*
Kathy Erickson
P.O. Box 666
Mohall, N.D. 28761
(701)268-3390

*State Parent Group:*
Pat Strait
1609 S. Norton
Sioux Falls, N.D. 57105
(605)336-8145

## OHIO

*State Director:*
Frank New
Division of Special Education
Director
Ohio Department of Education
933 High St.
Worthington, Ohio 43085
(614)466-2650

*Regional Resource Center Parent
Representatives and Federally
Funded Parent Training Grants:*
Margaret Burley
Ohio Coalition for the Education
of the Handicapped
933 High St., Suite 200H
Worthington, Ohio 43085
(614)431-1307

Thomas Murray
Executive Director
Tri-State Organized Coalition
3333 Vine St., Suite 604
Cincinnati, Ohio 45220
(513)861-2400

## OKLAHOMA

*State Director:*
Jimmie Prickett
Special Education Section Director
State Department of Education
Room 215, Oliver Hodge
Memorial Bldg.
2500 N. Lincoln
Oklahoma City, Okla. 73105
(405)521-3352

*Regional Resource Center Parent
Representative:*
Cherry Taylor
4113 N.W. 59th St.
Oklahoma City, Okla. 73112
(405)946-8734

*Federally Funded Parent Training
Grant:*
Martie Buzzard
UCP, Inc.
P.O. Box 996
Norman, Okla. 73069
(405)947-7641

*State Parent Group:*
Homeward Bound, Inc.
Mary Ann Becker
2415 S. Urbana
Tulsa, Okla. 74114
(918)789-7153

## OREGON

*State Director:*
Patricia Ellis
Associate Superintendent
Special Education and Student
  Services Division
Oregon Department of Education
700 Pringle Pkwy. SE
Salem, Ore. 97310
(503)378-2677

*Regional Resource Center Parent
  Representative and Federally
  Funded Parent Training Grant:*
Dr. Cheron Mayhall
Coordinator
COPE Project
999 Locust St., NE #42
Salem, Ore. 79303
(503)399-7966 or 373-7477

*State Parent Groups:*
William Moore
Research Professor
Oregon State System of Higher
  Education Teaching Research
345 N. Monmouth Ave.
Monmouth, Ore. 97361
(503)838-1220

Roz Slovic
Parents Graduation Alliance
University of Oregon
135 College of Eduation
Eugene, Ore. 97403

## PENNSYLVANIA

*State Director:*
Gary Makuch
Bureau of Special Education
  Director
Pennsylvania Department of
  Education
333 Market St.
Harrisburg, Pa. 17126
(717)783-6913

*Regional Resource Center Parent
  Representative and Federally
  Funded Parent Training Grant:*
Louise Thieme
Parent Education Network
John F. Kennedy Center
Hay Meadow Dr.
York, Pa. 17402
(717)845-9722

*Federally Funded Parent Training
  Grant:*
Christine Davis
Parents Union for Public Schools
401 N. Broad St., Room 916
Philadelphia, Pa. 19108
(215)574-0337

*State Parent Group:*
Ellen Siciliano
1900 Clairton Road
West Mifflin, Pa. 15122
(412)469-2540

## PUERTO RICO

*State Director:*
Lucila Torres Martinez
Assistant Secretary of Special
  Education
Department of Education
P.O. Box 759
Hato Rey, Puerto Rico 00919
(809)764-8059

*Regional Resource Center Parent
  Representative and Federally
  Funded Parent Training Grant:*
Carmen Selles Vila
Asociacion DePadres
  Pro Biene Star Ninos
  Impedides De Puerto Rico, Inc.
Box 21301
Rio Piedras, Puerto Rico 00928
(809)765-0345 (o) or
  (809)763-8485 (h)

## RHODE ISLAND

*State Director:*
Robert Pryhoda
Special Education Program Services
Unit Coordinator
Rhode Island Department of
Education
Roger Williams Bldg., Room 209
22 Hayes St.
Providence, R.I. 02908
(401)277-3505

*Regional Resource Center Parent*
*Representative:*
Nancy Husted-Jensen
Old Boston Neck Road
P.O. Box 456
Narragansett, N.Y. 02882
(401)789-9484

*State Parent Group:*
Parent to Parent
Joy Benson
204 Aldrich Bldg.
Rhode Island Hospital
593 Eddy St.
Providence, R.I. 02902

## SOUTH CAROLINA

*State Director:*
Robert Black
Office of Programs for the
Handicapped Director
State Department of Education
100 Executive Center Dr., A-24
Columbia, S.C. 29201
(803)758-6122

*Regional Resource Center Parent*
*Representative:*
Betty Smith
120 Tupper Lane
Summerville, S.C. 29483
(803)871-5545

## SOUTH DAKOTA

*State Director:*
George Levin
Section for Special Education
Director
State of South Dakota Department
of Education
Richard F. Neip Bldg., 3rd Floor
700 N. Illinois St.
Pierre, S.D. 57501
(605)773-3315

*Regional Resource Center Parent*
*Representative:*
Virginia Conlee
P.O. Box 220
Kadoka, S.D. 57543
(605)837-2211

*Federally Funded Parent Training*
*Grant:*
Jan Van Veen
South Dakota Parent Connection
McKennan Hospital, Room 4509
P.O. Box 5045, 800 E. 21st St.
Sioux Falls, S.D. 57117
(605)338-3009

## TENNESSEE

*State Director:*
Joleta Reynolds
Assistant Commissioner
Special Programs
State of Tennessee Department of
Education
132 Cordell Hull Bldg.
Nashville, Tenn. 37219
(615)741-2851

*Regional Resource Center Parent*
*Representative:*
Lindy Gaughn
1078 Overlook Dr.
Hendersonville, Tenn. 37075
(615)824-5287

*State Parent Group:*
Harriett Darryberry
EACH, Inc.
P.O. Box 121257
Nashville, Tenn. 37212
(615)298-1080

## TEXAS

*State Director:*
Jill Gray
Special Education Programs
    Director
Texas Education Agency
William B. Travis Bldg., Rm. 5-120
1701 N. Congress
Austin, Texas 78701
(512)463-9414

*Regional Resource Center Parent*
    *Representative:*
Alfonso Cervantes
150 Dexter
San Antonio, Texas 78226
(512)432-3200

*Federally Funded Parent Training*
    *Grant:*
Janice Foreman
ARC/TX
Early Parent Intervention
9109 Seventh St.
Orange, Texas 77630
(409)883-3324

## TRUST TERRITORIES OF THE PACIFIC ISLANDS

*State Directors:*
Haruo "Winney" Kuraei
Federal Program Coordinator
Trust Territory of the Pacific Islands
P.O. Box 27 CHRB
Capitol Hill, Saipan CM 96950
(670)322-9870

Daniel Nielsen
Special Education Coordinator
Department of Education
Special Education Programs
Lower Base
Saipan, CM 96950
(670)322-9956

## UTAH

*State Director:*
R. Elwood Pace
Coordinator of Special Education
Utah State Office of Education
250 East 500 South
Salt Lake City, Utah 84111
(801)533-5982

*Regional Resource Center Parent*
    *Representative:*
Keith McMillan
5079 W. 3500 St.
West Valley City, Utah 84120
(801)966-1498 (o) or
    (801)969-6370 (h)

*Federally Funded Parent Training*
    *Grant:*
Jean Nash
Utah Coalition for Education of
    Handicapped Children
4984 South 300 West
Murray, Utah 84107
(801)265-9883

## VERMONT

*State Director:*
Theodore Riggen
Executive Director
Division of Special and
    Compensatory Education
Vermont Department of Education
120 State St., State Office Bldg.
Montpelier, Vt. 05602
(802)828-3141

*Regional Resource Center Parent
Representative:*
Elizabeth Milizia
239 Northgate Apts.
Burlington, Vt. 05401
(802)658-7419

*Federally Funded Parent Training
Grant:*
Joan Sylvester
Vermont Association for Retarded
Citizens
37 Champlain Mill
Winooski, Vt. 05404
(802)655-4014

## VIRGIN ISLANDS

*State Director:*
Maureen Wynter
State Office of Special Education
Director
Department of Education
P.O. Box 6640
Charlotte Amalie, St. Thomas
Virgin Islands 00801
(809)773-1095

*Regional Resource Center Parent
Representative:*
Sarah Johansen
P.O. Box 6240
Sunny Isle, Christiansted
St. Croix, Virgin Islands 00820
(809)778-1600

## VIRGINIA

*State Director:*
N. Grant Tubbs
Administrative Director
Office of Special and Compensatory
Education
Virginia Department of Education
P.O. Box 6Q
Richmond, Va. 23216
(804)225-2402

*Regional Resource Center Parent
Representative:*
Jane Nott
8 Charnwood Rd.
Richmond, Va. 23229
(804)285-0907

*Federally Funded Parent Training
Grant:*
Winifred Anderson
Project Director
Parent Education Advocacy Training
Center
228 S. Pitt St., Room 300
Alexandria, Va. 22314
(703)836-2953

## WASHINGTON

*State Director:*
Greg Kirsch
Special Education Section Director
Superintendent of Public Instruction
Old Capitol Bldg.
Olympia, Wash. 98502
(206)753-6733

*Regional Resource Center Parent
Representatives:*
Barbara Patterson-Lehning
Parent/Community Relations
4160 86th St. SE
Mercer Island, Wash. 98040
(206)233-3396

Renee Nowak
Chairperson
Washington State Special Education
Coalition
3847 48th St. SW
Seattle, Wash. 98116

*Federally Funded Parent Training
Grant:*
Martha Gentilli
Director
Washington PAVE
1010 S. I St.
Tacoma, Wash. 98405
(206)272-7804

## WEST VIRGINIA

*State Director:*
William Capehart
Special Education Director
W. Va. Department of Education
Bldg. #6, Room B-304
1900 Washington St. East
Charleston, W.Va. 25305
(304)348-2696

*Regional Resource Center Parent Representative:*
Helen Wilson
Early Education and Early Intervention
3309 Duley Ave., Box 4246
Parkersburg, W.Va. 26101
(304)428-8312 or 422-3151

## WISCONSIN

*State Director:*
Victor Contrucci
Assistant State Superintendent
Division of Handicapped Children and Pupil Services
Department of Public Instruction
125 S. Webster, P.O. Box 7841
Madison, Wis. 53707
(608)266-1649

*Regional Resource Center Parent Representative:*
Margie Gunderson-Ostroot
P.O. Box 7851
Madison, Wis. 53707
(608)266-3047

*Federally Funded Parent Training Grant:*
Liz Irwin
UCP of SE Wisconsin
152 W. Wisconsin Ave., #308
Milwaukee, Wis. 53203
(404)272-4500

## WYOMING

*State Director:*
Ken Blackburn
State Department of Education
Hathaway Bldg.
2300 Capitol Ave.
Cheyenne, Wyo. 82002
(307)777-7414

*Regional Resource Center Parent Representative:*
Harriett Kepler
1436 Ashley
Laramie, Wyo. 82070
(307)745-9260

# Federal Telephone Directory

*The Office of Special Education Programs of the U.S. Education Department is located at 330 C St. SW, Washington, D.C. 20202. Key officials of the office can be contacted at the telephone numbers listed below.*

G. Thomas Bellamy, Director
(202)732-1007

> Patricia J. Guard, Deputy Director
> (202)732-1007

> Max Mueller, Director
> Division of Assistance to States
> (202)732-1014

>> Jeff Champagne, Branch Chief
>> Program Administration Branch
>> (202)732-1056

>> Etta Waugh, Branch Chief
>> Program Assistance Branch
>> (202)732-1052

>> Max Mueller, Acting Branch Chief
>> Program Review Branch
>> (202)732-1014

> Thomas Behrens, Director
> Division of Educational Services
> (202)732-1154

>> Mac Norwood, Branch Chief
>> Captioning and Adaptation Branch
>> (202)732-1172

Thomas Finch, Branch Chief
Early Childhood Branch
(202)732-1084

William Halloran, Branch Chief
Secondary Education and Transitional Services Branch
(202)732-1112

Paul Thompson, Branch Chief
Severely Handicapped Branch
(202)732-1161

Martin Kaufman, Director
Division of Innovation and Development
(202)732-1106

Nancy Safer, Branch Chief
Directed Research Branch
(202)732-1109

Jim Johnson, Branch Chief
Research Development Project Branch
(202)732-1123

Lou Danielson, Acting Branch Chief
Special Studies Branch
(202)732-1119

Norman Howe, Acting Director
Division of Personnel Preparation
(202)732-1070

William Peterson, Branch Chief
Leadership Personnel Branch
(202)732-1083

Harvey Liebergott, Branch Chief
Related Personnel Branch
(202)732-1082

Edward Moore, Branch Chief
Special Education Personnel Branch
(202)732-1048

Paul Ackerman, Director
Division of Programs, Analysis and Planning
(202)732-1155

Cathy DeLuca, Acting Branch Chief
Program Operations Branch
(202)732-1093

Bill Wolf, Acting Branch Chief
Program Planning and Information Branch
(202)732-1009

*Source: U.S. Education Department*

# Use This Coupon To Order
## FROM BIRTH TO FIVE:
## SERVING THE YOUNGEST HANDICAPPED CHILDREN

☐ **YES,** I need to know what I can do to comply with new provisions of the Education of the Handicapped Act. Please rush me _____ copy/(ies) of **FROM BIRTH TO FIVE: SERVING THE YOUNGEST HANDICAPPED CHILDREN** at **$34.95** per copy.

☐ Check enclosed (payable to Capitol Publications, Inc.)
☐ Bill me/my organization _____
Purchase order number
☐ Charge    ☐ VISA    ☐ MasterCard
            ☐ American Express

Account number _____ Expiration date _____

Signature (required for billing and credit orders) _____

Telephone _____

Name _____

Organization _____

Address _____

City _____ State _____ ZIP _____

For fastest service, call
**TOLL-FREE 1-800-327-7204**
M-F, 9-5 EST. In Virginia, call
collect (703) 739-6500.

**Education Research Group, Capitol Publications, Inc.**
1101 King St., P.O. Box 1453, Alexandria, VA 22313-2053

# Use This Coupon To Order Additional Copies Of
# . . . And Education For All:
# Public Policy and Handicapped Children

☐ **YES,** I want to learn more about how the last two decades of public policy have affected handicapped children. Please rush me _____ copy/(ies) of **. . . AND EDUCATION FOR ALL: PUBLIC POLICY AND HANDICAPPED CHILDREN** at **$29.95** per copy.

Name_____

Organization_____

Address_____

City_____ State_____ ZIP_____

**Education Research Group, Capitol Publications, Inc.**
1101 King St., P.O. Box 1453, Alexandria, VA 22313-2053

☐ Check enclosed (payable to Capitol Publications, Inc.)
☐ Bill me/my organization_____
Purchase order number

☐ Charge   ☐ VISA   ☐ MasterCard
              ☐ American Express

Account number_____ Expiration date_____

Signature (required for billing and credit orders)_____

Telephone_____

For fastest service, call
**TOLL-FREE 1-800-327-7204**
M-F, 9-5 EST. In Virginia, call
collect (703) 739-6500.